COMPREHENSIVE
APPROACH
TO
CORPORATE
GOVERNANCE

COMPREHENSIVE APPROACH TO CORPORATE GOVERNANCE

Tri Junarso

iUniverse, Inc.
New York Lincoln Shanghai

COMPREHENSIVE APPROACH TO CORPORATE GOVERNANCE

iUniverse books may be ordered through booksellers or by contacting:

iUniverse
2021 Pine Lake Road, Suite 100
Lincoln, NE 68512
www.iuniverse.com
1-800-Authors (1-800-288-4677)

ISBN-13: 978-0-595-40160-4 (pbk)
ISBN-13: 978-0-595-84540-8 (ebk)
ISBN-10: 0-595-40160-0 (pbk)
ISBN-10: 0-595-84540-1 (ebk)

Printed in the United States of America

Contents

FOREWORD. xiii

ACKNOWLEDGEMENT. xv

INTRODUCTION 1

- *History in brief of Corporate Governance.* *2*
- *Corporate Governance: Introduction* *3*

CHAPTER I   COMMUNICATION AND INVOLVEMENT . . . 7

- *The use of communication in business* *7*
- *Communications Framework* *9*

    Information Pack 9

    Annual Survey. 10

    Complaint and Comment. 10

    Brainstorming. 11

    Community/Public Question Time 13

    Sales/customer service interface. 14

    Feedback loop between marketing and operations. 14

    Seamless information from shift to shift 14

    Other interdepartmental interfaces 14

    Management review for communication 15

    Communication to media. 15

    Intra-department meeting. 15

    Inter-department meeting. 16

    Suggestion Program 16

    Employee Meeting 16

- *Medium of Communication* *17*

Memo 18

Bulletin 18

Brochure 18

Banners 19

Voicemail. 19

Voice-enabled e-mail 20

Internet 20

E-mail 23

Call center 24

Intranet 25

Extranet. 25

Pager 26

Handy Talkie. 26

Interoffice mail 27

Telephone 27

Cellular Telephone 28

Teleconference. 28

CHAPTER 2   POLICY AND PROCEDURE 30

- *Policy*. *31*

Culture, Vision, Value, Mission, and Goal Policy 33

Corporate Beliefs 33

Corporate Values. 34

Corporate Culture 35

Vision 36

Mission 37

Goal. 38

Strategy 39

Communication Policy 39

Social Accountability Policy. 40

Corporate Governance Policy 42

Code of Conduct and Ethics Policy. 42

Anti Fraud and Corruption Policy. 43

Financial Policy 43

Compensation Policy 44
Audit Policy 44
• *Procedure* *45*
Employee Handbook 46
Financial Manual 48
Revenue 49
Expenditure 49
Payment 49
Authority 50
Financial Statement and Report 50
Environment, Safety and Health Manual .53
Audit Manual 54
Purchasing Manual 58
Standard Operation Procedure (SOP) 61
Governance Manual 62
Board Governance 64
Code of Conduct and Ethics 65

CHAPTER 3 CORPORATE REPORT .67
• *Annual Report* *67*
10-K 68
10-Q 69
8-K 70
• *Annual Review* *70*
Best Value Review 70
Audit Review 72
Corporate Governance Review 74
Corporate Performance Review 76
Key Performance Indicator (KPI) 76
Balanced Scorecard (BSC) 77
Corporate Social Accountability Review 79
• *Financial Report* *80*

CHAPTER 4 CORPORATE PERFORMANCE
MANAGEMENT 84

- *Corporate Manifesto Management* *85*
  Corporate Culture, Values, Vision, Mission, and Strategy 86
  Vision 88
  Mission Statement 89
  Setting Goals and Objectives 89
  Corporate Strategy 89
- *Communication Management* *92*
- *Marketing Management* *94*
  Market Goals, Targets and Objectives 97
  Market Policy Statements 97
  Market Research 97
  Compiling the Market Plans 98
  Product Management 98
  Brand Management 99
  Pricing Management 102
  Pricing strategy 104
- *Budget Management* *106*
- *Financial Management* *108*
- *Procurement Management* *113*
- *Audit Management* *115*
  Responsibilities 117
  Audited Subjects 119
  Management Review 120
- *Customer Complaint Management* *121*
- *Production Management* *122*
  DMAIC 123
  DMADV 123
- *Quality Management* *123*
  Total Quality Control 124
  Quality Standard 125
- *Technical Management* *128*
- *Environmental Management* *130*
- *Investment Management* *131*

- *Safety Management* *133*
- *Best Value Management*. *136*
- *Risk Management* *137*
- *Compensation Management* *141*
- *Anti Fraud and Corruption Management* *146*
  Prevention. 146
  Tackling 147
- *Management Information System* *148*
- *Project Management* *152*
  Defining Goals 154
  Defining Requirement 154
  Estimate and Track Project Cost. 154
  Project Tracking 156
  Project Closure 156

CHAPTER 5   CODE OF CONDUCT AND ETHICS 157
- *Corporate Codes*. *158*
  Ownership 158
  Transaction and Accounting 158
  Payment 158
  Corporate Opportunities. 159
  Corporate Properties. 159
  Record 160
  Quality 160
  Report. 160
  Finance 161
  Audit. 161
  Employment. 161
  Tax 162
  Corporate Citizenship. 162
- *Personality Codes* *162*
  Conflicts Of Interest 162
  Integrity 164
  Respect 165

Accountability 165

Decision Making 166

Leadership 166

Equality 166

Harassment 167

Confidentiality 168

Violence 170

Drugs and Alcohol 170

Research 171

• *Business Codes* *171*

Customer 171

Supplier 172

Competitor 172

• *Regulatory Codes* *174*

Patent and Intellectual Property 174

Securities Laws 175

Compliance with Procedures 175

• *Corporate Related Political Codes* *176*

• *Reporting Illegal or Unethical Behavior* *177*

CHAPTER 6   GOVERNANCE AND ORGANIZATIONAL
STRUCTURE 179

• *Governance* *179*

• *Authority and Delegation* *179*

Scheme of Delegation 181

• *Stakeholders Meeting* *181*

Shareholders Meeting 182

Supervisory Board Meeting 183

Executive Board Meeting 184

Customers Meeting 185

Contractors and Vendors Meeting 186

Marketing Group Meeting 186

Company's Lawyers Meeting 187

Mother/Sister Company Representative Meeting 188

Labor Union Meeting 189

Investor Meeting 190

Creditor Meeting 190

• *Committees* *190*

Corporate Governance Committee 192

Compensation Committee 192

Committee for Operation and Technical 193

Audit Committee 194

Risk Management Committee 194

Cooperative Development Committee 195

Community Development Committee 196

Suggestion System Committee 197

Housing Colony Committee 197

Security Committee 198

Safety Committee 199

Standards Committee 199

MEP (Margin Enhancement Program) Committee 200

Human Resources Development Committee 201

Project Management Committee 203

Shut Down Committee 204

Environmental Committee 204

• *Organizational Structure* *205*

• *Organizational Change* *207*

• *Hierarchy* *208*

Shareholder 209

Supervisory Board 209

Executive Board (Board of Directors) 211

Responsibility 212

Authority 212

Senior Executive/Executive 213

• *Boards Qualification* *213*

• *Assessment* *214*

• *Succession* *215*

CHAPTER 7   HUMAN RESOURCES MANAGEMENT 217

- *Recruitment* 219
- *Induction* 220
- *Performance Management* 220
- *Stakeholders Assessment* 224
- *Training* 226
- *Competency Management* 228
- *Career Development* 228
- *Succession Management* 230

    Identification 232

    Development 233

    Evaluation 234

CHAPTER 8   CORPORATE COMPLIANCE 236

- *The Auditor-Company Relationship* 238
- *Auditing the Auditors* 242
- *Independent Directors: Role, Remuneration and Training* 243

    Independent directors on audit committee of listed companies 249

- *Shareholders* 256
- *Stakeholders* 260

REFERENCES 263

FOREWORD

Now and onwards the success of a corporation is not devoted to shareholders only. Most of the work on corporate governance in the past has been done keeping shareholders as the main point. Shareholders are not the only owners who matter. Employees, customers, suppliers, investor, creditor, community and government who also make investments no less at risk than the equity capital, are equally important. Transparency, accountability, integrity, equity and responsibility in the governance of corporations can have a transformational effect not only on corporate performance financially, but also the social agenda. Equity in corporate governance means participation and involvement of all stakeholders. It is therefore imperative that the role of corporate governance is extended beyond disclosures and compliance.

This book contains comprehensive study about corporate governance, which is newly understood as a philosophy for performing corporation. Corporate Governance still needs more improvements and innovations. Corporate Governance is about complexity of communication and involvement, policy & procedure, report, performance management, code of conduct & ethics, governance, human resources management, and corporate compliance (by law). Corporate Governance is not identical to company by law or code of conduct. This book offers differences in which the Readers find aspects of corporate governance, i.e.: detailed information about communication, policy and procedure, corporate risk, code of conduct and ethics (not only conflict of interest), corporate social accountability (rather than social responsibility), and stakeholders' assessment (that covers specifically supplier and corporate interest as part of assessment). This book refers to various sources, i.e. governments, corporations, books and articles. Therefore, it can be used as a common handbook for those entities.

The Author is an executive of PT South Pacific Viscose, which is a member of Lenzing Group, Austria. His experience in engineering and financial fields has inspired him to compile this book from different corners. The Author expects the Reader of this book for the biggest challenge before the corporations, is how to replace greed as a driver of corporate agenda with something more substantial. This may call for a progressive shift in the corporate culture.

Tri Junarso

ACKNOWLEDGEMENT

The Author understands there will be errors, misspellings, or omissions. For the time being it is the best the Author could do. If you find any error, please do not hesitate to let us know so that we can improve this book performance in future.

The Author would also like to thank the many people who have inspired, supported, and helped with this book, especially my family, and my wife; also Mangeng Bruno, and SBY for his speech of corporate governance in many occasions.

INTRODUCTION

Corporate governance has succeeded in attracting a good deal of public interest because of its apparent importance for the economic health of corporations and society in general. However, the concept of corporate governance is poorly defined because it potentially covers a large number of distinct economic phenomena. As a result different people have come up with different definitions that basically reflect their special interest in the field. It is hard to see that this 'disorder' will be any different in the future so the best way to define the concept is perhaps to list a few of the different definitions rather than just mentioning one definition.

Corporate governance is important, not only due to the changed regulatory climate that all organizations must function in today, but because letting shareholders, employees, partners and customers know that you have the right tools, policies and processes in place for good corporate governance is becoming a crucial advantage. Applying enterprise content management lets organizations focus on their objectives and increase the value they bring to all of their stakeholders.

Corporate governance describes all the influences affecting the institutional processes, including those for appointing the controllers and/or regulators, involved in organizing the production and sale of goods and services. Corporate governance deals with issues that result from the separation of ownership and control. But corporate governance goes beyond simply establishing a transparent and responsible relationship between managers and owners. The presence of strong corporate governance standards provides increased access to capital and thereby aids economic development.

Good corporate governance attracts investors by assuring them that the business environment is fair and transparent; that companies can be held accountable for their actions or lack thereof; and those investments can be protected and contracts enforced. Corporate governance is about commitment to values and ethical business conduct, how an organization is managed, includes its corporate and other structures, its culture, policies and the manner in which it deals with various stakeholders; accordingly, timely and accurate disclosure of information regarding the financial situation, performance, ownership and governance of the company; improves public understanding of the structure, activities and policies of the organization; able to attract investors, and enhance the trust and confidence of the stakeholders

History in brief of Corporate Governance

The Cadbury Report was about financial aspects of corporate governance, published in the United Kingdom in 1992. It was known a landmark. This report inspired the publication of the Viénot Report in France in 1995. The General Motors Board of Directors Guidelines in the United States and the Dey Report in Canada proved to be influential in the evolution of other guidelines and codes across the world. The Sarbanes-Oxley Act, which was signed by the U.S. President George W. Bush into law in July 2002, has brought about sweeping changes in financial reporting. This is perceived to be the most significant change to federal securities law since the 1930s. Besides directors and auditors, the Act has also laid down new accountability standards for security analysts and legal counsels. In November 2003, the Securities and Exchange Commission (SEC) approved changes to the NYSE and NASDAQ listing requirements. The changes focused mainly on Board independence, independent committees of the Board, audit committee composition, code of business conduct and ethics and related party transactions. The Higgs Report on non-executive directors and the Smith Report on audit committees, both published in January 2003, form part of the systematic review of corporate governance being undertaken in the U.K. and Europe. The recommendations of these two reports are aimed at strengthening the existing framework for corporate governance in the U.K. Enhancing the effectiveness of the non-executive directors and switching the key audit relationship from executive directors to an independent audit committee are part of this. In April 2004, the governments of the 30 Organization for Economic Co-operation and Development (OECD) countries approved a revised version of the OECD's Principles of Corporate Governance adding new recommendations for good practice in corporate behavior with a view to rebuilding and maintaining public trust in companies and stock markets. The principles include increased awareness among institutional investors, enhanced role for shareholders in executive compensation, greater transparency and effective disclosures to counter conflicts of interest.

CORPORATE GOVERNANCE: INTRODUCTION

Good governance involves effective communication, such as management and the board of directors, to share information and produce the documents they need and facilitate communication with internal and external stakeholders, such as employees and shareholders, etc. Level of corporate governance can be recognized by evaluating the acceptance of stakeholders on how the Board of Director (Executive Board) governing the company, i.e. communication is running effectively; stakeholders get involved; policies and procedures are well-followed; report and variances are systematically followed up; focus in corporate performance management; stakeholders respect on code of conduct; organization is properly structured; and departments are able to manage resources. Corporate can create a communication system, in which stakeholders are able to access information and give their views (i.e. telephone, internet, intranet, etc). The Management as a totality has to ensure the corporations' communications with the stakeholders is accurate, timely, and consistent. Communication should be also built up by initiating meetings, where all their concerns communicated and solved. It will prevent miscommunication and misunderstanding. Meeting must be held effectively.

The governance policy should define the Executive Board's responsibilities, authority, and administration: determine and regularly review the strategic direction for the corporation; use information from a wide range of sources including key persons, employees, partners, customers, and external experts; review, approve, and monitor the annual corporate objectives, ensuring they are consistent with the strategic direction and reflect the beliefs and values of the company; govern the corporation according to vision, mission and targets, corporation's culture, beliefs and values; ensure their continued importance and appropriateness in supporting the mission and vision. Policies should provide general guidelines for solving problems and making decisions in pursuit of specific goals. A policy's main purpose is to ensure consistency and control across the operations and to avoid unnecessary repetition in decision-making.

For the purpose of governance, the Executive Board should direct and authorize to provide: review of the company's priorities, achievements and future targets;

progress report of a development and succession plan; projects status review; risk evaluation report; report of compensation and benefits to employees; budgeting and expenditure report; investment and revenue report; internal and external audit report. It is important that Board of Director reviews company performance, so that they know if it is on track or not, and in the long term makes improvements. Focus on the processes to ensure effective service delivery and performance management, by: making clear the management processes (development, implementation and review), monitoring and control, as well as the financial regulations; arranging the independent review of financial and operational reporting processes; making arrangements for allocating resources; set up systems that provide information to measure the company's performance and systems to monitor and report performance against agreed standards and develop performance plans; developing and maintaining systems for identifying and evaluating risks and put in place effective risk management systems. All staffs should be clear about the functions of the organization, their own role and the roles of others. And decisions are made in a clear and accountable way.

Corporate governance is about commitment to values and ethical business conduct, how an organization is managed that includes corporate and other structures, corporate culture, policies and the manner in which it deals with various stakeholders. Accordingly, timely and accurate disclosure of information regarding the financial situation, performance, ownership and governance of the company is an important part of corporate governance. This improves common understanding of the structure, activities and policies of the organization. Consequently, the organization is able to attract investors, and enhance the trust and confidence of the stakeholders. The Management, in compliance with legal requirements and good practice, needs to establish formal guidelines for how the Management and staff should work together; establish procedures to answer question, provide advice, investigate allegations of wrongdoing and arrange for appropriate corrective or disciplinary action for violations of acceptable business conduct; set standards of personal behavior, which the Management and staff should adhere and to put in place procedures to make sure the company conforms with appropriate legal requirements and ethical standards, and to monitor how it complies in practice; keep a record of delegated or reserved powers, including matters specifically reserved for the decisions of Board of Director or other named individuals or groups and to make sure the roles of Board of Director up to executive staff are formally defined in writing. Executive Board should ensure appropriateness of organization structure (roles and responsibilities of each position and staff are clearly defined and that individuals act in a way consistent with these roles; procedures are followed and that the company complies with relevant regulations and good practice); and human resources capacity (all staffs are trained and experienced; employees have access to advice and resources in order to carry out their roles effectively; equality of opportunity in the recruitment process).

Directors should be focus on strategic direction of the corporate, not on the administrative or programmatic means of attaining those results; be responsible for the performance of the company, and monitor results through approved corporate objectives and performance measures; measure the performance through approved corporate objectives and performance; act in accordance with approved governance policy; establish and approve the corporate beliefs and values; determine the strategic direction of the corporation; assess relevant risks; approve the investment principles and policy; approve the funding policy; review and approve audited financial statements; approve policies. The organization would have a complete records management file plan and would always know that their records could pass any audit or review that might be required.

The system would also ensure that any document or record required to respond to a shareholder request or to provide a board member with additional information would be available when it was needed. The organization would have a shareholder correspondence management system in place, ensuring that all messages from shareholders were recorded, tracked and responded to. The system would ensure that the right person is assigned to respond. The designated responder could use the knowledge management tool to search all the documents and records in the organization to formulate the response. The responses would be recorded and tracked, both in substance and in time, to create a full audit trail. The system would link to the agenda and issues management system so that issues raised by the shareholders could be placed on the board's agenda. By ensuring that the organization has a set of policies and a process for the identification of records and their subsequent disposition (along with a secure document repository for active documents) the management team and the board of directors can be assured that they have the correct documents and records and that they can communicate their trust in the information that they are providing to all stakeholders.

Governance is a philosophy, an approach, and a process. Governance also reflects the personality of a corporation. It must be molded to suit the needs of a corporation, to fit with its vision, its mission, and beliefs and values. It must encompass both internal and external relationships. Fundamental to governance is the clarity, which brings to decision making, accountability, and the roles of the board and management. Governance model is driven by the principle, legislation, and the corporation's beliefs and values. Decisions, strategies and results should be measured, in part, within the framework of these beliefs and values. This may provide the foundation for all policies. Corporate governance is becoming even more important. It is essential that standards on corporate governance converge in the interests of rebuilding the stakeholders' confidence and ensuring better corporate behavior. Complying with the requirements involves operational compliance with best practice, including a review of internal controls and risk management, and drafting the precise wording of the disclosure required in the financial statements. Executive Board can decide to survey the opinion of stakeholders on corporate governance. It will give consideration in a comprehensive way before acting. Survey is as a detailed critical inspection, place a value on; judge the worth of something. A consultant may be needed to do this activity, if internal resources are not appropriate.

1

COMMUNICATION AND INVOLVEMENT

An industrial company has multiple accountabilities to stakeholders in term of communication and involvement, i.e.: making company achievement and policy more open and accessible; encouraging individuals to get involved ; ensuring clear communication; ensuring that employees are involved in developing company vision; encouraging constructive relationships and partnerships. Stakeholders are all parties who have an interest in or are affected by the entity's existence and operations that consist of: shareholder, management, employee, investor, creditor, customer, government, marketing group, community, supplier, etc.

In general, The Management (Director and Executives) have to ensure the corporations' communications with the stakeholders is accurate, timely, and consistent; represents to government, outside parties, partners, the media; speak with a unified voice in communications to stakeholders, once a decision is made; undertake dialogue with stakeholders focusing on strategic issues and policies and to ensure understanding of issues.

THE USE OF COMMUNICATION IN BUSINESS

The purpose of communication is to get organization message across to stakeholders. This is a process that involves both the sender of the message and the receiver. This process leaves room for error, with messages often misinterpreted by one or more of the parties involved. This causes unnecessary confusion and counter productivity. By successfully getting the message across to others, people convey their thoughts and ideas effectively. When not successful, the thoughts and ideas that they convey do not necessarily reflect their own, causing a communications breakdown and creating roadblocks that stand in the way of the goals—both personally and professionally. Illustration of the all-pervasive nature of communication, includes: exchanging ideas; announcing investment plans; producing a report with the monthly management accounts comparing actual results against budget; giving instructions to the production and purchasing departments about the new product plans for next year; delivering a presentation to the marketing department following the results of some quantitative, primary market research; announcing the annual trading results and future strategy to company investors and analysts, etc.

Communication flows in three main directions in a business are:

a. Vertical Communication: e.g. from managers to sub-ordinates, from shop floor workers to supervisors, from the Chief Executive to all other management and employees. Vertical communication flows are mainly used for reporting information (e.g. results, plans) and obtaining feedback (e.g. an employee survey summarized for the Board of Directors;

b. Horizontal Communication: this is between people of the same "level" in a business—usually in the same department, but sometimes communication between departments. This is sometimes known as "peer communication". It is normally used to co-ordinate work. E.g. Sales Managers for different regions circulate details of potential customers to each other and allocate based on the customer location; or accounting staff in different departments share information to help prepare the annual budget on a consistent basis;

c. Diagonal Communication: this involves interdepartmental communication by people at different levels.

People are also constantly involved in some sort of information exchange, whether it's within themselves or with others. They take part in four primary types of communication:

a. Interpersonal communication takes place between a few people who can interact face-to-face. When people are involved in interpersonal communication, they can both talk and listen, they can respond to each other in a direct and personal way.

b. Group communication is often called "back-of-the-head" communication, because most of the people involved in the communication process are looking at the backs of the heads of the people in front of them. The group can be a small group, or it can be a large group. When an electronic device—a medium—is involved, the communication is called mediated.

c. Mass communication is different from group communication because the primary communicator is physically removed from the receiver. A medium is required for this type of communication to be completed. The size of the receiver or communicator is not important here; the important thing is that they cannot see each other, so they can't respond to each other.

COMMUNICATIONS FRAMEWORK

The communication framework is aimed at optimizing communication patterns. The framework is primarily useful for most intra-organization communications and well-structured inter-organization communication. Communication framework is a plan for communicating with company stakeholders, i.e.:

Information Pack

Information pack should explain what the company is, how it works, what it does and how people can get in touch with, which contains:

(1). Company profile: contains basic information on public and private companies such as address and telephone number, executive names and titles, line of business, organization status, and year and location of incorporation, also details such as annual sales figures and sales growth rate, number of employees, size of facility and net worth; (2). Organization structure: organizational element at the company, and any changes to the proposed structure; (3). Company history: how it all started; (4). Map to the factory/office: diagram of location of site, showing geographical and other features, e.g. the position of towns and roads; (5). Resources/career opportunity: inform vacancy, offered compensation and benefits; (6). Annual report: information such as basic financial statements, management's opinion of the past year's operations, and the corporation's future prospects; (7). Financial report: information of income statement and a balance sheet; (8). Business plan: defines the business, goals, and corporate resume; (9). Corporate manifesto: culture, value, vision, mission, goal and strategy; (10). Interactive consultation: consultation relates to technical, product, human resources, etc; (11). Feed back: feed back on past consultations, and other related information;

(12). Poll/Survey: information on the annual company survey; (13). Resources: guidance, advice and information about job vacancy; (14). People question time: chance to question company and management; (15). Your-Views: give information about consultation on company's work and how members of the public may make their views known; (16). Take Part. Register to take part in future activities; (17). Calendar/event agenda: inform current and future activities; opportunity for stakeholders to take part; (18). Visitor's visit: serves everybody interested in the operation of the company with an exhibition open to all visitors; (19). Ownership: inform share ownership; (20). Key Figures/Achievements: cost centers, activity types, orders, and profit centers; (21). Research and Development: refer to future-oriented, longer-term activities in science or technology; (22). Memo of understanding: inform agreements

Annual Survey

Annual sample survey can be distributed to employees requesting information and opinion on company services. Survey includes a set of core questions repeated each year which allows changes in attitudes to be tracked. This is complemented by a set of new and topical questions on key issues. Every employee who participates will answer a common set of questions about services and supports available to them. As well, some departments may ask department-specific questions. Samples should be drawn randomly. A summary of results will be used to further develop, and measure progress on, current government-wide human resource management strategies and cross government priorities, including the Corporate Human Resource Development Strategy. Survey results will also be used departmentally to enhance the quality of your work environment. Employees will be asked to indicate their level of satisfaction or agreement with a number of statements and questions. These will relate to employee experiences as an employee as well as their own skills, abilities and knowledge. Employee will also have the opportunity to suggest improvements. The survey may take approximately 10–15 minutes to complete.

Complaint and Comment

Corporate should have complaint policy and procedure that provides a method for stakeholders to issue formal complaints. It is important to corporate that if in any way stakeholders are dissatisfied with the service or products then they have the opportunity to express their concerns, including complaints, and have them addressed. Corporate should be committed to enhancing customer satisfaction by creating a customer-focused environment, which is open to feedback, resolving any complaints, and continually improving the product delivery and service. Complaints procedure should be: publicly displayed, monitored regularly, reviewed and evaluated periodically.

The objective of complaints policy and procedure is to dedicate to developing and maintaining high levels of customer service, honesty, integrity and trustworthiness; handle complaints as part of the overall strategy to satisfy the needs of people using company's product/service. Any expression of dissatisfaction will be treated as a complaint and dealt with accordingly; treat complaints: confidentially, fairly, and promptly; endeavor staffs to: be courteous to the complainant; respond positively, offer constructive solutions; ensure complaints is recorded, acknowledged within reasonable time, notified to Senior Executive.

The principles of the policy is to be: visible (information about how and where to complain are published to customers, and other concern executives); accessible (complaints handling process is easily accessible to all complainants); responsive (receipt of each complaint should be acknowledged immediately and complaints should be addressed promptly in accordance with their urgency); objective (each complaint is addresses in an equitable, objective and unbiased manner through the complaints handling process); confidential (a customer's desire for confidentiality is respected and protected); accountable (executives take responsibility for their decisions and actions). Organization should understand customers' responsibilities and rights when making a complaint, if the products and services have not met their expectations. Corporate should acknowledge its responsibility to establish a complaint system and procedures that will subject the employees to corrective action when improper conduct has occurred. The purpose of the procedure is to provide prompt, just, and open disposition of complaints.

Brainstorming

The basis of brainstorming is a generating idea in a group situation based on the principle of suspending judgment. Brainstorming is used for solving problems in which issues are simply defined in terms of cost and product reliability. Brainstorming is a process that works best with a group of people. This group should: have a well-defined and clearly stated problem; have someone assigned to write down all the ideas as they occur; have the right number of people in the group; have someone in charge to help enforce the guidelines, i.e.: suspend judgment, every idea is accepted and recorded, encourage people to build on the ideas of others, encourage way-out and odd ideas.

Brainstorming as a traditional approach to do deliberate creative thinking with the consequence that people think creative thinking can only be done in groups. The whole idea of brainstorming is that other people's remarks would act to stimulate group member's ideas in a sort of chain reaction of ideas. Groups are not at all necessary for deliberate creative thinking. In a group, the members have to listen to others and they may spend time repeating their own ideas so they get sufficient attention. Thinking as a group using brainstorming can certainly produce ideas, but individual thinking should be employed. Group should strongly believe that individuals can be just as good at generating ideas and fresh directions. Once the idea has been born, then a group may be better able to develop the idea and take it in more directions than can the originator.

Organized brainstorming sessions using employees, friends and outside consultants can extract a long list of prospective new ideas from the collective minds of the session members. The members should consist of the most creative persons within the company and should be selected to provide an appropriate blend of backgrounds. Since all sections of the company can participate in the idea development including each department contributes to more cooperation. During the session the members are given some basic information focus areas and are encouraged to express as many ideas as they can regardless of how "wild" they might seem.

There are no restrictions for the ideas generated. They might seem to be outrageous, shortsighted, or even dangerous. They may be an old idea or something entirely new. It does not matter. The important thing in the first part of the session is the quantity of ideas not the quality. The group is discouraged from making negative judgmental comments. They are told to concentrate on only the positive aspects of each idea. The most difficult task in organized brainstorming sessions is to keep the ideas flowing.

One person should be appointed as the session leader. He may be the Director or just a good idea man. His/her primary function is to coax the formation of ideas and redirect the groups' thoughts whenever they seem to stagnate. He/she helps the group remove some of the social and mental blocks that normally restrict the imaginative portion of the brain. He/she asks the member to look at things from different perspectives by adding a "what if" in connection with the ideas. When the group seems to be out of ideas, word association can be used to stimulate ideas. The leader supplies a word and asking for ideas in association with that word. Words that conjure up mental images seem to work the best.

When ideas are generated, the members are directed to explore and develop each one to its outer limits. The session takes on a game-like atmosphere. Each idea is tossed around and examined from every possible angle. It is manipulated, exaggerated simplified, stretched and turned inside out. The ideas that take tangible form are then examined more closely to determine which ones seem to hold potential as prospective outcome.

The sessions end with a list of potential conclusions. The methods trick people minds to view the objectives from many different vantage points. The net result is the stimulation of mental pictures of new products. As the group draws on the collective experiences of the individuals the pictures are reshaped and new ideas emerge. They are asked to use metaphors to describe certain concepts. They may add a "what if" in front of some proposed idea. They can even break some long standing rule or custom in the name of imagination. During the idea brainstorm no idea is too rash. When a workable list of new ideas has been generated, the group is ready to explore in more detail some or all of the ideas that seem promising.

Community/Public Question Time

Meeting with representative of the community where Management communicates decisions/policies and answers questions. The Board of Director should welcome questions from the public which may be asked in Public Question Time. Questions may also be asked in writing. Any written answer or summary of that answer to a question in writing is recorded in the minutes of the meeting at which it is asked. The following regulations and procedures may apply to the Community/Public Question Time, i.e.: a member of the community may give written notice; the chairperson may invite any member of the community/public present at the meeting to ask questions relating to activities of the corporate; answer to that question may not to be debated; if a question is refused to accept, the chairperson is to give reasons for doing so.

Sales/customer service interface

Sales and customer service should be provided information timely, complete, objective, and accurately; sales should understand the processes involved in servicing customers; present clear and accurate information about pricing, services, and products. Not exaggerate, mislead, omit, or lie.

Feedback loop between marketing and operations

Marketing should communicate customer needs to the employees who could improve customer perceptions through their own actions. The reason given for disconnect is that by informing employees of the problems causing customer dissatisfaction, the competition may gain access to the information and use it against them. In the meantime, employees complacently keep doing the same things the same way—and keep losing more customers to the competition.

Seamless information from shift to shift

Shift-to-shift information transfer should be done smoothly; shift to utilize overlap time between shifts to communicate with each other information that might be helpful for the following shift. It can be solved by identifying a supervisor on each shift who has the additional responsibility of being the information conduit between his or own shift and the preceding and following ones. This person gathers input from the other supervisors about information that could affect upcoming shifts and passes that along to the next shift, either to the next shift's information supervisor or to a quick meeting of all the shift's supervisors. This person also is the main information liaison with other groups that can affect the shift's work. This can be either a rotating or fixed assignment; having a clipboard attached to each piece of equipment on which a log is kept of how the machinery is performing; having a desktop computer in the supervisors' area on which each supervisor enters information about the shift for other supervisors to skim through when beginning a shift.

Other interdepartmental interfaces

Communication should be done both vertically as well as crossing within departments; avoid countermanded by another department against a memo; provide access for different departments to see each other's schedules

Management review for communication

The review should identify the operational processes with potential bottom-line impact that seem to have communication gaps; identify the potential financial impact of the current miscommunication; observing the selected operational processes up close and talking to the employees who do them while they are at their normal work locations; implementation of potential solutions and involve concern employees; recommendations to senior management; track the improved operational outcomes

Communication to media

An authorized person must have responsibility for studying and making appropriate recommendations on the use of mass communication, and for overseeing programs involving their use. All communication directed to or received from media must be coordinated with the executives within departments. Communication with media includes,: news releases, media advisories, backgrounders, opinion editorials, letters to the editor, pitch letters, materials prepared for distribution by media such as public services announcements or advertising, or any other communication to media transmitted in person, in writing, or electronically.

Intra-department meeting

Intra department meeting is a communication within individual department members. Executives need to conduct Intra-departmental meeting within their respective staffs, prior to the Inter-departmental meeting. The purpose of the Intra-Departmental meetings is to enable executives to gather relevant information from their staff, so that they are able to present a clear picture of their operating units understanding of the issues and solutions at the Inter-Departmental meeting. Intra department meetings should be held as needed; agenda should be distributed before preceding the meeting. Minutes of meeting shall be documented and distributed to all concerns. It will carry out of departmental initiatives; communicating departmental needs and management decisions, actions, and directives.

Inter-department meeting

Inter department meeting is a communication among separate departments. Inter department meeting is to review problems and solutions that is documented in the intra-departmental meetings. Executives need to bring the Intra-Departmental matters from their internal meetings. Each executive is required to present issues and the accompanying solutions. This will enable the executives to follow up actions and decisions, as well as be aware of any issues not previously mentioned. All issues/solutions that are brought for discussion will be recorded and documented.

Suggestion Program

Employee suggestion programs run the gamut, from a suggestion box to programs with their own office space and budgets. The biggest problem with all of these programs is that employee enthusiasm tends to drop quickly, as do the number and quality of suggestions. Employees were encouraged to get together in teams to generate ideas for increasing revenues or decreasing expenses. For whatever ideas the team members developed, they had to investigate the potential savings or impact on costs, and to develop quantitative justifications supporting those assessments. The suggestion had to be accompanied by a detailed cost-benefit analysis showing how much money would likely be saved if the idea was implemented by the company.

Ideas that can improve operations or safety are to be welcomed and, in some cases, rewarded. Director must be willing to support the suggestions that come out of it; kick off the program with a splash; train program participants well; create worthwhile rewards.

Employee Meeting

The purpose of employee meeting is to make sure everyone in the company has a clear vision of the company's goals. Sometime, director may decide completely shuts down the factory and closes all offices so everyone can attend employee meeting. It should be done at least once a year, although most locations hold meetings more frequently. It's an opportunity for every employee to see how their contribution makes a huge difference in corporate success.

Employee meeting as part of the company's ongoing strategy is to drive improved business performance through total employee engagement. The meetings, combined with other vehicles for two-way communications are designed to better align employees' efforts to corporate goals and objectives. Good communication between management and employees is the hallmark of a well run company. Poor communication between management and employees can be a source of concern and lost productivity. Executive may see each of their employees daily, but if he/she doesn't have regular, ongoing communication with employees as a group, those relationships will not live up to their potential. Executives should make all employees feel that they have something important to offer the business. The feeling of team participation can be increased through employee meetings.

At employee meetings, Management provides the big picture. Employees may deal with executives daily regarding specific tasks. However, they may not be exposed to the larger goals for the company and progress toward those goals. An employee meeting provides a forum for sharing this information. Give employees an opportunity to ask questions or make suggestions. Gain employee buy-in by including employees as participants, not just as an employee meeting audience. Encourage the employees to come up with new ways to operate or to improve current systems. Recognize and reward success publicly. Recognition in front of fellow employees at an all-employee meeting has value. Never underestimate the value of praise, thanks and public recognition. People want to feel valued and appreciated. Even though employees do get paid for their labor, it's up to you to make sure they feel that their efforts are meaningful and appreciated. Take time to say thank you.

Upon occasion, executives may wish to discuss or share news about challenges within the business. This open, honest discussion can help mobilize employees to take action. Be careful not to criticize anyone directly. Executive should always try to end an employee meeting on a positive note, even if serious business issues were discussed during the meeting. Executives need to set the tone and course of the meeting from start to finish.

MEDIUM OF COMMUNICATION

Communicating a message requires careful attention to the strengths and weaknesses of the communication medium (verbal (face to face, video, audio), web, screen, print, broadcast). Each medium is appropriate in various contexts, and has its own strengths and weaknesses in how the communicator attracts and keeps the viewer's attention and conveys the intended message to the intended audience. Identify appropriateness of the medium to reach the intended audience. Following medium is effective for reaching the audience, i.e.:

Memo

Whether on paper or through e-mail, memo should be appropriate. Otherwise, system will get overloaded. A communicator may be needed, as e-mail editor, to send an e-mail or memo to all employees/stakeholders. Depending on the volume of information, these e-mail editors send out daily or weekly e-mail bulletins with easily scan-able headlines and crisply written summaries. Anyone who needs more information is either directed to additional sources or provided with a hyperlink to get there. Not only is everyone better informed, but they're using less work time to do so.

Bulletin

Bulletin of brief items can be delivered in print format or electronically to employees/stakeholders. Bulletin is a media for the exchange of information between organization and the population. At its best, communication helps organizations to gain the trust of their stakeholders by informing them of corporate activities in an honest and forthright manner, disclosing incidents immediately and sharing reliable information. The articles and case studies in this issue explain the importance of communication. Bulletin will help the reader gain a better understanding of corporate activities and objectives. It endeavors to keep all stakeholders informed of what's going on throughout the organization. The bulletin is a very effective way for corporate to exchange.

Brochure

Practically every business creates a brochure, but it's often an exercise in futility. Brochure needs following consideration: purpose of the brochure—define the objective up front. Brochure can be made for each purpose, or each segment of the market; get the reader's attention—make a provocative question or declaration, an appeal to the emotions, needs, and wants, or a benefit-laden statement; focusing to customers instead of corporate name; tell the brochure's reader (customer) exactly what company wants them to do when they're finished reading;

writing active verbs and enthusiastic words. If the corporate already has a large collection of printed materials, it may need to get text and images for the online brochure.

Banners

Banners can either be expressive and/or simple and effective at delivering a message. The message should be simple, just a few words, and unambiguous. On line banners can be displayed through internet. The primary purpose of the on line banners is to increase awareness of the business. The advantage to on line is that customers are only one click away from finding out what they need to know about the corporate. When customers see the on line banner and are interested in it, they can click on it to find out more information, or link directly to corporate web site.

Voicemail

Voice mail is a computerized system for receiving, recording, and sometimes forwarding audio messages. A voice mail system plays a prerecorded message to the caller when the line is not answered, and may provide choices such as paging, talking to an operator, or selecting a number by touchtone to choose between message boxes. Voice mail is a service provided by a phone network to store and manages voice messages for individual users. Like an answering machine, voice mail can handle a call by playing a greeting message and recording a voice message from the caller.

It digitizes incoming voice messages and stores them on disk or flash memory. It usually provides auto attendant capability, which uses prerecorded messages to route the caller to the appropriate person, department or mailbox. Voice mail systems may also offer directory lookup by name. A voice-mail system is a complex phone answering machine (run by a computer) which allows individuals to send and receive telephone voice messages to a specific "mailbox" number. A person can call the voice-mail system (often a 1–800 number) and leave a message in a particular person's mailbox, retrieve messages left by other people, or transfer one message to many different mailboxes in a list. Usually, anyone can leave messages, but it takes a password to pick them up or change the initial greeting. The system turns the user's voice into digital information and stores it until the addressee erases it or another message overwrites it. The server for the voice mailboxes is usually located in the message system computer of the commercial vendor which supplies the voice-mail service. Sometimes it can be found on the customer-organization's computer server at the location called.

Voice-mail messages can be written on magnetic disk or remain in the computer's memory, depending on the vendor's system.

Voice-enabled e-mail

Voice-enabled e-mail (sometimes referred to as voice-activated e-mail) uses voice recognition and speech synthesis technologies to enable users to access their e-mail from any telephone. In general, the various products available work similarly: The subscriber dials a phone number to access a voice portal, then, to collect their e-mail messages, they press a couple of keys and, perhaps, say a phrase like "Get my e-mail." Speech synthesis software converts e-mail text to a voice message, which is played back over the phone. The user may navigate through options (such as skipping messages, or hearing a list of senders, for example) through voice commands or key selections. Users dictate their replies, which are delivered to the recipients as voice messages.

Voice-enabled e-mail is especially useful for mobile workers, because it makes it possible for them to access their messages easily from virtually anywhere (as long as they can get to a phone), without having to invest in expensive equipment such as laptop computers or personal digital assistants (PDAs). Proponents hope that new services like voice-enabled e-mail and unified messaging will turn out to be the killer apps that will dissolve the perceived barriers between data networks and traditional voice networks.

Internet

Almost everyone has heard of the internet. They cruise the web, they watch the valuation of internet companies on the stock market, and they read the pundits' predictions about what will happen next. But not many people actually understand what it is and how it works. Take away the hype, and the basic operation of the Internet is rather simple.

The Internet is a communications facility designed to connect computers together so that they can exchange digital information. For this purpose, the Internet provides a basic communication service that conveys units of information, called packets, from a source computer attached to the Internet to one or more destination computers attached to the Internet. Additionally, the Internet provides supporting services such as the naming of the attached computers. A number of high-level services or applications have been designed and implemented making use of this basic communication service, including the World Wide Web, internet e-mail, the Internet "newsgroups", distribution of audio and video information, and file transfer and "login" between distant computers. The design of the Internet is such that new high-level services can be designed and operated in the future.

The Internet differs in important ways from the networks in other communications industries such as telephone, radio or television. In those industries, the communications infrastructure has been put in place to serve a specific application. It may seem obvious that the telephone system was designed to carry telephone calls, but the Internet had no such clear purpose. To understand the role of the Internet, consider the personal computer, or PC. The PC was not designed for one application, such as word processing or spreadsheets, but is instead a general-purpose device, specialized to one use or another by the later addition of software.

The Internet is a network designed to connect computers together, and shares this same design goal of generality. The Internet is a network designed to support a range of applications, depending on what software is loaded into the attached computers, and what use that software makes of the Internet. Many communication patterns are possible: between pairs of computers, from a server to many clients, or among a group of co-operating computers. The Internet is designed to support all these modes.

Since the Internet is a facility matched to the computer, it shares many features of that industry sector. One important example is that the Internet evolves at the pace of the computer industry, a much faster rate than the telephone industry. This has implications for technical features, depreciation cycles, the demand for capital, and the strategic alliances that tend to form.

Another important difference between the Internet and other networks is that providers of internet service do not usually capitalize and install their own communications links, for example fibers, microwave, and cables, but instead make use of transmission capacity installed by others, such as the telephone and cable TV industries. There is little communications technology that was specifically designed to support the internet, with the exception of the router, discussed below. Only now are people beginning to see communications infrastructure specifically designed for the internet.

In addition to the many information tools on the internet, the readily available and easy to use communication tools helped in large part to make the Internet so popular. The scientists and researchers who first used the Internet realized that the increased communications capabilities that they had would benefit not just academics, but all sectors of society. Today, tools such as electronic mail, newsgroups, chat, and even Internet phone are providing supplemental ways to communicate with people around the world. Each tool has pros and cons which people will want to weigh before deciding which tool bests suits the purpose for communicating. Information, through internet on the corporate activities, will communicate about events in the company in an open manner and promotes public knowledge how corporate works; encourage the fullest participation and engagement by all company communities in developing the policies and strategies; improve company to be more competitive, effective and efficient; it provides an opportunity to give feedback about the results of any past consultations; ensure the stakeholders' awareness of the necessity, properties and environmental impact of corporate operations. The company acts as a good corporate citizen.

Internal communications ensure that the employees are swiftly informed about any special events that may influence the operation of the plant and the company, and are always aware of the company's policies and decisions as well as of both financial and production status

Web based application tools, i.e.:

a.   E-mail: POP/SMTP; IMAP; HTML mail

b.   Newsgroups: NNTP as URL protocol; Supported by most browsers

c.   Web-based discussion forums: Web Board (O'Reilly); Hyper News; Collabra Share (Netscape)

d.   Real-time chats and conferences: Rooms (iChat); eShare Expressions (eShare Technologies)

e.   Internet Telephony/Video Conferencing: Internet Phone (Vocaltec); CU-SeeMe (White Pine); Net Meeting (Microsoft)

f.   Links with customers, suppliers, partners: Extranets; Virtual Private Networks

E-mail

E-mail is the transmission of electronic messages over communications networks. E-mail can travel within a local business network or across the Internet. Electronic-mail (e-mail) is the most popular Internet technology. It is least expensive to implement while being easy to use, fast and reliable. Due to its popularity, e-mail makes it possible to communicate with a broad audience. Although e-mail can include graphics, audio and video, most often it is used to send plain text-based messages with or without documents attached. Using e-mail, businesses can communicate with their customers and suppliers to exchange business information and documents for every day processes including providing sales information, booking appointments, providing customer support, providing documents, placing orders, sending invoices and checking on overdue accounts.

E-mail may be the most important, unique method for communicating and developing relationships since the telephone. First of all, it is easy to use. People also find it familiar and safe because it is similar in many respects to writing letters—minus the annoyances of addressing envelopes, licking stamps, and trips to the mail box. Of all the methods for developing relationships on the internet, it is the most common—and perhaps the most powerful. Even when other online tools improve greatly by becoming more effectively visual and auditory, e-mail will not disappear. E-mail is not just electronic mail sent via the internet. E-mail communication creates a space in which people—or groups of people—interact. It creates a context and boundary in which human relationships can unfold.

Most e-mail programs allow you to cc people or create a mailing list. These features make it very easy to expand a dyad conversation into a group discussion. Large groups of dozens or more people can be managed through several online services that offer e-mail group services. The membership boundary of the e-mail interactive space is as flexible as its members want it to be. Sometimes the boundaries are hidden: people can be dropped from a discussion without their even knowing it. Many of the ideas discussed in this article apply to e-mail dyads as well as groups. But the topic of mailing lists is a whole universe unto itself, involving all the subtleties and complexities of group dynamics. E-mail is able to communicate quickly and efficiently with employees and customers in order to conduct corporate business. Benefits of e-mail are:

a. Quick to Write and Deliver: An e-mail message can reach its destination anywhere in the world often in less than a minute. The informal style typically used in e-mail correspondence makes it much faster to prepare than a formal memo or letter. E-mail programs allow reply messages to quote the original text. Thus correspondents can reply point by point without re-stating a lot of information, resulting in quick, unambiguous replies to requests for information or discussion points.

b. Versatile: Since the message is digital, it is simple to copy, forward, and paste into other applications. Messages can be archived and searched to find key pieces of information quickly. Documents and files created with other applications can be attached to e-mail messages, making e-mail an easy choice for electronic document distribution and file sharing.

c. Convenient: As e-mail works on a store-and-forward basis, it is not necessary for the recipient to be present to receive the message. This eliminates telephone tag, and eases communication across time zones. Messages can be sent or received at any time of the day or night.

d. Inexpensive: Messages can be sent and received anywhere in the world for the price of the Internet connection. A single message can be sent to a list of recipients for no additional cost.

Call center

A call center is the focal point of customer service for most companies today. Using a variety of technologies, call centers connect the customer and the organization, in real-time, to provide customer service. Call centers take on different forms. A call center can provide pre-sales, sales and sales support or a variety of other types of service. A definition of "call center": Call (verb): to make a request or demand. Center (noun): a point, area, person or thing that is most important or pivotal in relation to an indicated activity or interest. The definition of call center is changing, but the core fundamentals of a customer making a call (via a phone, email, web site, IVR or fax) to a center (point, area, person or thing (e.g. IVR)) will remain constant because the customer views the call as an important or pivotal activity to themselves.

Call center, contact center or customer interaction center, operate on near identical principals of meeting customer needs in real-time or near real-time. Call Centers will contribute following purposes: to assist callers with obtaining marketing information; to assist callers with customer or product issues; to evaluate callers' experiences with marketing programs, products, service, and sales; to comply with any requirement of law or request of a governmental authority; to return calls or follow-up with third parties to provide the caller with assistance; to keep an accurate record of calls; to train employees and improve service

Intranet

The intranet can result in a reduction in traditional forms of communication, such as print and person-to-person communication. To justify the investment in the intranet, it can measured from how much it costs to carry out a particular activity or process using traditional forms of communication. To establish a more comprehensive business case, corporate need to measure how the organization currently communicates internally, i.e.: time to find and digest information; time for responding to requests for information from other staff and/or customers; number of response can be delivered in a more formal, repeatable manner; shared-knowledge to do job in more effective way; whether the organization effectively communicates important strategic issues to employee, etc. In many organizations, staffs simply don't trust information on the intranet, because they feel it's out-of-date and badly written.

Many intranets are poorly organized, making it difficult for people to find information quickly. A successful intranet requires a long-term strategy. Intranets seek to change a core activity within the organization: communication. The cornerstone of all communication is trust. It's bad enough trying to change someone's habits. It's not always feasible to quantify in strict financial terms the benefits of an intranet. An intranet can improve how an organization internally communicates. This can result in: more loyal, committed staff, because they feel that they are being kept informed of important developments; an organization which is more capable of quickly adapting to a changing environment.

Extranet

Extranet is a web technology used for inter-organization communications. Extranets are used to share information with vendors and customers. An extranet can greatly reduce the amount of money spent on overnight delivery services and travel. If documents are posted to a web server, so that they are securely accessible to any authorized person with a web connection and a browser, you may be able to cut your courier bill. Extranet is a community based communication; therefore executives need to defining the communities within and around an organization and the interactions between them. It will be potential for altering the nature of the work flow process and streamlining business operations.

Pager

Pager is an instant messaging system used to communicate within organization. It is one-way communication system, but an excellent way to communicate quickly. Integration of paging technology adds the capability to receive and display advertising, news, voice-mail indication, and text messages. Users could respond to the advertising, voice-mail, or text messages by dialing phone numbers that were downloaded with the messages. Pagers have many uses, not least of which is the ordinary user who wants to be reachable at all times, whether for personal reasons or work. Executives may rest easier leaving their duty with a supervisor if they have a pager on them; the executive can be paged in emergency. The pager is adapting to the needs of these companies and employees who must be mobile, yet in constant touch with the office.

Pagers are simply a beeper displaying a phone number. The reason for profiling the pager is that it continues to develop into a tiny, more general purpose, portable communication system. Pager allows the user to receive messages written in text, a simple numeric page or coded message. Paging systems use radio waves to transmit or broadcast one-way messages. The pager itself is small, allowing for accessibility at all times, and can be carried or clipped to clothing. Each pager has a number, like a phone number, which the caller dials. The pager is then contacted, and informs the user that he/she is being contacted, with a beep, a vibration, or other signal.

Handy Talkie

Handy talkie technology converge a wireless phone, alphanumeric messaging and internal access into mobile devices. The purpose of the technology is to present 2-way communication system in a compact structure. With features like voice recording, voice activation and wireless modems, it allows you virtual access to your business all the time. It is a reliable backup for emergencies and when going on other duty to remote places.

Interoffice mail

Inter-office mail consists of mail that is picked up from one office and delivered to another office. This mail should be identified quickly by using the inter-office envelopes. Caution is to be exercised when using an inter-office envelope taking care that all previous markings have been masked out completely to ensure proper delivery. The mail code will help the Mail Center get the mail piece to the proper building and department. The persons name will let the department office manager get the piece to that person. To ensure proper delivery of inter-office mail, sender should designate the name and department or staff to whom the correspondence is being sent. Including the box number will facilitate processing. These envelopes are used repeatedly for in-house or internal mailings. When using inter-office envelopes, mark or blot out the previous addressee to ensure proper delivery to the intended recipient.

Telephone

Telephone communication is a routine, but important, component of corporate activities. Everyone in the office should approach telephone communications as an opportunity to provide customers with good service and to obtain important information. A customer first and lasting impression of the corporate is often from a telephone call.

Absent or improper documentation of telephone contacts and messages can negatively impact the customer claim. Therefore, it is essential that telephone calls be documented with the same detail as an office visit. Corporate should have policies and procedures to enhance and monitor the quality of employee practice's telephone communications with customers. All staffs share in the responsibility to provide customers with courteous and efficient telephone communication.

Effective telephone communication will need: training all office staff in telephone etiquette, including handling an angry or dissatisfied customer. The attitude of the person who answers the telephone will set the first impression of the corporate; develop a protocol, and monitor staff compliance with the protocol; document every telephone communication with a customer, including date, time, complaint, and advice/prescription given.

The use of corporate telephone services is limited to official business only. The corporate should recognize that there may occasionally be times when personal calls must be made or received during business hours. Such calls must be held to a minimum, however, and must not interfere with the employee's work. Employees should make reasonable use of the corporate telephone systems and, simultaneously, to guard against abuse of telephone usage.

Cellular Telephone

Cellular telephony can be an effective resource for corporate to conduct the business when employees are away from their office. In general, cellular telephones (i.e., telephones connected to a commercial cellular telephone) may be assigned to employees for whom the nature of their work requires wide mobility and simultaneous access to the public telephone network.

Teleconference

Teleconference is a conference held among people in different locations by means of telecommunications equipment, such as closed-circuit television. The teleconference that includes video communications; pertaining to a two-way electronic communications system that permits two or more persons in different locations to engage in the equivalent of face-to-face audio and video communications Teleconference is to hold a conference via a telephone or network connection. Once a teleconference is established, the group can share applications and mark up a common whiteboard.

There are many teleconferencing applications that work over private networks. The system is conducting a conference between two or more participants at different sites by using computer networks to transmit audio and video data. For example, a point-to-point (two-person) video conferencing system works much like a video telephone. Each participant has a video camera, microphone, and speakers mounted on his or her computer. As the two participants speak to one another, their voices are carried over the network and delivered to the other's speakers, and whatever images appear in front of the video camera appear in a window on the other participant's monitor. Multipoint videoconferencing allows three or more participants to sit in a virtual conference room and communicate as if they were sitting right next to each other.

Corporate should address the use of teleconference technology, i.e. for Board meetings, customers meeting, etc. Teleconference will provide an opportunity to discuss current concerns, and promote a more interactive atmosphere. Good communications are essential within a business if it is to prosper. In any business, the communication of information is an essential part of three key business activities: management decision-making (without relevant, timely and accurate information, decision-making at any level becomes quite tricky!); co-ordination of departments, teams and groups—e.g. making sure that marketing, production and administration know what each other is doing, when and why; motivation of individuals

2

POLICY AND PROCEDURE

Policies and procedures are integral to the planning process and are essential tools for managerial direction and control of the operating environment. Policies and procedures pervade an entity and may differ depending on function and level. Boards (Executive Board and Supervisory Board) use policies to guide their managerial deliberations. Line supervisors are more concerned with the application of policy to the direction and control of daily operations. Some policies and procedures address internal management processes, such as travel reimbursements, time sheets, and personnel matters. Other policies and procedures address the entity's external operating environment.

Procedures tend to be more numerous and detailed at the lower levels of the entity. The development and implementation of procedures can be prescribed, limited, or otherwise directed by such norms and standards as legislation, rules, regulations, technical criteria, professional or ethical standards, or organization structure.

Standardization of procedures governing recurrent processes is generally a precondition for improving operations. Standardization allows management to apply "best known" operating procedures to a given process and enables management to track and gather baseline data on performance. Such measurement provides the starting point for analyzing operations to improve quality and efficiency. Integrating and coordinating policies and procedures are difficult because: this is often unwritten; the interpretation may vary within and across entities; the intent may be unclear or at odds with actual practice; underlying legislation, mission statements, or planning documents may be vague or subject to change during the operating cycle.

Both policies and procedures will ensure that entity operations are consistent, conform to applicable legislation, regulations, plans, and technical, professional or ethical standards, and promote achievement of the entity's mission, goals, and objectives; provide general guidelines for problem-solving and decision-making in certain situations; specify protocols for the execution of recurring tasks.

POLICY

Policies provide general guidelines for solving problems and making decisions in pursuit of specific entity goals. A policy's main purpose is to ensure consistency and control across entity operations and to avoid unnecessary repetition in decision-making. Policies should integrate with policies at higher levels and policies governing related internal operations; clarify the nature and scope of entity plans; provide sufficient flexibility to anticipate and resolve problems associated with managing the entity; prevent repeated or duplicate analysis of management or operational issues; avoid excessive operational detail; permit executives to delegate authority while maintaining control; be well-formulated, communicated, understood, updated, accepted, and used. Policies should support the mission, goals, and objectives of the entity while providing prudent and sufficient managerial and operational control. Policies exist at all levels of an entity—entity-wide, functional area, department, program, or project. Regardless of level, policies must permit some degree of managerial discretion, otherwise they become procedures. Well-designed policies encourage yet appropriately limit discretion and initiative.

Policy strategy involves gathering, analyzing, reporting, and acting on information on those political, economic, demographic, social, cultural, and technological factors which affect the present and projected operations and results of the entity; include information on past, present, and future entity performance; forecast outputs, outcomes, and key measures for the five-year period of the strategic plan; set the stage for entity strategic planning and help the entity identify and respond to current and future issues which might affect operations and results; inform all entity decisions about goals, objectives, strategies, and performance measures; specify the entity's current position and its expectations for internal and external change; address both positive and negative factors affecting the agency, including: strengths, such as improved client relations or higher efficiency in resource use; weaknesses, such as shortages of qualified staff or inability to meet performance targets; opportunities, such as improved technology or possibilities for requesting changes in legislation; threats, such as significant increases in service demand or possible resource reductions.

Corporate should set policies that support goals, ethical practices, ensure accountability, and demand performance. The management is responsible for communicating, enforcing, and evaluating these policies. Executive management carries out corporate policies, directs daily operations, and provides Directors with necessary information. Directors, however, are ultimately accountable for achieving desired results and avoiding unacceptable outcomes. The specific criteria related to the basic phases of the policy design are as follows:

a. Review and interpret applicable rules, regulations, and other statutory requirements which limit or control entity operations and results. Characterize and determine the expectations of stakeholders.

b. Scan the internal and external policy environments. Consider its relationships with other organizations. The entity should also gather, analyze, report, and act on such internal environmental variables as organization structure, organization culture, policies and procedures, resource availability and appropriateness, technological infrastructure, and problem-solving and decision-making capabilities.

c. Review and analyze information collected on the policy environment; determine and prioritize factors to which the entity should adjust. This analysis should consider the rate of change in the factors, windows of opportunity, and other information that can be used to evaluate the relative importance of the various factors.

d. Provide information to all entities for the mission and strategic planning processes. Corporate goals and objectives for all units should relate appropriately to the entity's mission, goals, and objectives.

e. Monitor and maintain alignment of policy and entity mission, goals, and objectives. Monitor interfaces: actively develop and manage its relationships with other organizations and forces in its environment to minimize conflict and encourage cooperation.

Management should view policies as extensions of the planning process, which seek to link goals and objectives to strategies and operations. Policies should ensure consistency between and align with the entity's goals and objectives and provide appropriate benchmarks for managerial action and decision-making. Procedure that is to design a policy requires determine where the policy resides in the entity, who participates in the process, and how the participants are selected; obtain and review any manuals, policies, and forms that could document any phase of the policy, including its relationship to entity goals, objectives, strategies, and plans; determine the assumptions, criteria, methods, processes, and techniques used in the policy; obtain and review available documentation on the assessment of risks, costs, and benefits; determine the derivation, scope, and use of information about stakeholders/beneficiaries gathered in policy; determine tools to transfer information to the entities; obtain information to review, evaluate, and adjust the effectiveness of policy.

Policy is defined as a plan or course of action intended to influence and determine decisions, actions, and other matters. It can be a guiding principle, or procedure considered expedient, prudent, or advantageous. As a rule, the closer the policy is to the level of goals and objectives, the broader should be the policy statement. Conversely, the closer to the tactical or operational level, the more specific should be the policy statement. Just as policies should tie to goals and objectives, procedures should connect with strategies and operations.

Culture, Vision, Value, Mission, and Goal Policy

Company should believe that continued growth is impossible without the trust of all of the stakeholders. Corporate manifesto, i.e. culture, vision, mission, value and goal will sharpen the trust, which needs to describe why does the corporate exist; who should benefit most from all the effort that is put into the corporate; why should an employee do more than the minimum required; who owns the corporate, how corporate behave, importance of the corporate, etc; articulate credible, realistic attractive future for the organization; stretch the organization beyond its current comprehension and capabilities; be clear, focus on action and interface with the strategy of the organization

Corporate Beliefs

Beliefs and values enable the success of the corporation. The entity must properly interpret and translate its statutory mandate into a reasonable, obtainable mission, goals, and objectives to meet the identified needs addressed in the statutes. The entity should provide only those services necessary to fulfill its statutory mandates and provide these services at the lowest possible cost. Corporate believes, i.e.:

a. The corporation must be financially secure; people must be treated with dignity;

b. In communication that is open, honest, timely, and defined;

c. In the fair and equitable compensation of workers' in the fair assessment of employers;

d. Healthy, energized, and informed staff enables the corporation to be effective and agile.

This policy is accomplished by creating an environment that: applauds learning, welcomes new ideas, capitalizes on differences of opinions, understands and deal with risks.

Corporate Values

Value management framework focuses on customer requirements. It is action oriented rather than compliance based—it focuses on optimizing customer value. Value management encourages innovative thinking, business problem solving and performance improvement. Corporate Values is defined as activities, those are most important to the company that includes (1). Partnerships: work together in partnerships, both internally and externally, to achieve shared goals; encourage teamwork; believe that an active, well-informed and independent Board is necessary to ensure the highest standards of corporate governance; excellent Service; provide customers with excellent service and products; (2). Achievement: fulfill commitments and achieve desired results; (3). Respect: treat everyone with dignity and interpersonal sensitivity; share information with staff, customers, and partners; act with integrity and as trustees of the workers' compensation system; listen and respond to the needs of our customers; (4). Learning and Growth: demonstrate continuous personal and corporate improvement; apply this knowledge to provide the best services and products; individual performance & employee development; passion for customers, for partners, and for technology; (5). Dignity: treat with respect and consideration; maintain respect for employees, customers, partners & shareholders; communicate externally, in a truthful manner, about how the company is run internally; (6). Fair: treat equally and without prejudice or bias and in a timely manner; (7). Honest: treat truthfully; honest communication throughout the company; adhere to Code of Ethics & Business Conduct Guidelines; open; easy to access and to understand; decisions and actions are clear, reasonable and open to examination; practice open; be transparent and maintain a high degree of disclosure levels; (8). Accountable: decisions and actions are clear, reasonable and open to examination; committed; accountability to customers, shareholders, partners, and employees for results, and quality; the Board, which oversees how the management serves and protects the long-term interests of all the stakeholders of the company; challenge; taking on big challenges and seeing them through; continuous improvement; (9). Personal integrity: constructive; self-criticism; self-improvement and personal excellence; proactive; responsibility; (10). Professional: deliver professional services in accordance with relevant technical and professional standards

Corporate Culture

Corporate culture can be defined as behavior, habit, and rule which stakeholder uses to interact with each other or moral, social, and behavioral norms of a corporation based on the beliefs, attitudes, and priorities of stakeholders.

a. Behavior, the manner in which corporate behaves, i.e. emphasis on innovation and commitment to cost containment; non-discriminatory; committed to a safety culture of a high standard; have a simple and transparent corporate structure driven solely by business needs; compete vigorously, engaging only in practices that are legal and ethical; maintaining a work environment that is free from discrimination or harassment; act in a socially responsible manner, within the laws, customs and traditions of the countries in which we operate, and contribute in a responsible manner

b. Habit, a mental attitude of corporate, i.e. fast is better than slow; Chinese people sometimes like to give expensive corporate gift companies. Chinese people think the more expensive corporate gift company they give, the more they care. That's actually not a good habit. A great corporate gift company should be expressing your thought and not costing a fortune; a habit of innovation, coming together, will make an organization more innovative. The habit of innovation at an individual level (personal brilliance) is the differentiator.

c.   Rules which a group of coworkers uses to interact with each other; i.e.: make money without doing evil; satisfy the spirit of the law and not just the letter of the law; make a clear distinction between personal conveniences and corporate resources; management is the trustee of the shareholders' capital and not the owner

Corporate culture refers to both formal, written company policy concerning everything from dress code to employee relationships as well as the informal behavior.

Vision

Vision describes the desired future to which a corporation aspires, i.e.: struggling to find a means of accurately understanding the availability and performance of the fundamental pillars of their business—resources, costs and time; provides business management information based on the two fundamentals of time and capability (both resources and skills). Example of vision jargon, e.g. preferred choice product; model of the new/desired environment; value through innovation—recognize that in a competitive and fast changing world, the values of products, services and companies are constantly changing. In order for things to have real value to the customer; exceeding the expectation of customer—by embracing best practice; unique corporate supplier model—with the proprietary information systems to save customers time and money throughout the procurement process; delivering business value; cutting development costs—without any doubt, cutting development costs is the key benefit provide Return on Investment (ROI) calculations that make technology investments easier to justify; smart code generation—provide faster and cheaper application development, higher quality applications, more predictable and consistent results, faster product development cycle times, faster time to market for commercial application development, reduced project costs, and reduced project risks—ensures that the focus is solving business problems; created by developers for developers—mean that the product developers also have experience as product users; trusted by leading corporations—products are to be used in major corporations; information is no border world—anything can be done through information for world betterment; fit to future—risk readiness, challenge, equality, critics and conflict readiness; world-class company; be recognized as the pioneer and global leader in the development

Mission

Mission articulate broadly the purpose, intent, and beneficiaries of entity operations while remaining consistent with the expectations of applicable governing bodies. The mission statement identifies what the entity does, why and for whom it exists, and the nature and scope of its unique contribution. It provides the foundation for the entity's strategic plan. Beneficiaries are a subset of stakeholders. While a mission statement is typically found at the macro level, any operational or administrative level should consider developing and periodically evaluating its own mission statement to assess and specify the purpose for its existence. Mission defines the reason for the corporation's existence, i.e. ensure customer satisfaction, minimize complaint; provide the right service, at the right time, and be cost-effective in our processes; act with dignity and treat everyone with respect; conduct the business in a fair, open, honest and professional manner; bring about positive relationships with workers, employers, and others affected by the workers' compensation system; communicate distinct identity, benefits and values; expect and recognize individual and corporate achievements and contributions to the company; ensure the financial integrity; ensure not only to be economically viable, but at the same time socially responsible and ecologically sustainable; continuously working to adapt and improve the way in which we operate, minimizing environmental, safety and health risks, and fostering an open and constructive dialogue with organizations and individuals. In all company activities Management will protect employees, facilities and the environment from harmful influences, conserve natural resources and promote environmental awareness; develop and promote injury prevention programs; build relationships; planning the process that anticipates and responds to the environment, and that integrates operational planning, and that results in service and management excellence and efficiency; follow risk management process that identifies and mitigates risks that jeopardize the implementation of the strategic plan; promote pride in company's employees; ensure accountability for individual and corporate achievements, and responsibility for how work is accomplished; build a company founded on the principles of profitable business through integrity, commitment to customer, to organization; demonstrate to customers substantial savings in both the actual cost of the product and the hidden procurement costs. Reducing the number of vendors, and buying all non-production goods and services from one source, select manufacturers, utilizing sophisticated ordering and inventory systems and a vast delivery network, and receive the best prices from suppliers; provide the highest quality services, comparable with the best in the industry; support customers and business partners in meeting their critical needs for the current as well as for the future; maintain trust and long term relationships with clients, in the spirit of partnership; providing the most cost-effective and efficient systems to its clients by using state-of-the-art technology in software development; establish a culture of innovation and provide the very best working environment and growth potential for its highly valued employees; in all company activities Management will protect employees, facilities and the environment from harmful influences, conserve natural resources and promote environmental awareness; the operating principle of the company is to supply high quality products and services to customer to the maximum amount, as safely and economically as possible.

Goal

Goals are general statements of purpose that establish the direction for a component of the mission. Goals may have multiple objectives. Objectives are more detailed than goals, have shorter time frames, and are measurable, quantifiable, and achievable. Objectives are clear targets for specific actions. An integral part of the planning process is to review the entity's goals, objectives, and strategies to maintain their alignment with the entity's mission. If the goals, objectives, and strategies are not in alignment with the mission and the mission statement is still valid then the goals, objectives, and strategies must be adjusted. Goal should be specific, measurable, agreed, realistic, and track-able (SMART), i.e. minimize the number of customer complaints and maximize customer loyalty; superior product performance compared to competitors as judged by customers; minimize raw material consumption and waste; maximize process and technical availability; maximize profit margin; minimize overtime and absenteeism, etc

Goal needs to be rolled down up to the operation level, i.e.: Goal Roll Down (GRD); Key Performance Indicator (KPI); Balanced Scorecards (BSC). Evaluation is also required to track the progress, i.e. set allowable variance and deviation; set standard; set maximum, nominal, expected capacity; provide control and inspection; communicate the problem

Strategy

Strategies are the means for transforming inputs into outputs and outcomes and should allocate the use of budgetary, human, and other resources. Strategies are methods to achieve goals and objectives. For example:

a.   Customer satisfaction: identify the needs of customers; communicate these needs to all relevant company functions; set and review quality objectives based on the customer's requirements; plan, conduct, measure and control all activities necessary to achieve these Objectives and fulfill the needs of the customers in a structured and economical way; continually improve the performance of the company on all levels of operations; produce added value

b.   Superior product: identify key processes that are technology-based or serviced, or impacted by new or upgraded technology; identify facility and work/workspace environment; that should not deteriorate product and quality; identify information flows within the organization which would influence process, technology selection, design, or implementation; define the parameters of and for change the customer in future; operate in a safe, reliable and economical manner with minimum impact on the environment

Communication Policy

Business communication encompasses a huge body of knowledge including marketing, branding, customer relations, consumer behavior, advertising, public relations, media relations, corporate communication, community engagement, research & measurement, reputation management, interpersonal communication, employee engagement, online communication, and event management direct and open communication is fundamental to corporate culture.

The business communication message is conveyed through various channels of communication including the internet, print (publications), radio, television, ambient, outdoor, word of mouth, etc. Good communication means a healthy environment of mutual trust and respect exists in which stakeholders can comfortably communicate work issues or employment concerns, and business. Communication technology is putting more employees in direct contact with suppliers, customers and colleagues in foreign lands. Strong business communication skills are critical to success and in order to succeed in today's competitive environment, organization must communicate effectively, efficiently, and with confidence. Communication policy shall describe corporate vision, mission, and objectives; communication framework; medium of communication; ownership; conditions (confidentiality, access, authorization, etc); responsibility and usage

Social Accountability Policy

Social accountability policy covers the environment, purchasing, personnel, health, safety, community, security and communications. Accountability implies the willingness to acknowledge responsibility to others, and the willingness to fully accept responsibility for one's actions and their implications. Therefore, it's more than participative plans, which will be honest, transparent, and ethical. It should:

a. Environment: (1). Follow the principle of sustainable development for the environment by minimizing the harmful effects of the corporate operation and by ensuring appropriate management of the generated waste; observes and studies the state of the environment and takes immediate corrective action when required (2). Maintain the employees' competence and expertise on environmental issues at a high level (3). Aspire to act as a pioneer in the management of environmental issues. (4). Reduce the already low waste in compliance with the principle of prevention and continuous improvement. Any changes caused by the plant process are monitored proactively and in readiness to fight any harmful environmental impact caused by them. (5). Accept responsibility for securing and developing living conditions in the regions near the factory areas (6). Minimize the amount of generated waste by ensuring efficient use of energy, supplies and raw materials and by developing practical reuse of waste (7). Products and services shall meet the quality and environmental requirements. Corporate should also be committed to conducting business in a manner which respects, preserves, and improves the environment, that includes: conduct services in an environmentally responsible manner; use energy wisely and, improve the energy efficiency of the operations; comply with all environmental laws and regulations, company policies, and standards of good industry practices; use technologies and operating procedures designed to minimize health and safety risks; encourage employees to report any condition that may pose an environmental, health, or safety hazard and provide a confidential means for them to do so; safeguard the environment and natural resources; commit to being responsible corporate citizens of the communities in which we reside;

support organizations which improve education, health, and the well being of others

b. Personnel: perform work tasks in a responsible manner, displaying motivation, competence and commitment to observing procedures that have been agreed on; availability of competent professional staff is ensured by a competitive pay scale that encourages effective performance of work, good daily practices and achievement of long-term objective; work community based on equality, where no discrimination is allowed and where the achievement of equality is promoted. All employees are offered equal opportunities for professional and career development regardless of their sex or age. Provides opportunities to the personnel to maintain and develop their working ability; company and the staff is prohibited for discrimination, harassment or bullying in the work place

c. Safety and health: promote health and occupational safety in compliance with the zero-accident philosophy; maintain a good work place atmosphere and working conditions; everybody working in the plant area is to look after their own safety and the safety of their colleagues

d. Purchasing. Buy local policy that informs local businesses what corporate expects from suppliers; seek to package contracts in a way that does not necessarily restrict opportunities for local businesses to compete for the work,; include the requirement to employ local people if the terms of the contract allow this, e.g. out of hour response times; help local businesses achieve "approved supplier" status

e. Communication: commitment to ensure that all personal information of individuals in its possession is protected and used in accordance with the law

f. Security: accountability for security risk management (analyze and assess threats and risks to which sensitive information and assets are exposed, select risk-avoidance options, implement cost-effective safeguards)

g. Community: facilitating, promoting and ensuring quality development making community a better place to live, work and play.

Corporate Governance Policy

Corporate governance helps to make company as a good place for employees to work, a good provider of products and services for customers, a good investment for stockholders, and a good citizen in the communities. The fundamental to corporate governance policy is establishing the roles of management and the board, with a balance of skills, experience and independence on the board appropriate to the nature and extent of company operations; a basic need for integrity among those who can influence a company's strategy and financial performance, together with responsible and ethical decision-making; meeting the information needs of investment community is also paramount in terms of accountability and attracting capital. Presenting a company's financial and non-financial position requires processes that safeguard, both internally and externally, the integrity of company reporting; provide a timely and balanced picture of all material matters; the rights of company owners, that is shareholders, need to be clearly recognized and upheld; every business decision has an element of uncertainty and carries a risk that can be managed through effective oversight and internal control; keeping pace with the risks of business and other aspects of governance requires formal mechanisms that encourage enhanced board and management; rewards are also needed to attract the skills required to achieve the performance expected by shareholders; the impact of company actions and decisions is increasingly diverse and good governance recognizes the legitimate interests of all stakeholders

Code of Conduct and Ethics Policy

Company should value honesty, integrity and adherence to the highest ethical standards. The Code embodies corporate values and sets forth the principles to guide corporate behavior. Therefore, Executive Boards should possess the highest personal and professional ethics, integrity and values, and be committed to representing the long-term interests of the company's shareholders. Organization must also have an inquisitive and objective perspective, practical wisdom, and mature judgment, include: to ensure that all persons to whom this code is applicable are aware of such standards, both legal and ethical; to identify areas of ethical risk for directors, officers, and employees; to provide guidance in recognizing and dealing with ethical issues, provide mechanisms to report unethical conduct, and help foster a culture of honesty and accountability; anyone who engages in prohibited conduct is subject to appropriate disciplinary action or criminal act

Anti Fraud and Corruption Policy

Sound systems of accountability are vital to effective management and in maintaining stakeholder's confidence. Minimizing of losses to fraud and corruption is essential for ensuring that resources are used for their intended purpose. Anti-Fraud and Corruption Policy outlines the company commitment to creating an anti-fraud culture and maintaining high ethical standards in its administration of finance. The policy should describe:

a.   Creation of an anti-fraud culture, monitoring the effectiveness of internal controls, commitment to tackling fraud and corruption

b.   Defining roles and responsibilities, for dealing with the threat of fraud and corruption, both internally and externally, i.e. councilors, employees, contractors, consultants, suppliers, service users, staff and committee

c.   Consistent treatment of information regarding fraud and corruption, proper investigation by an independent and experienced audit team, the optimum protection of the witness, and appropriate action to be taken against fraud and corruption

Financial Policy

The Management has responsibility for assuring that business practices and financial systems are in compliance with financial policy. Delegation of responsibility and accountability for the financial management is only given to qualified person who be actively involved in the tasks being performed; have the appropriate knowledge and technical skills to perform those tasks, including knowledge of relevant regulations and policies. Financial policy should cover providing appropriate financial authority to discharge responsibilities, and accountable for the financial management; ensuring the efficiency and effectiveness administrative processes, financial transactions are appropriate and are accurately recorded; effectiveness of internal controls; assuring that business practices and financial systems are in compliance with the policy, regulatory, and other requirements; effective use of technology that is secure, reliable, responsive and accessible; monitoring expenditures which must operate within the budget; risk management and professionals with appropriate knowledge and technical skills

Compensation Policy

Corporate should reevaluate the total rewards and remuneration program periodically, not just in light of the new corporate climate but in light of changing economic conditions, business performance and strategy, and organizational design. It is not just how much, but, more importantly, how a company pays its executive talent. If it just tries to match or exceed what other companies pay, the company will miss some important opportunities to use executive compensation as a management tool. The company can use compensation to influence business decisions and outcomes in accordance with its strategic plan.

Compensation policy will describe

a. Form and amount of compensation is determined in accordance with good principles; i.e. consideration of economic conditions, business performance and strategy, organizational design, competitiveness, and regulatory requirements

b. The relationship between rewards earned and individual and corporate performance

c. Compensation package that can attract, retain and motivate people to the long-term success, growth and profitability of the corporate. Therefore, it should be reasonable, defensible, and appropriate

Audit Policy

Auditing is an independent appraisal activity established within the company to examine and evaluate its activities. Both internal and external audits may include financial, performance, operational, information and compliance audits. The auditors will assist Director and executives in the effective discharge of their fiduciary and administrative responsibilities by providing analysis, appraisals, counsel, information and recommendations concerning activities reviewed and by promoting effective controls for the recording and reporting of operational activities and for the custody and safeguarding of assets. Audit policy describes: assessments about adequacy, efficiency, and effectiveness of management practices, control systems, and information, in keeping with good principles and contributing to continuous improvement and accountability; ensuring effective, independent and objective audit; incorporating audit results into action, i.e. priority setting, planning and decision-making processes

PROCEDURE

Procedures derive from and conform to policies but are more tactical, specific, concrete, and detailed than policies. Procedures serve as a management control mechanism by standardizing daily operations to ensure consistent processing of recurrent tasks. Procedures specify how recurring tasks are to be executed and enumerate both the steps and sequence to be followed. Since they address future scenarios, procedures are also a form of standing plans.

Procedures are more effective control tools if the entity consciously assesses their relationship to its policy and operational systems. Procedures often extend to more than one functional area or department. This increases their importance as controls. Characteristic of procedure, includes: exist at all entity levels; organize operation and control of the entity; reduce the need for managerial direction of routine matters; improve efficiency by standardizing actions; delineate and sequence task steps; facilitate personnel training. Procedures should provide sufficient flexibility to handle both daily operations and reasonably foreseeable abnormal situations; allocate and use resources efficiently and not cost more to develop and implement that the risk(s) they seek to avoid; be clearly understood, thoroughly delineated, and easily accessible in writing; add value to the service or product delivered to internal or external customers.

The specific criteria related to the basic phases of the policies and procedures process are as follows: within the context of the entity's goals and objectives, identify those management decisions and recurring tasks which require standardization; develop policies for the management decision areas and procedures for the recurring tasks based upon input from appropriate internal and external stakeholders; document the policies and procedures; to minimize exposure to risk and facilitate both internal and external reporting and control, entities should document both the process and product of policy and procedure development; disseminate and communicate policies and procedures in writing to appropriate stakeholders. Policies and procedures should be communicated in writing in a timely fashion to all appropriate internal and external stakeholders. Optimally, internal stakeholders should receive both verbal and written notification of newly developed policies and procedures. Entity-wide policies and procedures, such as sick leave policies and time keeping procedures, should be distributed to every employee. Updates and revisions should be communicated in a timely manner; implement, monitor, and review policies and procedures for appropriateness, compliance, and alignment with entity goals and objectives; adjust policies and procedures as necessary.

Employee Handbook

An effective employee handbook will provide employees with an understanding of their roles in company's success, which can make the company a better place to work. An employee handbook's primary function should be to serve as a communication tool within your organization. It provides answers to employees' questions about insurance and other benefits, attendance, safety, compensation and harassment, as well as facilitates consistent policy enforcement and legal protection for your company. An employee handbook also can help new employees gain insight into company's culture by emphasizing the company's ethics and philosophies. Before implementing company's employee handbook, the organization should:

a.   Determine who will be responsible for the project. He/she should be familiar with the management philosophies and company's operating practices; understand the expectations and deadlines.

b.   Determine whether to implement an employee handbook or employee handbook and policy manual. A policy manual typically is more comprehensive than an employee handbook because it contains written guidelines. A policy manual may contain information and procedures specific to each policy. Employee handbooks are distributed to all employees. The employee handbook must include language that legally will protect the company and avoid including policies or benefits that only apply to management, such as executive compensation policies and perks. This information may cause negative employee relations issues.

c.   Gather memos, letters, copies of procedures, posted policies and directions currently relevant to the organization, and determine which policies and procedures will be included in the employee handbook.

d.   Articulate both employees and company's rights, embrace policies and procedures that will provide legal protection for the company; and demonstrate company commitment to employment laws.

e. Employee handbook's format should be consistent. A narrative format is the most common. Tone, tense and language also will influence employees' perceptions of the policies and company. The employee's handbook also should be published in languages spoken by the employees. It also should consider whether to present the handbook to employees in paper form, electronic form or a combination. The handbook format should accommodate revisions.

f. Before publishing and distributing the employee handbook, the employment attorney's advice should be taken because he will be defending your company if any policies are scrutinized or questioned government agencies. If employees are represented by a labor union, items in the collective-bargaining agreement may conflict with items in the employee handbook. The handbook should be presented to the union representative—to respond their concerns about specific policies. And employee handbook is a communication tool and not subject to negotiation. Finally, after made changes, the employee handbook should be presented to the Management for review and approval. The better communication to employees, the more they will take ownership of the policies.

The employee handbook should demonstrate as a communication tool. New hires will benefit from an individual handbook overview as part of their new employee orientation. The handbook should provide a positive message about two-way communication within the organization. The most efficient way to familiarize current employees with employee handbook is to hold a group meeting when the handbook is distributed to each employee. An employee handbook should be organized into several sections that will make it easy to use. Consideration includes the following sections:

a. Introduction: includes a company's history and growth, management and operating philosophies, and organizational structure.

b. On the job: explains every regulatory and administrative policy that affects employees' daily duties. Some topics included in this section should be attendance, equal employment opportunity, internet and technology use, harassment, performance evaluations, and personal appearance and demeanor.

c.   Payroll: explains timekeeping particulars and how compensation is determined and overtime is calculated and paid. This section also should include information about payroll, such as paydays, pay advances, pay deductions, travel time, final wages, and cashing of payroll and expense checks.

d.   Time away from work: contains policies related to time away from work, including holidays, vacation days, sick leave, disability, funeral leave, military leave and medical leave of absence.

e.   Benefits: discusses health and welfare benefits and special benefits programs, such as tuition reimbursement and professional development.

f.   Communication: discusses whether a company considers different types of information and communication proprietary, customer-related or employee-related; include information about how employees are expected to communicate with each other and customers; problem-solving and grievance policies; supervisors' roles; and policy addressing third-party intervention during disputes.

g.   Safety and security: contains a company's safety policy, its drug- and alcohol-free workplace policy, drug-testing program, and smoking and workplace-violence policies.

Financial Manual

Finance Manual sets out policies and procedures needed for the efficient and effective management of the agency and effective operation of internal controls. Particular responsibilities documented in the Manual, are generally assigned to various officers by reference to certain functions or job title. This is done to accommodate differences in job responsibilities between entities. It does not imply that additional positions are warranted.

To ensure there is a clear allocation of responsibilities to officers, each entity should substitute the name of the actual position that is responsible for the function specified. For smaller entities, this may mean nominating one position to undertake several roles. Where this is done, incompatible duties should be kept separate to the extent practicable to maintain internal control. (Incompatible duties are duties which, when done by a single officer, facilitate losses through fraud, etc.).

Revenue

The primary objective of any revenue management process is to collect what is owed, and accomplishing this in an effective and efficient manner, so that resources are not wasted. It should:

a.   Be formal, written, and supported by top management. Ensure everyone understands and agrees with the procedures. Training of staff is also enhanced where procedures are clearly documented. Record and report revenue transactions

b.   Include the nature and location of the revenue process in the organization structure. Identify and develop methods to obtain the information needs of the revenue management process

c.   Treat all payers consistently: Provide information to enable payers to know when, where, how, and how much to pay.

d.   Comply with legal requirements. Develop a plan to collect revenues in compliance with legal authority or obligation to collect revenue.

e.   Monitor and evaluate the revenue management process; ensure that entity goals are being met

Expenditure

The proper management of expenditure is fundamental to ensuring value-for-money in delivering services to the community. As well, having cost-effective internal controls within the purchasing and payments system plays an important part in ensuring that waste of funds, over-expenditures and corruption do not occur.

Payment

An entity should analyze its payment patterns (including length of time to process payments and the time taken for warrants to be presented) to see if the timing or flow of purchases should be changed. This data and information bearing on the type of payment methods used, along with the location of disbursement facilities (remote location disbursement), should be easily retrievable from the accounting system. The process should maximize profitable cash flow and contain controls that will ensure that transactions are properly recorded and reported; prevents unnecessary prepayments; facilitates prompt payment of debt; avoids duplicate payment

Authority

The process should clearly document the authority and procedures to commit funds. All statutory and regulatory limits must be acknowledged and the process designed for compliance. In governmental accounting, the encumbrance is used to track funds committed so that appropriations budgeted to the entity will not be over-committed. When purchased items or services are delivered, the encumbrance entry is credited with a debit to the appropriate expenditure.

Financial Statement and Report

Financial reporting is used to disclose information about the corporate to investors, creditors, governments, and other interested parties; information about the corporate is used to determine what has been accomplished in the past and forecast what is likely to be accomplished in the future; a corporation constructs an annual report that includes a general discussion about the corporate activities during the past year as well as developments that are expected to be implemented in the near future (i.e., next year) and the financial statements of the firm for the most recent years (the year just ended and up to four previous years).

The annual report generally includes the following financial statements:

a. Income Statement—provides a summary of the revenues recognized and the expenses incurred during a particular operating period

b. Balance Sheet—records the financial position of the firm at a particular point in time by showing the assets (investments) and the liabilities and equity (financing) of the firm; include:

i. Cash versus other assets—on the assets side of the balance sheet, only cash represents actual funds that can be invested

ii. Liabilities versus stockholders' equity—the liabilities of a firm represent the debt, or money, the firm owes to lenders, while equity represents the ownership position of the stockholders;

iii. Preferred versus common stock—all corporations have one type of stock called common stock;

iv. Common equity account—the common equity section of the balance sheet generally is divided into three accounts: common stock, which equals the number of shares outstanding times the par value of each share; paid-in capital, which represents the amount above the par value for which common stock was issued; and retained earnings, which represents income the firm earned in the past that was "retained" and reinvested in the firm, not paid to stockholders as dividends;

v. Accounting alternatives—inventory valuation can be based on either the FIFO (first-in, first-out) method or the LIFO (last-in, first-out) method;

vi. Time dimension—the balance sheet is a "snapshot" of where the firm is at a specific point in time, while the income statement (the statement of cash flows also) shows the results of the firm's activities over a period of time.

c. Statement of Retained Earnings—shows the change in the retained earnings account since the last balance sheet was constructed.

d. Statement of Cash Flows—reports the effect of the firm's activities—operating, investing, and financing—over some period on its cash position: (A). Income versus cash flows—the revenues and expenses that appear on the income statement are recognized when incurred (1). Non-cash items—some non-cash items appear on the income statement, such as depreciation; (2). Accounting profit—net income, generally is not the same as the net cash flows. (3). Operating cash flows—cash flows generated from the normal operating activities of the firm—that is, the manufacture and sale of inventory. (B). Cash flow cycle—general operating activities affect various balance sheet accounts and cash flows; for example, selling a product on credit immediately decreases inventory, immediately increases accounts receivable, generates a profit that is recognized in retained earnings (assuming the product is sold for more than it cost to manufacture), and, when the customer pays for the product at some future date, decreases receivables and increases cash.

e. Ratio Analysis—often referred to as financial statement analysis, ratio analysis provides a method to evaluate how financial positions (1) change on a year-to-year basis for a single firm and (2) compare between two firms, even if they differ in size; such analysis are useful to managers inside the firm and investors and creditors outside the firm who want to try to predict future financial positions of firms. (A). Liquidity ratios—give an indication of how well the firm can meet its current obligations; (B). Current ratio—shows the relationship between current assets and current liabilities; (C). Quick, or Acid-Test, Ratio—similar to the current ratio, except the value of inventories is subtracted from current assets in the numerator; (D). Asset Management Ratios—give an indication of how well (effectively) the firm manages its assets; (E). Inventory turnover—shows how many times during a period (e.g., a year) the average inventory is turned over due to sales activities: (1). Days sales outstanding (DSO)—indicates the average time, in days, (2). Fixed assets turnover—gives an indication of how efficiently the firm uses its fixed assets (excludes current assets) to produce revenues; (3). Total assets turnover—similar to the fixed assets turnover, except the value of total assets (includes current assets); (F). Debt management ratios—indicate how the amount of debt the firm has affects its financial position: (1). Debt ratio—provides an indication of the capital structure of the firm; (2). Times-interest-earned (TIE) ratio—indicates whether the firm generates sufficient operating income (not cash) to meet its interest obligations each year; equals to EBIT (Earnings before interest and taxes)/interest charges; (3). Fixed charge coverage ratio—like the times-interest-earned ratio, except all fixed payments related to financing; (4). Profitability ratios—show how the firm's management of its liquidity position, assets, and debt has affected normal operating activities, and vice versa: (a). Net profit margin—shows what percent of sales revenues is left over after expenses related to operations and financing and taxes; (b). Return on total assets (ROA)—a measure of the return on investment earned by the firm; (c). Return on common equity (ROE)—similar to ROA, ROE is a measure of the return on the original funds invested by stockholders; (5). Market Value ratios—measures that consider the value of the firm stock in the financial markets; (6). Price/earnings (P/E) ratio—gives an indication of how much investors pay for each dollar of income generated by the firm; high growth firms generally have higher P/E ratios; (7). Market/book ratio—indicates the relationship between the selling price of the common stock and its book value;

f. Trend and comparative analysis—ratios should be evaluated (1) at a particular point in time in comparison to some norm, such as an industry average, to determine the current financial position of the firm (comparative analysis) and (2) over time to determine whether the current financial position is improving or deteriorating (trend analysis); such analyses will help interested parties forecast the future financial position of the firm.

g. Du Pont equation—shows the relationship between the return on investment and both the total assets turnover and the net profit margin; can be used to determine in more detail where weaknesses or strengths exist; if ROA is relatively low, it might be due to a low profit margin, a slow turnover of assets, or both

Environment, Safety and Health Manual

The Environment, Safety & Health (ES&H) manual is a compilation of ES&H-related requirements and policy information. The requirements in the ES&H manual are for the specific work and associated hazards and environmental aspects, and corporate practices that management has determined are requirements. The ES&H manual also describes the implementation of the ES&H Management commitments. Individuals responsible for the work activities must ensure that the hazards and environmental aspects associated with these activities are analyzed and controlled in accordance with the requirements in the Manual. In instances where the ES&H requirements for a work activity are not covered in the Manual, workers should contact their ES&H Department. The ES&H and experts (health, safety, and environmental, or professionals) will help in determining the requirements that apply to the specific work activity. The ES&H manual may consist of:

a. ES&H Management: worker responsibilities, Safety Management System, and managing ES&H (general responsibilities of the Management and workers, subcontractors, and government and local agencies with regard to work conducted at the company; how work is to be performed based on Safety Management System)

b. Health and Safety: controls and hazards (i.e. personal protective equipment; and specific requirements for work activities)

c. Environment: environmental aspects and controls (specify regulatory requirements and controls for protecting the environment and for implementing the Environmental Management System (EMS)). It includes requirements for identifying and minimizing negative impacts of environmental aspects, setting environmental targets and objectives, and developing plans for managing environmental aspects in such a way as to provide responsible stewardship of the environmental resources in our care.

ES&H requirements and policies should be reviewed for possible incorporation into the Manual, and the ES&H executive ensures that employees are following the latest requirements and policies.

Audit Manual

Corporate internal audit program consists of the policies and procedures that govern its internal audit functions, including risk-based auditing programs and outsourced internal audit work. Audit plan should include:

a. A mission statement or audit charter outlining the purpose, objectives, organization, authorities, and responsibilities of the internal auditor, audit staff, audit management, and the audit committee.

b. A risk assessment process to describe and analyze the risks inherent in a given line of business.

c. An audit plan detailing internal audit's budgeting and planning processes. The plan should describe (1). Audit goals, schedules, staffing needs, and reporting. (2). Identify the frequency of audits. (3). Set out for each audit area the required scope and resources, including the selection of audit procedures, the extent of testing, and the basis for conclusions

d. Informing the board and management of individual department or division compliance with policies and procedures. The audit report should state whether (1). Operating processes and internal controls are effective, and describe deficiencies as well as suggested corrective actions; (2). Clear support for all audit findings and work performed; (3). Disposition of any agreed-upon actions to correct significant deficiencies.

e. Audit manual also describes the roles and responsibilities of the Executive Board, executives, and internal or external auditors; identifies effective practices for audit programs; and details examination objectives and procedures.

An effective audit program should: identify areas of greatest risk exposure to the institution in order to focus audit resources; promote the confidentiality, integrity, and availability of information systems; determine the effectiveness of management's planning and oversight of corporate activities; evaluate the adequacy of operating processes and internal controls; determine the adequacy of enterprise-wide compliance efforts related to the policies and internal control procedures; and require appropriate corrective action to address deficient internal controls and follow up to ensure management promptly and effectively implements the required actions.

The Executive Board should ensure that written guidelines for conducting audits have been adopted; and assign responsibility for the internal audit function to a member of management who has sufficient audit expertise and is independent of the operations of the business. The Board should give careful thought to the placement of the audit function in relation to the corporate management structure; have confidence that the internal audit staff members will perform their duties with impartiality and not be unduly influenced by senior executives/executives of day-to-day operations.

Accordingly, the internal audit executive should report directly to the Board or its audit committee, whom responsible for reviewing and approving audit strategies (including policies and programs), and monitoring the effectiveness of the audit function. The board or its audit committee should be aware of, and understand, significant risks and control issues associated with the corporate operations, including risks in new products, emerging technologies, or information systems.

Audit program is essential to evaluate risk management practices, internal control systems, and compliance with corporate policies. Effective audit programs are risk-focused, promote sound internal controls, ensure the timely resolution of audit deficiencies, and inform the board of directors of the effectiveness of risk management practices. An effective audit function may also reduce the time examiners spend reviewing areas of the institution during examinations. Ideally, the audit program would consist of a full-time, continuous program of internal audit coupled with a well-planned external auditing program. Scope of audits involves:

a.   Self Audit: business competency, personality (energetic, enthusiastic, willing to learn, deliver responsibility and make decisions, motivate subordinates); ability to listen stakeholders; monitor market behavior (monitor changes, information relevant to business and trade); maintain relation with other business owners or business organization; attend seminars relevant to business and management; take active roles in the community; evaluate compensation and payback

b. Strategic Planning: i.e. clear statement of corporate mission; corporate target market; define customer's characteristics; strategy to keep the corporate ahead of the competition; measurement of corporate performance; policies to guide action and decision making; identify potential opportunities for increased sales and profits (new products, new markets, or new locations); foresee future conditions and changes that have a significant impact on the business; assessment of corporate competitor

c. Organizational Structure: current organization chart; evaluate relationship between individual and function; indicate authority, responsibility, and accountability for each function; clear current job description that define accurately all work responsibilities

d. Human Resources Management: compliance with laws and regulation (employment, training, job safety and health, performance appraisal, wage, working hour and working condition); personnel records; job specifications; induction program; copy of current company's policy and procedure

e. Accounting System: accounting system that provides full range of data sufficient to make management decisions; monthly statements; every element of the accounting statements is understandable; annual audit by an independent public accountant; apply break-even analysis and opportunity cost analysis; accounts receivable is aged regularly; provide for the funds and statements needed for payroll taxes and deposits, income tax deposits, and deposits and payments of unemployment compensation taxes and workmen's compensation liabilities; adequate for present business and immediately foreseeable growth; reconcile bank statements monthly; adequately managing cash through cash budget

f. Budgeting and Expense Control: expenditures that based on allocations established by budgeting system; budgets is tied to set time periods, performance standards, and incentives; require a budget proposal for future business operations; budgets are used to control the amount and rate of expenditures; budgets provide a record for improved performance; require discussing budgets with key employees; analyze the costs that are fixed for a period (such as rent and salaries of clerical and supervisory personnel);

attempt to construct a break-even model for the business; require to compare cost, revenue, and profit figures against industry data; review both actual operations and forecast at the end of each accounting period

g. Cash Management: all cash receipts are deposited to the company's bank account; cash receipts records are processed by two or more people working independently; all withdrawals of cash controlled by adequate checks; continuously monitor and reconcile all cash disbursements against the original authorization; all checks and purchase orders are pre-numbered and accounted for; invest seasonal excess cash productively; use lines of credit to decrease the demands for cash; calculate cash flow regularly

h. Taxes and Legal Obligations: maintain tax calendar showing when the various requested national, state, and local reports are to be filed or payments made; someone specifically is responsible for all tax reports and payments; keep adequate individual payroll records; require to prepare the payroll kept up-to-date on maximum wages for payroll tax purposes; making timely deposits If the payable withholding is above the minimum amount; records are adequately differentiate between taxable and nontaxable sales; adequate equipment records, giving the date purchased, basis of the asset (cost or otherwise), estimated useful life, method of depreciation, accumulated depreciation, and location of the asset; require to confer with attorney regarding reporting requirements to the government and to the employees, if company has a pension plan or a profit-sharing plan; require to up to date business licenses

i. Risk and Insurance: analyze the risks of business and employees are exposed to under normal operations; require to assume unnecessary risk; require a professional insurance broker inspection to help identifying areas where risks can be reduced; require insurance on key personnel; take advantage of all premium cost-cutting possibilities; periodically review insurance program

j. Purchasing: regularly review the quality of products purchased, their timely delivery, and the quality of other services provided by company's suppliers; solicit bids on purchases; require to have more than one source of supply for any critical item; purchases are to be made at the "right" price; require to buy by specification, rather than by brand name; adequate policies and procedures regarding authorization; review existing purchase procedures

k. Marketing and Sales: identify the specific segment; review products or services against the competitors; review other products/service that have a good reputation in the minds of customers; require to attempt to meet competitors head-on or sell differentiated products that carry a different price/value relationship; ensure marketing and promotion efforts honest and straightforward; ensure all aspects of marketing and promotion coordinated with production planning and scheduling; ensure marketing and promotion efforts controlled by budgets

l. Location: review operation convenient and easily accessible to the target market; ensure transportation facilities such as access, parking, loading and unloading, public transportation, and lighting well developed

m. Pricing: ensure prices competitively based on the quality and services; require to use break-even analysis in computing cost for price setting; ensure economies of scale in the operation which enable company to sell at a lower price than competitors; require to develop pricing strategy that allows to adjust prices to meet competitive situations

n. Planning for Growth: require to review opportunity for advance planning; able to thoughtfully analyze recurring crises; require a succession planning

Auditor's Report may tell responsibilities of the auditor and directors in general and lists the areas of the financial statements that are audited; lists how the audit standard is applied, and what areas of the company are assessed; give the auditor's opinion on the financial statements of the company being audited. This is simply an opinion, not a guarantee of accuracy.

Purchasing Manual

The Purchasing manual contains the policies and procedures governing purchasing within the corporate that are a compilation of purchasing practices and interpretations of the laws, rules and regulations. The procurement process includes:

a. Define and document the goals and objectives for the procurement process. Goals for the procurement process should link to the entity's strategies, goals, and objectives. Procurement goals and objectives should be documented and address planning, acquisition, standards and quality assurance, contract administration, and disposition programs. The entity should publish and maintain a current procurement user's manual which contains applicable central procurement agency guidelines.

b. Determine the nature, scope, and location of the procurement process in the organization structure: establish a central procurement office responsible for management of all procurement activities; define the organizational placement of the central purchasing function at a management level to ensure that sufficient authority, independence, and safeguards are provided to foster the goals and objectives of the procurement program; define the accountability, responsibility, and authority of central procurement; authorize central procurement to have responsibility for the content and correctness of solicitations, contracts, specifications, and terms and conditions.

c. Identify, document, and implement the policies, procedures, and controls needed for the procurement process: document all procurement processes, rules, and regulations in manuals which are regularly reviewed and updated; document the relationship of the statewide procurement process to procurement process delegated to other entities; delegated purchasing authority to adhere to procurement law and to central procurement rules, policies, and procedures; direct central procurement to monitor all delegated procurement activities. The entity should establish criteria which prevent abuse of authorized procurement thresholds and restriction. Lines of authority and separation of duties must be established.

d. The controls needed to manage the remainder of the procurement process will vary according to the nature of the item to be acquired. Each process step has general criteria and then a list of possible controls and data, organized by the control objectives of economy, efficiency, and effectiveness, i.e.: (1). Plan and schedule procurement activities: forecast requirements; assess time required to complete procurement action; assess lead time and seasonal variations that affect when procurement should be initiated; determine assignment of procurement officials needed; determine cost of procurement action and analyze resources for adequacy to accomplish anticipated work load; (2). Receive requisitions and develop specifications: identify minimum requirements (design, performance, or both); develop requisition; send requisition to purchasing function; purchasing reviews requisition for accuracy and completeness; purchasing checks to see if item(s) are available from on-hand or excess; if not, purchasing determines methods of purchase; (3). Solicit bids from vendors: seek sources of supply through use of trade directories, yellow pages, commerce directories, professional organizations, etc; develop the bidders list using pre-qualification procedures to avoid unnecessary disqualifications and protests; publish requirements in the public advertising; develop standard formats and clauses for contract administration and monitoring; develop instructions for the preparation and submission of proposals; distribute invitations for bids; (4). Evaluate and award bids: equitable evaluation requirements must set forth any factors, other than initial price, that will be used in evaluating the bids or proposals; if award is made for other than the low initial price, the reasons must be documented as future record); provide for an equitable award at the lowest possible cost; adherence to legal criteria; ability of vendor to perform satisfactorily; (5). Receive, inspect, inventory, and store the items: identification of the types of knowledge, skills, and abilities which quality assurance staff require for their task; identification of the types of testing available and when each should be used; identification of the basic sampling methods and how they are applied; provisions for describing the different types of documentation and reporting procedures which should be used and why, what each report should contain, and how the information should be used; procedures for handling supplier nonperformance and complaints; (6). Monitor and evaluate the procurement process. The entity should evaluate the various procurement processes for effectiveness and efficiency. This information should be used to enhance or modify current processes; Input indicators (the number of requisitions received); output indicators (the number of contracts completed; the percentage of business from historically underutilized businesses; the number of requisitions filled; the number of new annual contracts developed; the number of annual contracts revised; special savings achieved; number of purchase orders issued; number of single-bids received); outcome indicators(amount of backlog; number of awards challenged; number of specifications challenged by vendors)

Purchasing and contracting is a complex process subject to governing laws, operating rules and regulations, court decisions, administrative law rulings, recommendations, recommended practices, designated procedures, specific conflict-of-interest provisions, and the overall proprieties that attach to customers' service. The fundamentals of successful public purchasing are competition, impartiality, conservation of funds, and openness.

Standard Operation Procedure (SOP)

The primary purpose of the Standard Operating Procedure (SOP) is to identify hazards associated with a specific operation and document the means by which those hazards will be mitigated. The person most familiar with the operation should prepare the SOP. This is for the benefit and welfare of the employees involved in the operation. The SOP is to be written in a manner and language that is appropriate to the personnel and the nature of the operation.

Standard Operating Procedure (SOP) includes the following element:

a. Purpose. State the intent and objectives of the SOP, i.e. communicate the hazards associated with this operation; document the control measures that will be used to control the hazards; document the precautions and limitations applicable to this operation, and define the required qualifications of personnel performing the operation.

b. Scope. This would include applicable information concerning the location of the operation, the organizations involved, and the equipment involved.

c. Responsibilities. List the titles or persons, and organizations responsible for specific aspects of the SOP.

d. Hazards. List and briefly describe the hazards associated with this operation that could result in harm to: personnel, the general public, equipment and materials, the facility, and the environment. Possible hazards for consideration include: radiation, high temperatures, high pressures, chemicals, electrical shocks, excessive noise levels, confined spaces, moving equipment, lasers, flammable materials, compressed gases, explosives, dangerous fauna, extreme environmental conditions, etc.

e. Hazard control measures and limitations. Address the administrative, engineering, and/or personal protective equipment measures that will be used to control each of the hazards. This section should include safety rules, precautions, and limitations applicable to this operation that define operating boundaries that are not to be exceeded.

f. Procedural steps. Necessary where specific procedural steps should be followed to ensure the safety or quality of specific tasks associated with the operation covered by the SOP. It should be consequential step-by-step instructions for completing the tasks. The procedure should be organized in a logical sequence that is compatible with task performance.

g. Training requirements. List qualifications and training requirements for individuals performing all or specific tasks covered by the SOP.

h. Emergency procedures. Explain what is to be done in case of an emergency that sufficient for most operations performed on-site at the factory. Operations at remote locations or with unusual hazards may require different or more specific response information.

Governance Manual

Governance manual makes reference to the principles of corporate governance generally accepted by the international community. The Manual focuses on the laws and practices that take into account applicable; commitment to values and ethical business conduct; how an organization is managed (includes its corporate and other structures, its culture, policies and the manner in which it deals with various stakeholders); accordingly, timely and accurate disclosure of information regarding the financial situation, performance, ownership and governance of the company; This improves stakeholders understanding of the structure, activities and policies of the organization. Consequently, the organization is able to attract investors, and enhance the trust and confidence of the stakeholders. Governance manual should contain general principle includes (1). Rights of and equitable treatment of shareholders: Organizations should respect the rights of shareholders and help shareholders to exercise those rights. They can help shareholders exercise their rights by effectively communicating information that is understandable and accessible and encouraging shareholders to participate in general meetings; (2). Interests of other stakeholders: Organizations should recognize that they have legal and other obligations to all legitimate stakeholders; (3). Role and responsibilities of the Board: The Board needs a range of skills and understanding to be able to deal with various business issues and have the ability to review and challenge management performance. It needs to be of sufficient size and have an appropriate level of commitment to fulfill its responsibilities and duties. There are issues about the appropriate mix of executive and non-executive directors. The key roles of chairperson and CEO should not be held by the same person; (4). Integrity and ethical behavior: Organizations should develop a code of conduct for their directors and executives that promotes ethical and responsible decision making. It is important to understand, though, that systemic reliance on integrity and ethics is bound to eventual failure; (5). Disclosure and transparency: Organizations should clarify and make publicly known the roles and responsibilities of board and management to provide shareholders with a level of accountability. They should also implement procedures to independently verify and safeguard the integrity of the company's financial reporting. Disclosure of material matters concerning the organization should be timely and balanced to ensure that all investors have access to clear, factual information

Governance Manual may contain mechanisms and controls that are designed to reduce the inefficiencies that arise from moral hazard and adverse selection. A control system should regulate both motivation and ability, i.e.:

a. Internal corporate governance controls: monitor activities and then take corrective action to accomplish organizational goals, i.e.: (1). Board of Director (Executive Board), with its legal authority to hire, fire and compensate top management, safeguards invested capital; (2). Performance-based remuneration is designed to relate some proportion of salary to individual performance. It may be in the form of cash or non-cash payments such as shares and share options, superannuation or other benefits; (3). Audit committee

b. External corporate governance control: encompass the controls external stakeholders exercise over the organization, i.e.: debt covenants; external auditors; government regulation

Corporate governance encompasses the framework of rules, relationships, systems and processes within and by which fiduciary authority is exercised and controlled in corporation. The Manual provides framework for governing the corporate, i.e.:

a. Governance framework: review and recommend corporate governance framework generated by management.

b. Governance activity: review corporate governance activities and approve changes.

c. Disclosure policy: review management's compliance with corporate disclosure policies and procedures.

d.   Governance disclosure: prepare corporate governance disclosure for corporate annual reports and management proxy circulars.

e.   Organizational structure: review and approve any proposed changes to corporate organization structure which have a material effect on reporting lines or the independence of key control groups such as internal audit, finance, legal, compliance and risk management.

Board Governance

Corporate governance also includes the relationships among the many players involved (the stakeholders) and the goals for which the corporation is governed. Systems and processes deal with matters such as delegation of authority, performance measures, assurance mechanisms, reporting requirements and accountabilities. This Manual outlines possible structures and procedures for setting up and maintaining effective corporate governance and shows how the various parts interact. It is intended to give the stakeholders enough information to know what needs to be done and what kind of expert help should be sought in order to accomplish it. The Manual is designed to inform shareholders, Boards, and Committee members alike of their rights and obligations within the corporate system, i.e.:

a.   Nomination or appointment of Boards: guide line for nomination or appointment to the Board.

b.   Committee appointments: guide line for the appointment of directors to Board committees.

c.   Removal of Director from Board Committee: guide line for the removal of a director from a Board committee.

d.   Director qualifications/competencies: criteria of the selection of Boards, and committee, including competencies and skills.

e.   Director development: guide line to oversee the development by management of a director development program.

f.   Director remuneration: set up remuneration with agreed terms of reference

g. Mandate review: review the mandates for the Boards, each Board committee, the Chief Executive Officer and the Chairman of the Board as well as the delegations of authority.

h. Performance assessment: guide line for assessing performance of the Boards and committee.

i. Succession planning: guide line for succession and emergency preparedness planning process for the Chief Executive Officer and the Chairman of the Board to the Board based on the applicable succession planning process.

Code of Conduct and Ethics

Employees and Board Members must be responsible for: complying not only with the letter but also the spirit of all applicable laws, rules and regulations; observing high ethical standards when conducting business on corporate behalf; asking questions when in doubt about the appropriateness of a situation; reporting known or suspected violations of any applicable laws, rules, regulations, policies and procedures; certifying their familiarity and compliance with the Code, its standards, policies and procedures. The Manual should detail the Code which involves:

a. Corporate codes: ownership, transaction and accounting, payment, corporate opportunities, corporate properties, corporate records, quality, report, finance, audit, employment, tax, corporate citizenship

b. Personality codes: conflict of interest, integrity, respect, accountability, decision making, leadership, equality, harassment, confidentiality, violence, drugs and alcohol, research

c. Business codes: customer, supplier, competitor

d. Regulatory codes: patent and intellectual property, securities laws, compliance with procedure

e. Government and political related codes

The corporate as an organization through these Manuals should be committed to observing the highest standards, continue to review and improve corporate best practices, and monitor developments in the field. Company's website should make the Manuals available for the stakeholders and be updated from time to time as the relevant practices change.

3

CORPORATE REPORT

Report examines corporate performance from the perspective of all of the company's stakeholders: investors, employees, customers and the communities where we live and work. A company that is financially strong is able to give a fair return to its investor; to provide good, well-paying jobs and benefits to its employees; to offer a broad tax base and philanthropy to its communities; to fund pensions and healthcare coverage for its retirees; and to invest in new products and new technology for its customers. In other words, strong financial performance drives a cycle of wealth creation with benefits that go well beyond those who own the stock of a company.

While demonstrating a commitment to operating in the stakeholders' interest and maintaining trust and knowledge which stakeholders and financial regulators need, the performance of corporate and transparency report shares information about the structure, policies, governance and performance of corporate itself. On the business level, corporate should emphasize that—in order to gain confidence—it is fundamental to present in total transparency all sides of the story and to talk about the company's success as much as about the remaining dilemmas and scandals.

ANNUAL REPORT

Annual report describes company's objectives and targets (service and products), achievement (commitments and desired results), learning and growth (continuous personal and corporate improvement to provide the best services and products). The purpose of the Annual Report is to provide the stakeholders with sufficient information to be able to gain an understanding of the corporate as whole, and to assess the results the corporate has achieved with available the resources. The document also reports on the corporate performance in relation the goals and objectives outlined in the Corporate Strategic Plan and actual results achieved in the year in comparison to the strategies set out in the Business Plans. A successful strategic plan acts as a blueprint for future policy and resource decisions. It guides day-to-day organizational choices, through the business planning process, and provides a measurement tool to evaluate progress.

The Annual Report consists of an annual review, and financial report. Annual review gives detailed information on corporate, its strategy, its divisions, and its activities related to stakeholders. The financial report contains the audited consolidated financial statements of the corporate. Annual report is a document which a company presents to its Annual General Meeting for approval by its shareholders. The details provided in the report are of use to investors in gaining an understanding of the company's financial position and future direction.

10-K

10-K is a report similar to the annual report, except that it contains more detailed information about the company's business, finances, and management. It also includes the bylaws of the company, other legal documents, and information about any lawsuits in which the company is involved. There are nine sections in most annual reports (10-K report). Not all reports will have all the sections or the same type and amount of information. These sections include:

a. Chairman of the Board Letter: contents changing conditions, previous objectives met or missed and upcoming objectives, and actions taken or not to be taken

b. Sales and Marketing: covers what the company sells, how, where and when.

c. 10 Year Summary of Financial Figures. Evaluate revenues and profits progress each year

d. Management Discussion and Analysis (MD&A): discussion of significant financial trends over the past few years. While this is not the guts of the financial statements, it does give investors a clearer picture of what the company does. It also points out some key areas where the company has performed well. It should be candid and accurate. If a company gives a decent amount of information in the MD&A, it's likely that management is being upfront and honest. It should raise a red flag if the MD&A portion of the financial statement ignore serious problems that the company has been facing. Withholding important information not only deceives those who read the financial statements, but in extreme cases also makes the company liable for lack of disclosure.

e. CPA Opinion Letter: written by the CPA firm (Certified Public Accountant. An individual who has received state certification to practice accounting), as an opinion on the company's financials. The job of the auditors is to express an opinion on whether the financial statements are reasonably accurate and provide adequate disclosure. By law, every public company with stocks or bonds trading on an exchange must have their annual reports audited by a Certified Public Accountant firm. An auditor's report is meant to scrutinize the company and identify anything that might undermine the integrity of the financial statements. Financial statements that have not been audited are essentially worthless. Un-audited financial statements have a higher probability of being misleading and fraudulent

f. Stock Price History: General trend of price over time.

g. Financial Statements: statements showing revenues, expenses, and income (the difference between revenues and expenses) of an organization over a period of time. It covers balance sheet, income statement, statement of retained earnings, and cash flow statement etc

h. Notes to the Financial Statements: specific comment relates to financial statements, i.e. audit, accounting principle etc.

i. Other information on the company's management, officers, offices, new locations, brands etc.

The 10-K must be filed within 60 days (it used to be 90 days) after the end of the fiscal year.

10-Q

10-Q (Quarterly report) is a comprehensive report of a company's performance that must be submitted quarterly by all public companies. It is a quarterly un-audited financial report. Firms are required to disclose relevant information regarding their financial position. The form must be submitted on time, and the information should be available to all interested parties. 10-Q is a less detailed, more frequently filed version of the 10-K. The 10-Q is due 35 days (it used to be 45 days) after each of the first three fiscal quarters. There is no filing after the fourth quarter because that is when the 10-K is filed.

8-K

8-K is an interim report which announces any material events or corporate changes that occur between 10-Q quarterly reports. 8-K is a report of unscheduled material events or corporate changes that could be of importance to the shareholders or the SEC. 8-K form must be filed by a publicly traded company when it sustains an event that may affect its financial condition or value of its stock. These events could consist of company acquisitions, bankruptcies, merger failures, resignations of a board of director, or alterations in corporate bylaws.

ANNUAL REVIEW

The Annual Review focuses on the progress organization has made towards meeting corporate objectives and highlights the main achievements during a year.

Best Value Review

Best value is a challenging new performance framework that requires Board to publish annual best value performance plans and review all their services. Best value describes the outcome of any acquisition that ensures corporate meet the best of corporate values, i.e. (1). Continuous improvement in the way in which its functions are exercised, have regard to a combination of economy, efficiency and effectiveness. Maximize performance, personalize customer service and deliver continuous improvement in value, quality, creativity and innovation; (2). Be the best possible quality, and value for money; (3). Put people first will seek to provide services which bear comparison with the best; (3). Deliver services to clear standards—covering both cost and quality—by the most effective, economic and efficient means available; (4). Responsive to community needs; subjected to regular community consultation; (5). Accessible to the people they are intended for; (6). Meet the customer's needs in the most effective, economical, and timely manner

Value management needs to provide training and consultancy to help people achieve best value. Value management is an overarching approach; which aims to improve effectiveness, efficiency and economy by team work and decision-making based on value in the round (not just finance). Value management is different; it is action oriented rather than compliance based; and focuses on optimizing customer value. Value management encourages innovative thinking, business problem solving and performance improvement. Best value is achieved by motivating people, developing skills, harnessing synergies and promoting innovation to improve performance, satisfy the customers and add value to the organization. This should be done through developing corporate performance management and monitoring processes; providing guidance and training in performance management; providing an objective assessment of corporate performance; bringing together the corporate best value performance indicators; providing performance information.

The Management must show that they have applied the 4Cs of best value to every review:

a.   Challenging: consider fundamentally why, how and at what level services are being provided, and functions are being undertaken

b.   Comparing their performance with others: actively encourage all departments to compare their performance with internally or externally. These comparisons will take into account the views of service users and potential suppliers. This approach implies not only an improved "baseline" database of performance and management information within corporate, but also an increased willingness to share this information and actively seek innovative comparisons. Departments will be encouraged to seek and investigate good practice, and to work towards adoption of clear and accountable service standards; embracing fair competition as a means of securing efficient and effective services; fully adopt the principle of seeking the best value option for product and service delivery, with no predisposition towards in-house or externalized delivery.

c.   Consulting: actively involve and engage in the review process and, wherever possible, when developing policies and approaches; setting standards and targets and making key decisions which affect relevant stakeholders. All consultation processes must include a mechanism to take into account the views and information obtained, and to provide constructive and open feedback to those taking part with stakeholders

d.   Competing: fully adopt the principle of seeking the best value option for service delivery, with no predisposition towards in-house or externalized delivery. Securing efficient and effective services.

The purpose of this review is to enable stakeholders to see whether best value is being delivered; enable the inspected department to see how well it is doing; enable the Management to see how well its policies are working on the ground; identify failing services where remedial action may be necessary; and identify and disseminate best practice; ensure all services are continuously improving in terms of the '3Es': economy (providing services at the lowest cost); efficiency (maximizing quantity and quality of work for the cost); effectiveness (delivering what is needed); secure the best possible services to meet the expressed needs of citizens and continually improve performance; act in the interests of the whole community by working in partnership; make the corporate a more attractive place to live and attract new investment and employment; provide opportunities for all citizens to develop their full potential without discrimination

A key method of achieving continual improvement in the services delivered by corporate is to providing departments with the support that they need to improve their performance. An important element of this management support i.e. resources used regularly to support corporate and departmental initiatives to meet external and internal demands for the improvement of corporate services; to ensure departments receive the best support possible, a best value review of management support at corporate has taken place.

Audit Review

The internal audit report should assure that internal controls within the company are effective. Monthly review of the existing internal controls associated with accounting functions within the agency is essential. The compliance officers must be independent of the accounting function that is being reviewed. The compliance officers shall prepare an internal control report and submit it to the accounting executive.

The report shall provide the following information:

a. All re-conciliations are up to date;

b. Financial information that is submitted on time;

c. Stock takes of physical assets, inventory and money have been carried out as and when required;

d. Status of unresolved audit issues;

e. Improvements in internal control, such as rotation of duties between staff, those have been implemented or are proposed.

Internal audit is an independent appraisal function that assesses the effectiveness and efficiency of management frameworks at all levels. It provides accounting executive and staff with information on the effectiveness and efficiency of systems, practices and built-in controls adopted to achieve stated objectives. Internal audit assists accounting executive and staff by identifying improvements to operational practices and systems that support the delivery of development assistance and contributes to the departments learning capacity by disseminating best management practices. Internal audits are conducted in areas of significance and risk; to provide the CEO and the Executive Board with credible, timely and objective information to enable them to determine the followings:

a. the effectiveness of program delivery activities and internal operations, including the economic and efficient use of resources;

b. the reliability and integrity of information for decision-making and reporting on accountability;

c. prudence and probity in the use of public funds and the safeguarding of assets;

d. compliance with statutes and regulations;

e. adequacy of follow-up action on key audit findings

During the performance of an audit engagement, the auditor may decide to use the work of a specialist. A specialist is a person with a special skill or knowledge in a particular field other than accounting or auditing. The specialist may be either engaged by the client or by the auditor, or employed by the audit firm or the client. Although the auditor is expected to be knowledgeable about business matters in general, the auditor is not expected to have or obtain the same level of understanding of a subject field as an expert in that particular field. Areas where specialists are utilized in audit engagements include:

a. Valuations of certain types of assets, for example: land and buildings, plant and machinery, works of art, minerals and precious stones.

b. Valuations of businesses and derivatives.

c. Information technology.

d. Determination of quantities or physical condition of assets, for example: minerals stored in stockpiles, and underground mineral and petroleum reserves.

e. Actuarial valuations.

f. Measurement of work completed and to be completed on construction contracts in progress for the purpose of revenue recognition. For example, providing corroborating evidence on the progress and possible obstacles to completing a hydroelectric plant.

g. Legal interpretations of contacts and agreements, statutes, and government and other regulations.

Corporate Governance Review

Corporate governance report deals with the following seven main areas:

a. The role of the shareholders and their interaction with the management of the company: under this area, special priority is afforded to creating greater interaction between the shareholders and the management of the company, who have a joint interest in the company being as competitive as possible and creating as much value as possible. This means that shareholders must have better access to company information and they must be given good opportunity to exercise influence at general meetings.

b. The role of the stakeholders and their importance to the company: another aspect of good corporate governance is that the company maintains good relations with anyone affected by the company's activities. For example, this may be employees, neighbors, customers, or interest organizations. Specific initiatives include drafting policies for relevant areas such as the environment and the social area, as well as ongoing dialogue with stakeholders.

c. Openness and transparency: this means that the company should report and provide information about both financial aspects and supplementary aspects such as the environment, health and safety, ethics, and social responsibility. This information is necessary for dialogue with both shareholders and stakeholders.

d. The tasks and responsibilities of the board: the board of directors should be more systematic in taking responsibility for the company's overall strategic management, financial and managerial control of the company, and ongoing assessments of the work of the board of management. This requires more information sharing and good dialogue between the board of directors and the board of management.

e. The composition of the board: in order that the board of directors can carry out its duties in an appropriate manner, it is also important that the board is composed so that it possesses all the relevant knowledge and competences. Moreover it is important that the board is changed regularly and that regular assessments are carried out of the work of the board, the board of management, and cooperation between the board of directors and the board of management.

f. Remuneration to the directors and the executives: performance-related pay is recommended based on results so that the interests of management better correspond to those of the shareholders.

g. Risk management: the establishment of systems for risk management is stressed as this is a requirement for creating the knowledge necessary to manage the company.

The basic philosophy in all seven areas is that good corporate governance should secure a triple win-win situation for the company's management, shareholders, and other stakeholders. Shareholders gain greater insight and more shareholder value. Stakeholders gain greater insight and their voice is heard by the company. The company earns goodwill from its stakeholders and is better able to raise capital from its shareholders.

Corporate Performance Review

Leading organizations do not stop at the gathering and analysis of performance data; rather, these organizations use performance measurement to drive improvements and successfully translate strategy into action. In other words, they use performance measurement for managing their organizations.

Operational performance management focuses on creating methodical and predictable ways to improve business results, or performance, across organizations. Performance management helps organizations achieve their strategic goals. Rather than discarding the data accessibility previous systems fostered, performance management harnesses it to help ensure that an organization's data works in service to organizational goals to provide information that is actually useful in achieving them. There are 2 (two) kinds of most popular methodology to measure corporate performance, i.e. Key Performance Indicator (KPI) and Balanced Scorecard (BSC).

Key Performance Indicator (KPI)

Once corporate has analyzed its mission, identified all its stakeholders, and defined its goals, it needs a way to measure progress toward those goals. Key Performance Indicators are those measurements. Key Performance Indicators, also known as KPI or Key Success Indicators (KSI), help corporate define and measure progress toward organizational goals. Key Performance Indicators are quantifiable measurements, agreed to beforehand, that reflect the critical success factors of an organization. Whatever Key Performance Indicators are selected, they must reflect the organization's goals, they must be key to its success, and they must be quantifiable (measurable).

Key Performance Indicators usually are long-term considerations. The definition of what they are and how they are measured do not change often. The goals for a particular Key Performance Indicator may change as the organizations goals change, or as it get closer to achieving a goal. Key Performance Indicators reflect the organizational goals. Key Performance Indicators must be quantifiable. If a Key Performance Indicator is going to be of any value, there must be a way to accurately define and measure it. Principle on the definition of Performance Indicators, i.e. develop relevant, robust and understandable performance indicators to cover all critical and user-priority aspects of the service, using corporate guidance where available; commit to providing performance and financial; develop service standards, and performance measures linked to these standards; report performance as regularly, transparently and openly as required, requested or as is practical; set challenging targets for performance; actively seek corporate of similar services and functions with which to compare performance, taking a cost-benefit approach to assessing the level of comparison to be undertaken

Balanced Scorecard (BSC)

Doing the right things and doing things right is a balancing act, and requires the development of good business strategies and efficient operations to deliver the products and services required to implement the strategies. Competitive pressures on private businesses, and performance improvement and reform pressures on public sector organizations; mandate that organizations continually worry about executing good strategy well. At the same time, they worry about running business operations efficiently. One framework that helps achieve the required balance between strategy and operations is the Balanced Scorecard.

The Balanced Scorecard is a performance management system that can be used in any size organization to align vision and mission with customer requirements and day-to-day work, manage and evaluate business strategy, monitor operation efficiency improvements, build organization capacity, and communicate progress to all employees. The scorecard allows organization to measure financial and customer results, operations, and organization capacity.

Balanced Scorecard systems give organization the ability to view three different dimensions of organizational performance: results (financial and customer), operations, and capacity. The figure also shows the components of a fully developed scorecard system: business foundations (including vision, mission, and values); plans (including communications, implementation, automation, and evaluation plans, to build employee buy-in and communicate results); business strategies and strategic maps (to chart the course and define the logical decomposition of strategies into activities that people work on each day); performance measures, to track actual performance against expectations; new initiatives (to test strategic assumptions); budgets (including the resources needed for new initiatives and current operations); business and support unit scorecards (to translate the corporate vision into actionable activities for departments and offices); and leadership and individual development (to ensure that employee knowledge, skills and abilities are enhanced to meet future job requirements and competition).

A Balanced Scorecard system provides a basis for executing good strategy well and managing change successfully. Building a Balanced Scorecard performance system using the framework described here will cause people to think differently (more strategic) about their organization and their work. For many, this is a refreshing change to "strategic planning as usual". But it will also bring change in the way things are done, as new policies and procedures are developed and implemented. For some, these changes can be troubling. The realization is that the Balanced Scorecard journey involves changing hearts and minds at least as much as it involves measuring performance.

The BSC presents a conceptual framework for translating an organization's vision into a set of performance indicators distributed among four perspectives:

a. Financial: Private sector financial objectives generally represent clear long-range targets for profit-seeking organizations, operating in a purely commercial environment. Financial considerations for public organizations have an enabling or a constraining role, but will rarely be the primary objective for business systems. Success for public organizations should be measured by how effectively and efficiently they meet the needs of their constituencies.

b. Customer: This perspective captures the ability of the organization to provide quality goods and services, the effectiveness of their delivery, and overall customer service and satisfaction. In general, public organizations have a different, perhaps greater, stewardship/fiduciary responsibility and focus than do private sector entities.

c. Internal Business Processes: This perspective focuses on the internal business results that lead to financial success and satisfied customers. To meet organizational objectives and customers' expectations, organizations must identify the key business processes at which they must excel. Key processes are monitored to ensure that outcomes will be satisfactory. Internal business processes are the mechanisms through which performance expectations are achieved.

d. Learning and Growth: This perspective looks at the ability of employees, the quality of information systems, and the effects of organizational alignment in supporting accomplishment of organizational goals. Processes will only succeed if adequately skilled and motivated employees, supplied with accurate and timely information, are driving them. In order to meet changing requirements and customer expectations, employees may be asked to take on dramatically new responsibilities, and may require skills, capabilities, technologies, and organizational designs that were not available before.

Corporate Social Accountability Review

Corporate governance, transparency and accountability remain the bedrock upon which corporate may ongoing pursuit of broad-based business excellence lies. While short-term economic performance must be balanced with social accountability commitments, the global environment today demands that corporate considers a longer-term horizon for overall sustainable development—taking into consideration the needs of all stakeholders. This review provides an outline of the approach to corporate accountability, covering systems and processes and major economic, social and environmental impacts. The operational management should be based on a solid foundation of core values, embed in its understanding of legal and regulatory requirements, stakeholder and societal expectations and current market practices. Corporate needs to utilize the resources to progress its activities, and co-opts management and technical specialist input to align the accountability agenda with those of the various strategic business functions and to ensure full representation and participation of all the business units. Corporate social accountability review will disclose following information:

a. Economic impacts: procure goods and services, that sustaining jobs in the local community.

b. Environmental impacts: measure against the outputs, using less water and energy, and producing less waste and pollutant; extend the environmental management systems and expand the reporting

c. Social impacts: assess on critical human resource management issues, engage with local communities, maintain relations with government and their various regulatory agencies, strictly enforce corporate ethical conduct policies

Reporting on corporate social responsibility is largely a voluntary effort. As such, some senior corporate managers fail to see the benefit of providing data on issues such as diversity, environment, workplace practices, product performance, and corporate governance. The companies should offer lots of information could open themselves up to criticism for the unfavorable data they provide, while those hiding in the weeds escape detection. In the social responsibility report the company must present good news as well as bad; last year's accomplishments as well as pending targets and—more importantly—the report serves to project the company's future and thereby re-affirm its commitment as a tool of communication. Corporate may also emphasize the importance of a transparent and socially responsible business; and postulate transparency as a tool to bolster credibility with the objective to gain stakeholder confidence.

FINANCIAL REPORT

A financial report meant to accurately reflect corporate financial condition. Various types include:

a. Balance sheet—a financial statement comprising a listing of the assets, liabilities and owner's equity of a business as of a particular date. Under the accounting equation, assets are always equal to (and thus in balance with) liabilities and owner's equity; hence, the term 'balance sheet.' The balance sheet is a snapshot of the company's financial standing at an instant in time. The balance sheet shows the company's financial position, what it owns (assets) and what it owes (liabilities and net worth). The "bottom line" of a balance sheet must always balance (i.e. assets = liabilities + net worth). The individual elements of a balance sheet change from day to day and reflect the activities of the company. Analyzing how the balance sheet changes over time will reveal important information about the company's business trends. In this subject we'll discover how you can monitor your ability to collect revenues, how well you manage your inventory, and even assess your ability to satisfy creditors and stockholders. Liabilities and net worth on the balance sheet represent the company's sources of funds. Liabilities and net worth are composed of creditors and investors who have provided cash or its equivalent to the company in the past. As a source of funds, they enable the company to continue in business or expand operations. If creditors and investors are unhappy and distrustful, the company's chances of survival are limited. Assets, on the other hand, represent the company's use of funds. The company uses cash or other funds provided by the creditor/investor to acquire assets. Assets include all the things of value that are owned or due to the business. Liabilities represent a company's obligations to creditors while net worth represents the owner's investment in the company. In reality, both creditors and owners are "investors" in the company with the only difference being the degree of nervousness and the timeframe in which they expect repayment.

b. Statement of cash flow—a financial statement that reports net cash provided or used as a result of a company's operating, investing, and financing activities and the net effect of those cash flows on cash and cash equivalents for a given period in a manner that reconciles beginning and ending cash and cash equivalents. Cash flow statements report a company's inflows and outflows of cash. This is important because a company needs to have enough cash on hand to pay its expenses and purchase assets. While an income statement can tell whether a company made a profit, a cash flow statement can tell whether the company generated cash. A cash flow statement shows changes over time rather than absolute dollar amounts at a point in time. It uses and reorders the information from a company's balance sheet and income statement. The bottom line of the cash flow statement shows the net increase or decrease in cash for the period. Generally, cash flow statements are divided into three main parts. Each part reviews the cash flow from one of three types of activities: (1) operating activities; (2) investing activities; and (3) financing activities.

c. Statement of income—a financial statement whose purpose is to show the results of a company's operations, i.e., whether or not the business has earned a profit for a specific period of time. The statement of income lists the various revenue and expenses of the business along with related net income. An income statement also shows the costs and expenses associated with earning that revenue. The literal "bottom line" of the statement usually shows the company's net earnings or losses. This tells how much the company earned or lost over the period. Income statements also report earnings per share (or "EPS"). This calculation tells how much money shareholders would receive if the company decided to distribute all of the net earnings for the period. (Companies almost never distribute all of their earnings. Usually they reinvest them in the business).

d. Statement of retained earnings—a financial statement that illustrates the change in equity resulting from earnings or losses and dividends declared. The statement of retained earnings is often combined with the income statement or incorporated into the statement of shareholder's equity, show how net income is derived, calculate earnings per share, and reconcile changes in retained earnings. Retained earnings or retained profits are profits that have not been paid to a company's shareholders as dividends. The decision of whether a firm should retain profits or disburse them as dividends depends on several factors including: the corporate judgment of its own investment opportunities relative to those available in the market and any difference in tax treatment of dividends paid now and capital gains expected to result from investing retained earnings. It is also called plow back, the act of putting earnings from sales back into the business operation. Unrestricted earnings should be retained only where there is a reasonable prospect. This will happen only if the capital retained produces incremental earnings equal to, or above, those generally available to investors.

e. Statement of shareholders' equity—a financial statement that illustrates the change in the various components of shareholder's equity for a given period, including change in the capital stock and retained earnings accounts. Shareholders' equity is the amount owners invested in the company's stock plus or minus the company's earnings or losses since inception. Sometimes companies distribute earnings, instead of retaining them. These distributions are called dividends. Included are: shares authorized and outstanding; additional paid-in capital; retained earnings; foreign currency translation effects; treasury stock. Statement of retained earnings, also known as Statement of owners' equity, explains the changes in company's retained earnings over the reporting period

f. Financial statements can be used as a roadmap on the business journey to economic success. Using numbers as navigation aids can steer reader in the right direction and help avoid costly breakdowns. Most business owners don't realize that financial statements have a value that goes far beyond their use to prepare tax returns or loan applications. Financial statements are required by law and must include a balance sheet, an income statement, cash flow statement, an auditor's report, and a relatively detailed description of the company's operations and prospects for the upcoming year. Financial statements should: be candid and accurate; involve discussion significant financial trends over past couple years; give clear comments; mention potential risks or uncertainties moving forward. How people analyze the financial statements really depends on their interest in the company. Management, creditors/lenders, partners and investors all use financial statements, buy each group is interested in different things. For example, an investor might assess profitability, growth, stability and the rate of dividends. On the other hand, a creditor is much more interested in the amount of debt that a company currently has and whether it has the ability to make repayments. Fundamental analysis is about using real data to evaluate a stock's value. The method uses revenues, earnings, future growth, return on equity, profit margins and other data to determine a company's underlying value and potential for future growth. Financial statement analysis is the biggest part of fundamental analysis. Also known as quantitative analysis, it involves looking at historical performance data to estimate the future performance. Quantitative analysis will focus on information that can be found on revenue, expenses, assets, liabilities, and all the other financial aspects of the company; and look at this information to gain insight on a company's future performance.

An annual report provides clearest window into the management, results and potential of a company. In fact the annual report can play a diverse range of roles in a company's messaging mix. The annual report can affirm communication to stakeholders; synthesize messages into memorable and re-purpose able sound bites or memes; put dimensionally company's potential relative to its performance; reinforce and amplify brand positioning or characteristics, be boldly used to affect market valuation; lead all of corporate strategy and message planning efforts.

4

CORPORATE PERFORMANCE MANAGEMENT

Focus on the processes and results will ensure effective and efficient service delivery and performance management. It is important that organization can review its performance, so that it knows on track or not, and in the long term, makes improvements. Corporate Performance Management helps organization formulate strategies for profitable growth, align strategies with operational plans, actively monitor day-to-day operations Performance management involves strategic management, corporate governance, performance measurement, process drivers, problem identification, value creation, goal alignment.

There were certain attributes which set apart successful performance measurement and management systems, including:

a. A conceptual framework is needed for the performance measurement and management system. Every organization, regardless of type, needs a clear and cohesive performance measurement framework that is understood by all levels of the organization and that supports objectives and the collection of results.

b. Effective internal and external communications are the keys to successful performance measurement. Effective communication with employees, process owners, customers, and stakeholders is vital to the successful development and deployment of performance measurement and management systems.

c. Accountability for results must be clearly assigned and well-understood. High-performance organizations clearly identify what it takes to determine success and make sure that all managers and employees understand what they are responsible for in achieving organizational goals.

d. Performance measurement systems must provide intelligence for decision makers, not just compile data. Performance measures should be limited to those that relate to strategic organizational goals and objectives, and that provide timely, relevant, and concise information for use by decision makers—at all levels—to assess progress toward achieving predetermined goals. These measures should produce information on the efficiency with which resources are transformed into goods and services, on how well results compare to a program's intended purpose, and on the effectiveness of organizational activities and operations in terms of their specific contribution to program objectives.

e. Compensations, rewards, and recognition should be linked to performance measurements. Performance evaluations and rewards need to be tied to specific measures of success, by linking financial and non financial incentives directly to performance. Such a linkage sends a clear and unambiguous message to the organization as to what's important. Performance measurement systems should be positive, not punitive. The most successful performance measurement systems are not "gotcha" systems, but learning systems that help the organization identify what works—and what does not—so as to continue with and improve on what is working and repair or replace what is not working.

f. Results and progress toward program commitments should be openly shared with employees, customers, and stakeholders. Performance measurement system information should be openly and widely shared with an organization's employees, customers, stakeholders, vendors, and suppliers.

CORPORATE MANIFESTO MANAGEMENT

Executives have the management prerogative to establish practices and set goals, and lead employees to share attitudes and values. The clearest indication of a strong corporate culture is that employees are aware of it. Involvement into corporate manifesto can be achieved by:

a.   Balanced Approach. Everyone has a hierarchy of things that are important to them, which one is prior to other. Corporate should believe it's a good business to help employees find and live out their own balance. The Management doesn't want employee to sacrifice their life outside of work for corporate. The organization needs to support them as a whole person. Corporate should not assume that employees will work long hours. It does happen, but when it does there should be very quick follow-up to recognize and honor the extra effort.

b.   Tooling and Training. People must never complain that they don't have the tools to do the job. Corporate should provide tool needed by employees to work easily and satisfactorily. The right tools mean less frustration and better career development, leading to greater job satisfaction and higher retention rates. A commitment to ongoing training is important. Corporate training program is to be done similarly aggressive. In-house classes are to be held weekly at least and include such business-oriented topics as competitors' offerings and product improvements.

c.   Motivate. Money alone doesn't make people get motivated. The employees should differentiate the organization from others. The executives should attract employees by caring work environment and top-quality coworkers.

Corporate Culture, Values, Vision, Mission, and Strategy

The culture of an organization defines what it is, what it wants to be and the way it is going to succeed. The culture of an organization can be changed to take account of new elements. A changed culture will also improve the image of the organization, its goals and its staff to stakeholders and the public. Improved culture can be achieved in a number of ways such as: introducing new products or operating methods, coaching new and existing staff, improving service provision, re-branding and improved communications. A change of culture may also be needed when working in a joint venture, or following the acquisition of other organizations. Understanding the corporate Culture of other organizations working methods can reduce problems between the partners, and provide methods of resolving them when they occur, thus helping to ensure success.

Corporate culture starts when the organization begins and develops as it grows. Culture reflects the values, ethics, beliefs, personality and traits of the company's founders, management and employees. Employees who feel comfortable and compatible with the company culture will stay; those who don't will leave or will not perform as well as they can.

Organizational values often include such traditional virtues as trust, loyalty and commitment, honesty and respect for one another, and avoiding conflicts of interest. Values may also include newer elements such as innovation, teamwork, customer focus and continuous improvement. Ethics codes generally deal with corporate values and guiding principles, and codes of conduct generally deal with actual behavior that is favored or prohibited. The focus of a code is to do business with integrity or just sets out some prohibitions.

In more specific, corporate values includes: customer satisfaction (anticipate and understand customers' needs, develop solutions and services that our customers need, continuously introduce value-added services, promptly respond to customer queries, continuously, follow-up on customer perceptions, never compromise and always deliver agreed service levels, external communications to shareholders); administrative excellence (properly document all policies, processes and procedures, properly document each transaction, constantly audit compliance to administrative excellence, and auditable documents); accountability (accountable and think through the consequences of our actions, truth in advertising, environmental protection); performance management (benchmark corporate behavior and processes against the best in class practices for all core processes, welcome being measured by all key constituencies, leadership by example); innovation (continuously measure process outputs, continuously improve business processes, participate in the implementation of new initiatives concerning process and technology); transparency and openness (encourage expression of opinions, encourage feedback on performance at all levels including leadership, give employees access to all information that they need to perform their tasks effectively, the balance between transparency and openness on the one hand and confidentiality on the other); value people (ensure that each member has the competence to perform his or her job, provide the environment and opportunity for growth and learning, treat people fairly and encourage diversity and expression of thought, provide fair compensation and welfare, provide a healthy, safe and enjoyable working environment, encourage occupational health and safety practices); teamwork (encourage the creation of case or project teams, encourage a multi-disciplinary approach to problem solving, encourage team leadership based on competencies rather than position, encourage open communication and coordination across functional boundaries, consultative decision making and networking); and ethical practices (follow and practice the ethical code of conduct, behave towards the customers, suppliers, partners and colleagues as we would like them to behave towards us, responsible business practice (prohibitions on bribery, gifts, nepotism, self-dealing)).

For the vast majority of companies, having well-defined visions and mission statements changes nothing. The exercise of crafting them is a complete waste of time and talent if visions and mission statements are used for nothing but being published in the annual report and displayed in a reception area. One of the reasons, for the failure of missions and visions to achieve the desired objective, is the naiveté of most company managers and executives. Nothing happens by magic. Executive should be able to energize employees to work towards corporate objectives, visions and missions should be more than a sign on the wall. Executives should live it, be seen living it, and constantly communicate it to their employees.

Vision

Vision is a short, succinct, and inspiring statement of what the organization intends to become and to achieve at some point in the future, often stated in competitive terms. Vision refers to the category of intentions that are broad, all-intrusive and forward-thinking. It is the image that a business must have of its goals before it sets out to reach them. It describes aspirations for the future, without specifying the means that will be used to achieve those desired ends.

The corporate success depends on the vision articulated by the Chief Executive or the top management. For a vision to have any impact of the employees of an organization it has to be conveyed in a dramatic and enduring way. The most effective visions are those that inspire, usually asking employees for the best, the most or the greatest. Make sure employees keep stretch in corporate vision, communicate it constantly, and keep linking the events of today to the vision. To choose a direction, an executive must have developed a mental image of the possible and desirable future state of the organization. This image, which is called a vision, may be as vague as a dream or as precise as a goal or a mission statement.

Mission Statement

A mission statement is an organization's vision translated into written form. It makes concrete the Management view of the direction and purpose of the organization. It is a vital element in any attempt to motivate employees and to give them a sense of priorities. A mission statement should be a short and concise statement of goals and priorities. In turn, goals are specific objectives that relate to specific time periods and are stated in terms of facts. The primary goal of any business is to increase stakeholder value. The most important stakeholders are shareholders who own the business, employees who work for the business and customers who purchase products and/or services from the business.

Setting Goals and Objectives

The major outcome of strategic road-mapping and strategic planning, after gathering all necessary information, is the setting of goals for the organization based on its vision and mission statement. A goal is a long-range aim for a specific period. It must be specific and realistic. Long-range goals set through strategic planning are translated into activities that will ensure reaching the goal through operational planning. Before setting corporate goals, be clear about individual goals; make sure the goals set are the true goals; convert the relevant personal goals into corporate goals; separate the corporate goals into short term and long term; incorporate the corporate goals into the action plan. Setting objectives involves a continuous process of research and decision-making. Knowledge the member of the unit is a vital starting point in setting objectives.

Strategic planning takes place at the highest levels; executives are involved with operational planning. The first step in operational planning is defining objectives—the result expected by the end of the budget (or other designated) cycle. The objectives must: be focused on a result, not an activity, be consistent, be specific, be measurable, be related to time, and be attainable

Corporate Strategy

Strategy is a very broad term which commonly describes any thinking that looks at the bigger picture. Successful companies are those that focus their efforts strategically. To meet and exceed customer satisfaction, the business team needs to follow an overall organizational strategy. A successful strategy adds value for the targeted customers over the long run by consistently meeting their needs better than the competition does. Strategy is the way in which a company orients itself towards the market in which it operates and towards the other companies in the marketplace against which it competes. It is a plan an organization formulates to gain a sustainable advantage over the competition.

Corporate strategy is concerned with identifying the future direction of the organization. A realistic and engaging vision should be provided to stakeholders. The strategy should also provide a number of goals and objectives for the organization, as well as indicating how they should be achieved. Once the strategy has been decided, it must be made available to stakeholders. This should be promoted, and advertised, by a variety of means, including briefings, documents and other communications methods. For long term strategies, the vision must be managed appropriately. This will ensure the vision is understood, as well as highlighting the interim goals, tasks and objectives required to achieve the vision. Corporate strategy involves:

a. Declaration: codification of the organization's basic values via a "Vision, Mission & Values" statement, a code of conduct or any document with equal significance. Such documents must be relevant and specific with regard to the organization, as well as fundamental with regard to its values. These documents define the central values of an organization in terms of its most important stakeholders

b. Strategic orientation: embed into the organization's specific business strategy. This allows for the necessity that relevance of the company and efficiency in applying it can only be ensured by reflecting the organization's present identity and its preferred development. The declaration of basic values has to meet specific factors and the character of the company (strategy, structure, culture). Projects for corporate development (strategy development, re-engineering, lean management etc.) have to reflect the declaration of basic values, guidelines, policies and procedures

c. Implementation: the declaration of basic values is implemented by internal and external communication, development of appropriate guidelines, policies and procedures, and training on all involved organizational levels. These measures are used to realize the declaration of basic values in specific business units or regions, and successively have to result in operative documents. There, central criteria of seriousness are the integrative consistency and an approach of guidelines, policies and procedures that comprises all organizational processes. It includes: internal and external communication of the declaration of basic values, communication of the guidelines to business partners, operational breakdown of the declaration of basic values in guidelines (for corporate areas or units) and realization of the guidelines in policies and procedures (for particular fields of activities), training of relevant employees, esp. in morally sensitive units and functions (e.g. sales, purchasing, internal auditing), information and consulting of employees and managers in conflict situations

d. Role model and autonomy: individual commitment and setting a good example on all management levels are a prerequisite for the success of the corporate. This also applies for qualifying and backing up employees' competency to make autonomous decisions in situations (of ethical conflict) where there are no explicit guidelines and procedures in the corporate. It takes into account the fact that it is impossible to issue precise policies and procedures for every thinkable situation in the daily business of an organization. It needs: competence and responsibility at top-management level, executives and permanent commitment for the aims of the corporate and their realization, specific trainings with regard to employees' particular fields of action

e. Resources: depending on the size of the organization and the extent and complexity of the corporate, resources (financial and human) are required for its realization. For the implementation period companies and groups of companies have to appoint a qualified person in charge who takes the operative responsibility

f. Communication: internal and external communication of the organization's values, guidelines, policies and procedures, along with evaluation, is the crucial medium of credible self-commitment by the corporate. It will include: publication in the company, talk with superior, group meetings, instruction of new employees, CD-ROM, house journal, intranet/internet communication to business partners, press reports, discussions with external stakeholders, etc.

g. Motivation: according to guidelines, policies and procedures, incentive structures are to be established that honor or promote exemplary acting in compliance with the values as well as sanction actions infringing the corporate and social values. It may need: inclusion of the corporate into employment contracts and/or job instructions and/or assessment systems for management and employees, measures to sanction actions that are illegal and infringe the values

h. Evaluation: procedures to evaluate the corporate aim at documenting and verifying the process and at sustaining its realization; self-assessment here is the fundamental concept.

i. Documentation: the documentation of the corporate and of its evaluation is used to retrace its implementation and realization. It is to be designed according to the organizational structure and the documentation systems that are already employed, and has to suffice legal requirements as for form and storage. It requires informative and comprehensive documentation about the corporate and all transactions that concern the corporate as well as about the procedure and results of its evaluation must be available.

j. Management Review: the executive board of an organization has the duty to carry out regular assessments of the corporate, with regard to its effectiveness and efficiency. The assessment serves to ensure the quality of the corporate and its adaptability to changing environmental conditions.

COMMUNICATION MANAGEMENT

Communication is a process that involves both the sender of the message and the receiver. This process leaves room for error, with messages often misinterpreted by one or more of the parties involved. This causes unnecessary confusion and counter productivity. In fact, a message is successful only when both the sender and the receiver perceive it in the same way. Communication principle involves:

a. Transformational approach: facilitates empowering opportunities for individuals to contribute to the shared values, mission and objectives

b. Consultative and open: supports a transparent approach and stakeholder engagement with the matter

c. Credibility: a credible communication approach engenders the community towards a belief that the end goal is achievable

d. To involve not just inform: supports a transformational approach and stakeholder engagement with the matter

e. Visible management support: an active management commitment gives credibility to communication. Support from management must be visible

f. Face-to-face communication: facilitates audience involvement and feedback

g. Avoid information 'overload': too much information leads to confusion and irritation. Accurate and timely information is essential.

h. Consistent messages: consistency enhances the professionalism and credibility of the project

i. Repeat messages and vary mechanisms: the more ways a message can be communicated, the more likely it is to be internalized. Using different mechanisms ensures repetition without individuals 'switching off' and has more chance to reach a wider stakeholder.

j. Respond to information demand (encourage team to seek the kind of information stakeholders need rather than management pushing it at them): ensures engagement with the change

k. Tailor communication to stakeholder needs: make information 'real' to the audience. The stakeholder is more likely to listen if the information is pertinent to their current frame of reference.

l. Central co-ordination: ensures consistent approach

m. Manage expectations: encourages audience to believe in what you to tell them. Need to be realistic not overly optimistic.

n. Listen and act on feedback: encourages support in the approach by being responsive to the needs of the audience; ensures approach meets changing stakeholder needs.

Good communications are essential to modern business. Organizations need to ensure that the most appropriate communications are used. They also need to ensure that the messages they give and receive are clearly understood by everybody. There are complex issues relating to the use of communications, together with the tools and systems used to convey the messages. These include the development of communications strategies and the integration of the tools and associated processes. It is essential that the most appropriate tools are available when communicating. These need to be taken into account when developing or improving the image provided to stakeholders. Organizations also need staffs, who understand the benefits of being able to communicate effectively. The themes, logos and publicity used for the product and service can communicate a lot about the organization its aspirations and its working practices. The selection of appropriate themes for product/service or organizations can be difficult. These themes should be capable of being used across the different types of media such as, web sites, press, video, brochures and forms.

Communication management needs: assessment of publicity techniques; development of communications plans; promotion of integrated themes for different product/service; consultancy relating to supporting publicity campaigns and afterwards; identifying and implementing improved communications facilities; review and health checks for communications and procedures; facilitating meetings and workshops; preparation for public relations & public speaking; preparing and communicating goals and objectives; provision of staff development, coaching and mentoring to staff.

MARKETING MANAGEMENT

Marketing activities and strategies result in making products available that satisfy customers while making profits for the companies that offer those products. It produces a "win-win" because: customers have a product that meets their needs, and healthy profits are achieved for the company. These profits allow the company to continue to do business in order to meet the needs of future customers. A focus on what the customer wants is essential to successful marketing efforts. This customer-orientation must also be balanced with the company's objective of maintaining a profitable volume of sales in order for the company to continue to do business. Marketing is a creative, ever-changing orchestration of all the activities needed to accomplish both of these objectives. Marketing is the process of planning and executing the conception, pricing, promotion and distribution of ideas, goods, and services to create exchanges that satisfy individual and organizational objectives. Marketing activities are numerous and varied because they basically include everything needed to get a product off the drawing board and into the hands of the customer. The broad field of marketing includes activities such as designing the product so it will be desirable to customers (using tools such as marketing research and pricing; promoting the product so people will know about it (using tools such as public relations, advertising, marketing communications; and exchanging it with the customer (through sales and distribution). It is important to note that the field of marketing includes sales, but it also includes many functions besides sales. Many people mistakenly think that marketing and sales are the same. These are the fundamentals of a true marketing mindset: producing what the customer wants should be the focus of business operations and planning; creating profitable sales volume, not just sales volume, is a necessary goal; coordinating between marketing activities and all other functions within a business that affect marketing efforts. Marketing activities is to consider the big picture of how they fit in with the other business functions involves: marketing efforts—what products (goods, services or ideas) are to be offered; to whom (the target market), and how (how to inform potential customers of the offering, how to make the transaction, etc); production efforts (create product); accounting-finance (capital and operating funds are managed and tracked); human resources (employees and the policies concerning them).

Marketing management is the practical application of marketing techniques. It is the analysis, planning, implementation, and control of programs designed to create, build, and maintain mutually beneficial exchanges with target markets. The marketing executives have the task of influencing the level, timing, and composition of demand in way that will achieve organizational objectives. Marketing Management involves: understanding the economic structure of corporate, identify segments within the market, identifying the target market, do marketing research to develop profiles (demographic, psychographic, and behavioral) of the core customers; understand the competitors and their products; develop new products; establish environmental scanning mechanisms to detect opportunities and threats; understand the company's strengths and weaknesses; audit the customers' experience of the brand in full; develop marketing strategies for each of the products using the marketing mix variables of price, product, distribution, and promotion; create a sustainable competitive advantage; understand where corporate wants the brands to be in the future, and write marketing plans on a regular basis to help staffs get there; setup feedback systems (
management information system) to help staffs monitor and adjust the process

Marketing management should: be focus on marketing strategies (i.e. market share/dominance, penetration & product advantage, innovation, growth, aggressiveness, offensive/defensive); build brands through a coordinated integrated marketing strategy that involves all points of contact between the company and the public; consider customer's lifetime value (i.e. acquisition cost, churn rate, discount rate, retention rate, time period); consider the whole value chain is as the unit of analysis, in order to meeting the end customers' needs; organize sales by customer segment; use all relevant market variables, especially behavioral variables like usage rate, loyalty, or benefit; emphasis on keeping existing customers; measure the marketing performance by financial, strategic, and marketing metrics; ensure stakeholders satisfaction; encourage everyone in the company does some marketing; optimize cross functional teams; speed up product development and implementation.

The structure of a market in terms of its suppliers is important when determining market strategy. To enter a market dominated by one or a few important suppliers could only be relevant if it is considered that the existing suppliers are inefficient and/or complacent, i.e.:

a.   If there is one of a few important suppliers, market share is more likely to be gained on service and quality or acquisition policies. To attempt to take market share by price, could lead to a price war.

b.   If a market consists of a few suppliers with a significant proportion of the market and then many other players, market share can be increased by increased sales and marketing activity (e.g. increased advertising and additional salespersons) and/or acquisition policies.

c.   If a market has many suppliers, none of whom are dominant, then market share can be increased by applying any combination of the policies mentioned previously. In this case the policies chosen should be aimed at presenting an image to the market that the directors feel best represents the company's aims and objectives.

Assessing competitors and rating their size, is an alternative method of estimating the total market. Information about competitors, can be obtained from yellow pages (identifies competitors); credit agencies; the local chamber of commerce; and legal (but not very ethical) direct approaches, without disclosing the true identity.

Market Goals, Targets and Objectives

Before setting business goals, the executive should be clear about personal goals; make sure the goals set are the true goals; convert the relevant personal goals into business goals; separate the business goals into short term and long term; incorporate the business goals into the marketing plan.

Market Policy Statements

The Policy Statement lists the policies that are considered necessary to achieve the marketing objectives. It states the basic policies and targets for the planning period, without evaluating these. The statements in the policy document must be realistic and have substance justifying their inclusion, covering such areas as: customer service objectives; the introduction of new products; rationalization of the product range; market share increase or decrease; pricing policy and anticipated real changes in prices; changes in product specifications

Market Research

Market research is an essential pre-requisite to creating a marketing plan. Without research the marketing plan cannot be compiled on a realistic and objective basis. Market research should be an ongoing, routine function of collecting information relating to; the market; the needs of the customer; the customer's perception of the company; its competitors and their activities. Market research can determine: the estimated market size and the company's market share objective; the growth factor; customers—why they specifically come to the company. Market characteristics and structure are important in determining a marketing plan. A market can be immature or mature. An immature market is where the product or service has not yet supplied the potential market. Market growth therefore consists of two factors, supplying the product or service to the "new" customer and replacing the product or of the "old" customer. An immature market exists, when: political and social changes create a new market; the wealth of the population of a market is increasing; technology provides new products; technology provides a superior replacement product; the price of the product is reduced and brought within the buying power of a greater proportion of the population. A mature market is a market where the potential market has been virtually fully supplied. Activity in the market is therefore largely confined to replacing the product or service at the end of its useful life. It will grow in accordance with population variations (both numbers and wealth), providing no alternative products or new competitive elements (e.g. imports) are introduced into the market. Marketing staffs need to compile the analysis of competitors on the following lines: list all important competitors in the market; analyze their strengths and weaknesses; list their products; rate their pricing structures; make assessment of their promotional activity; make an assessment of their distribution methods.

Compiling the Market Plans

Marketing executives should estimate the sales for the year as follows: estimate the frequency/number of each type of product/activity that will occur in the year; if the business is seasonal, split the year into seasons and estimate the frequency/number of each type of product/activity for each season; value each of the activities to determine the sales for the year; if the estimated sales for the year show an increase larger than the estimated market growth, write up the action plans which cause the change; If the estimated sales for the year fail to meet objectives, create action plans to generate the additional sales; if credible action plans, which justify the changes, have not been, or cannot be compiled, modify the marketing plan accordingly.

Market plan will help achieving a realistic goal. Consequently, it brings together all the corporate assets—plant, management, technology, finance, staff—to reach the goals. It may need to cutting administration costs, training staff, evaluating sales executive, setting up sales seminars for agents, correcting any ill-defined or wordy mission statements or overall strategic plans. Make the market plan a nuts-and-bolts action plan to achieve goals; bind and strong.

Product Management

Product Management is responsible for defining the products, pricing, promotion, and distribution. It deals with: products that are produced and sold; kind of new product to be added in the market; existing products that will be discontinued; time that will be needed for a product to penetrate the market; number of products to have in the product line; balancing a product portfolio; strategy to introduce a product to the market; apply product differentiation strategy; define the best product positioning; brand name to be used; consideration to apply individual branding (all a company's products are given different brand names) or family branding (one brand name is used for several related products); consideration to use product bundling or product lining; logo to be used; product life cycle considerations; planned obsolescence considerations. Product Management may also represent an organization's approach to the process of managing and marketing its products and services as smaller businesses inside the larger enterprise, supported by multi-function product teams (led by product executives) and a standard product development process.

Product executives are responsible for the marketing and development of products, includes: strategic (positioning a product, assessing the competition and thinking about the future); tactical (developing appropriate promotional campaigns, talking to reps about what customers want and think and doing the day-to-day sales tracking that's required for any major product category). Product management professionals are excited about their ability to manage and strengthen brands. They are at the vortex of company life because their decisions directly affect the success of a business. Product management as a discipline is about what the product should be. Product executives are advocates for the customer's needs and desires. A large product might have numerous product managers working towards its success at a variety of levels, all the way from the junior product manager writing specifications about single feature sets to a product strategy director who has overall responsibility to executive management for the product direction. The activities of product executives include the following: defining and planning product lines and product enhancements; managing product contracts and sales; setting strategic direction based on customer needs and business goals; interpreting strategic goals into operational tasks; making proposals to senior management regarding implications of proposed plans; serving as a representative to internal and external clients; taking the lead in establishing tactical plans and objectives; developing and implementing administrative and operational matters ensuring achievement of objectives; evaluating risks and trade-offs; proposing contingency plans; analyzing business processes and creating applications to improve or support those processes; branding; working with graphic designers to create look and feel; defining navigational flow and user experience; defining feature sets and scooping releases

Brand Management

Establishing a successful brand involves more than having a catchy brand name, it requires hard work and a good strategy. The payoff of a company's efforts may be a strong customer base that is not easily enticed by competitor's products.

Branding is about "delivering on a promise." That promise must be (1). Relevant: The brand has to mean something to stakeholders, especially today because consumers and employees are skeptical about brands; (2). Consistent and clearly focused: Strategies for delivering on a brand promise may change, but the promise must remain the same; (3). Defensible: The brand must stand up to certain measurable criteria; (4). Built from the inside out: An effective brand promise extends from the entire organization because everyone understands what the brand is. (5). Employees are aligned on different levels—from what that overall vision is to the management team understanding its strategy, structure and execution.

Building a strong brand pays off in a number of ways (1). Clarity of purpose: Employees will know where the company is going and what it represents. This kind of clarity brings executives unity and trust, which ultimately translate into high productivity, performance and quality; (2). Competitive differentiation: Clearly standing out is an important factor at the point of sale or consideration; (3). Loyalty: A strong brand creates "apostles" who keep coming back. These customers believe that the brand expresses them; (4). Premium price: Strong brands often survive longer and command higher prices, even in economic downturns.

Brand management is the application of marketing techniques to a specific product, product line, or brand. It seeks to increase the product's perceived value to the customer and thereby increase brand franchise and brand equity. Marketers see a brand as an implied promise that the level of quality people have come to expect from a brand will continue with present and future purchases of the same product. This may increase sales by making a comparison with competing products more favorable. It may also enable the manufacturer to charge more for the product. The value of the brand is determined by the amount of profit it generates for the manufacturer. This results from a combination of increased sales and increased price.

Good brand name should be legally protect-able; easy to pronounce; easy to remember; easy to recognize; attract attention; suggest product benefits; suggest the company or product image; distinguish the product's positioning relative to the competition. A brand is not merely a catchy name, an interesting logo or a clever tag-line. Brand needs to be organically developed and consistently positioned in the marketplace. Then this gradually is transformed from components (with no meaning) into attributes (meaningful). This occurs when the promise the brand makes is, in the end-users mind, consistently delivered and the brand attributes are emotionally embraced by the end user. Brand is differentiated into 3 (three) categories: (1). Premium brand that typically costs more than other products in the category; (2). Economy brand is a brand targeted to a high price elasticity market segment; (3). Fighting brand is a brand created specifically to counter a competitive threat. Branding establishes the direction, leadership, clarity of purpose, inspiration and energy for one of a company's most important assets, its corporate brand. Brand rationalization refers to reducing the number of brands marketed by a company. Companies tend to create more brands and product variations within a brand than economies of scale suggest they should. Frequently they will create a specific product or brand for each market that they target. But this can be a very inefficient strategy so a company may decide to rationalize their portfolio of brands from time to time.

Branding is a marketing tool wherein the executives create a distinct and memorable identity for a country, company, products, service or even an individual. The objective in branding is to capture a clear and compelling position in the mind of target user or consumer. A brand promise forges a relationship of trust and emotional satisfaction with the end-user. It is not so easy to calculate the change in shareholders' equity that can be attributed to a product or category. More complex metrics like changes in the net present value of shareholders' equity are even more difficult for the product executive to assess. In a diversified company, the objectives of some brands may conflict with those of other brands. Or worse, corporate objectives may conflict with the specific needs of the brand. Brands offer the confidence of quality and the assuredness of consistency. Brands can command a premium price, which increases margins and profits. Brands enable people to control, somewhat, the destiny at retail. Brands infuse their organizations and its people with a pride in workmanship and pride in association. This leads to greater productivity and output—as well as less turnover and absenteeism. Brands also provide added equity to a company's value by increasing the potential for licensing and the revenue it generates.

Brand conveys the essence, character and purpose of the company and its products and services. It is the heart and soul of the brand for which all outward expressions emanate. When effectively managed and communicated the brand has tremendous power. Branding is the process that will determine customer confidence, trust and perceived reliability. Branding is tough to do because organization cannot create it just by running an ad; it has to be expressed in the strategy of the product. Company needs focusing on establishing a company's leadership in

their business market through innovative positioning, product creation and promotional programs.

Pricing Management

Pricing is process of applying prices to purchase and sales orders, based on factors
such as: a fixed amount, quantity break, promotion or sales campaign, specific
vendor quote, price prevailing on entry, shipment or invoice date, combination
of multiple orders or lines, and many others. Pricing involves: amount of charge
for a product or service; the pricing objectives; applying
profit maximization pricing; consideration to set the price: (cost-plus pricing,
demand based or value-based pricing, rate of return pricing, or
competitor indexing); option of single price or multiple pricing; prices change in
various geographical areas or zone pricing; consideration of quantity discounts;
competitors price; consideration of using price skimming strategy or penetration
pricing strategy; image vs price; consideration to use psychological pricing; consideration of customer price sensitivity and elasticity issues; consideration to use
real-time pricing; consideration of price discrimination; legal aspects against retail
price maintenance, price collusion, or price discrimination.

A well chosen price should: achieve the financial goals of the firm (e.g.: profitability); fit the realities of the marketplace; support a products positioning and be
consistent with the other variables in the marketing mix (price is influenced by
the type of distribution channel used, the type of promotions used, and the quality of the product—price will usually need to be relatively high if manufacturing
is expensive, distribution is exclusive, and the product is supported by extensive
advertising and promotional campaigns—a low price can be a viable substitute
for product quality, effective promotions, or an energetic selling effort by distrib-
utors.

Market interdependence also is impacting pricing. Pricing is relatively simple
when markets can be separated and a price individually determined for each. Historically, pricing has tended to be a highly decentralized decision with individual
country managers setting prices in pursuit of their own objectives. Individual customers have moved to worldwide procurement, further narrowing the flexibility
of pricing managers as they try to set prices across markets. Related cause of complexity is information: better information creating smarter, more powerful customers.

Information technology allows for international tracking and transmittal of pricing information, creating the need for harmonized world pricing. Buying groups have formed in a wide variety of situations from independent funeral home operators sharing information and pooling casket purchases to major corporations joining with one another to negotiate ticket prices with airline companies. For many companies, purchasing has become a strategic function. The forces of interrelatedness and information have created more complex price schedules. No longer able to charge customers different prices just because of their geographic separation, firms attain price customization by applying the same pricing schedule to all customers; fully aware that because of the specific terms and conditions of sale different prices is received in the end.

The goal of price management is to help the corporate attain maximum financial performance by improving its pricing thinking and to show how that improved thinking can translate into improved net price realization.

Four dimensions help to define the pricing: viewpoint on pricing (profit is driven by sales volume, price, and costs Sales volume is seen as a controllable outcome of company actions. Costs should be managed vigorously. Pricing is often the third front in the battle for profitability, as the scarce resources of management time, energy, and imagination are siphoned off to the first two fronts of sales volume and costs); fact files to support pricing (data that are more accurate, timely, relevant, and disaggregated. It will give initial analysis, i.e.: competitive analysis—to identify differentiation opportunities, and consumer analysis—to identify consumer wants and important segmentation of the market. Based on this, decisions are made that create the perceived value of the firm's offering in the market place: first the target market is selected, and then the value-creating elements of the marketing mix assembled, i.e., the product itself, communication efforts to support its marketing and distribution to create convenient availability, and other support); tools and scope of analysis (undertake a systematic analysis of customers and competitors to enable him to assess the outcome of alternative pricing scenarios); determination and implementation (focusing on customer value; and overcome the tendency to too much uniformity in: prices across customers, prices over time, gross margin percentages across products).

Communications play an important role here. A differential pricing strategy can no longer be hidden. The media has seen to that. Therefore, the pricing options need to be communicated as something positive for the consumer. If lower prices are available then the consumer should be made aware of them prior to the purchase. Marketers are rethinking their entire value change in order to focus more on the final consumer. Target market segmentation has been used as a way to develop tighter marketing strategies. The consumer has changed and is far more aware of prices that are being charged in different areas. Furthermore, marketing tools are evolving fast and are becoming more sophisticated to enable pricing to be undertaken in different ways.

There are a number of ways in which differential pricing is being undertaken at present. The following identifies four main areas although these are not necessarily exhaustive: supply and demand (under this mechanism a higher level of demand for the product or service raises the price although the product or service itself may not change in nature); promotional activity (the use of price as a promotional instrument is more controversial. Price-led offers such as buy one-get one free or extra product are used commonly. A low price may also be used during an introductory period after product launch or to attract new consumers. The overuse of price as a promotional tool could have the effect of turning brands into commodities. A long-term low-price strategy changes the brand values. A brand can no longer be viewed as a premium product); geographic (a different price could be charged in different regions or in different countries. This is based on the assumption that different areas are able to afford different price levels or that the costs of marketing a product or service can vary by area); customer-focused (prices that vary according to the actual customer. It's more widespread in consumer marketing)

Pricing strategy

The dynamic supply and demand moves forward from existing pricing that makes the assumption that consumer demand is not static and that the value of a product and brand can change according to different criteria. The second scenario is where consumer aggregation applies industrial bulk buying to the consumer sector. This enables groups of consumers to buy in bulk to force down prices. The third scenario is based on the value of individual customers. It uses the assumption that different consumers have different buying behavior and price points. Good pricing decisions require facts about cost of doing business, the consumer's evaluation processes, and competitive activity. Pricing strategies include:

a. Competition based pricing. Setting the price based upon prices of the similar competitor products

b. Cost plus pricing. Calculate the cost of producing the product and adds on a percentage (profit) to that price to give the selling price.

c. Creaming or skimming. Selling a product at a high price, sacrificing high sales to gain a high profit, therefore 'skimming' the market.

d. Limit pricing. pricing adopted by firms in a contestable market in order to 'limit' the ability of new entrants to take advantage of economies of scale where by costs are low enough for them to become competitive

e. Loss leader. A product which is sold at a loss to attract customers to buy other full priced products sold by the business

f. Market orientated pricing. Setting a price based upon analysis and research compiled from the targeted market

g. Penetration pricing. Setting an initial low price at the stage of deployment of the product to attract initial customers. The price is likely to rise later as the product gains a market share

h. Price discrimination. Setting a different price for the same product in different segments to the market. For example, this can be for different ages or for different opening times, such as cinema tickets

i. Predatory pricing. Aggressive pricing designed or intended to drive out competitors from a market

Price change reviews should be regularly scheduled to review prices in light of such changes to keep the price-value equation from getting seriously unbalanced in either direction. Pricing strategy is the core element of pricing successfully. It can help companies achieve corporate, divisional, and product goals by ensuring consistency and transparency throughout its pricing process. Good pricing strategy must be clearly defined for the lifetime of a product, it must also be robust enough to adapt to changes in corporate objectives, market conditions, or sales results. Oftentimes, companies with weak pricing strategies find themselves making pricing decisions haphazardly, and in a reactionary rather than an anticipatory manner. Value pricing lies at the core of the most profitable pricing decisions. Companies must fully understand the value that they bring to the market before they can fully capture the profit potential of their products.

The best pricing processes are worthless if they are not implemented in practice. Profit improvements are only realized when optimal pricing decisions are brought to and enforced in the market. Therefore, it is essential that people responsible for implementing each step of the pricing process know the pricing strategy, understand their role in the process, and have the proper tools, resources, and training to conduct their portion of the process. Furthermore, it is essential that incentives/compensation are tied to both completing each phase of the pricing process and are linked to the pricing strategy. Price management is a fluid process that allows organization to adapt pricing decisions to changes in corporate/divisional strategy, market conditions, competitive situation, and throughout the product life time. Therefore, it is important to install a reliable and efficient way to monitor the effectiveness of pricing decisions and incorporate those results in future pricing decisions.

BUDGET MANAGEMENT

A budget is an organized proposal reflecting the conservatively estimated revenue and the carefully anticipated expenditures for the current year. Budget is a plan and it is subject to internal reallocations. It is not the authority to spend money. In normal circumstances, the treasurer has authority to spend budgeted amounts as bills are received and approved by the president. When it becomes evident that a certain outlay may cause an item to exceed the budgeted amount, the expense should not be incurred until referral has been made to the executive committee for proper disposition (such as a budget change).

An effective budget process should include alignment with strategic plans; formal, logical and integrated documentation; quantified planned objectives and the means selected for achieving them; consideration of all the events and activities needed to fulfill the goals of each entity function; integration with the accounting system; basis for coordinating the operating plans of all entity sub-units; means for communicating detailed work plans or action plans throughout the organization and to relevant oversight and other interested groups, both internal and external to the entity; input from lower level managers who have more detailed knowledge of actual program and service needs; basis for evaluation of performance by comparing actual to budgeted data. Such comparisons highlight variances between actual and planned results, and signal the need for possible managerial action

Steps to plan a budget:

a. Establish and communicate budget policies, direction and assumptions. Develop budget policy, direction and assumptions and communicate to those preparing budgets. To promote efficiency, the budget policy should be developed and documented in time for consistent application throughout the budget process. The policy should be distributed in a timely manner to all personnel involved in the process.

b. Plan the budget process. Review budget and actual financial statement from prior year

c. The budget should be reviewed by appropriate internal and external authorities. Internal budget review is a process through which various functional areas of the entity present their budget proposals to the appropriate level of management, i.e. justification of increases, explanation of decreases, requests at more than one possible level of funding

d. Budget allocations. Ensuring that the expenditure requests are in line with entity goals, objectives, and policies

e. Determine income. Calculate and record the income received from various sources. Income: revenues minus cost of sales, operating expenses, and taxes, over a given period of time. Income is the reason corporations exist, and are often the single most important determinant of a stock's price. Income is important to investors because they give an indication of the company's expected future dividends and its potential for growth and capital appreciation. That does not necessarily mean that low or negative earnings always indicate a bad stock; for example, many young companies report negative income as they attempt to grow quickly enough to capture a new market, at which point they'll be even more profitable than they otherwise might have been.

f. Determine expenses. This step is more time-consuming than the previous one, but also more important because it's the side of the equation that you probably have more control over. Begin by estimating how much you spend monthly on each type of expense: fixed expenses, variable expenses, discretionary expenses

g.   Implement, monitor and adjust budget as needed. The primary elements of this phase include managing and administering the budget, establishing policies for activities such as transfers and amendments to the budget, and establishing a control system to monitor expenditures and revenue collections. Effective management of entity funds requires periodic evaluation of the operational budget. Particular control mechanisms that pertain to the implementation and adjustment phase of the process include: (1). Periodic budget reports—Generally, functional units of the entity receive monthly budget reports which allow for monitoring of expenditures and revenues. These reports provide the financial data required by the entity to control and monitor its operations, to ensure compliance with legal and financial limitations, and to anticipate changes in financial resources and requirements because of factors which may have been unknown or unforeseen at the time of budget preparation. (2). Budget amendment process—This process also acts as a control mechanism in the budget process by ensuring that adequate fund levels exist within the various budget categories to support appropriate expenditures. The process includes not only reviews of expenditures but also approvals for transfers of funds.

FINANCIAL MANAGEMENT

Finance manual emphasizes that it is the responsibility of all managers to ensure that operating procedures and policies in their areas of responsibility are consistent with the requirements of the Manual and be accountable for the areas of responsibility under their control.

Executive advises their subordinates on financial policy and management of the company. They are responsible for: the interpretation and implementation of the financial policies of the company; the provision of advice on all matters associated with the financial management; and financial reporting for management and external users. The Financial executive also oversees the operation of budgets, investments and accounting systems.

Effective financial planning cannot take place without first establishing goals and objectives:

a. Goals are concrete—statement of what to achieve. The finance goal may be to increase revenues and reduce existing expenditures to have additional funds available for programs and member services.

b. Objectives are specific statements of steps to be taken to achieve the overall goals. They should be timely, realistic, attainable, and measurable.

c. Review prior year's goals, review prior year's finance section in annual report, review prior year's actual financial statements

Once goal and objective are set, decide how they are to be attained. Allocate resource, assign duties and set deadlines. Periodically, appraise progress toward objectives and goals, evaluate results and institute changes if necessary.

Implementing and maintaining internal financial controls are important aspects of running a successful business which includes:

a. Accounts Payable. Ensure that the accounts payable process disburses cash effectively and efficiently. The process should maximize profitable cash flow and contain controls that will ensure that transactions are properly recorded and reported. "Accounts Payable" is used in accrual-based accounting to record debts that have been incurred but not yet paid. Accounts payable are obligations (debt, liabilities) that will be settled at a future time. They are considered "current liabilities," which means that the debt will be settled with current assets during the current operating cycle.

b. Budgeting. To effectively identify, allocate and account for funds used to provide the necessary services and programs which support the entity's mission, goals, and objectives. Budgets are statements of expected results expressed in monetary or numerical terms, and are often an integral part of the entity's planning process. During implementation of services, the budget provides an accountability tool for comparing anticipated to actual outcomes. Consequently, budgeting serves as an important link between the strategic planning process and performance measurement process. Budgets are developed and implemented for various purposes: planning (budgets link goals, objectives, and strategies with resources); motivation (budgets establish parameters that guide work efforts toward accomplishment of organizational goals); evaluation (budgets are suitable tools for monitoring and verifying performance and providing feedback for planning); coordination (the budget process requires input and alignment from various components of the organization); communication (budget formulation and reporting provides an opportunity for direct exchange of information both internal and external to the organization); education (budgeting requires management and staff to periodically analyze their departments and overall operating environment, contributing to enhanced learning); ritual (budgets are often prepared out of habit, usually resulting in benefits that are far below the costs of performing the task

c.   Cash Management. To collect, maintain, and disburse funds in a way that minimizes the risk of misuse, maximizes profitable cash flow, and supports the entity's operations and mission. Cash is both a fundamental resource and the means by which the entity acquires other resources. To manage cash is to manage the entity's ability to purchase assets, service debt, pay employees, and control operations. Thus, effective cash management directly correlates with the entity's ability to realize its mission, goals, and objectives. The cash management process combines: cash management tools, such as cash budgets and cash forecasting, for controlling cash availability and maximizing the investment of idle funds; procedures for collecting, disbursing, and investing cash; internal controls for safeguarding, recording, and reporting cash. This process must comply with existing laws and regulations, both federal and state, and applicable professional and ethical standards.

d.   Debt Management. Ensure that debt is issued only for accepted corporate purposes, consistent with the entity's mission and legislative expectations and is prudently managed in conjunction with overall financial plans and related functions. Debt is issued to finance a wide variety of projects including infrastructure, general capital improvements, and utilities, and to encourage Margin Enhancement Program (MEP). The cost and long-term nature of these projects require that capital be raised from sources other than normal operating revenue. Capital may be raised by issuing short- or long-term debt, entering into capital leases, receiving capital contributed by other departments/units. Effective debt management is essential because of its far-reaching consequences. The decision to issue debt may commit an entity's revenues for several decades into the future and, as a result, limits the entity's flexibility to respond to changes in service priorities, revenue inflows, or cost structures. Legal and statutory restraints, voter or policy maker attitudes, market conditions, and anticipated revenue flows are some of the factors that will influence the strategy an entity follow to raise capital.

The debt management process involves several other management functions, i.e.: planning: identifying the types and timing of projects to be financed; investment management: investing proceeds and monitoring arbitrage earnings; cash management: expending proceeds and maintaining required account balances (e.g., minimum reserve and/or interest and sinking fund balances); asset management: building, acquiring, and maintaining project assets

e. Fixed Assets. Acquire, maintain, safeguard, distribute, and administer the fixed assets needed to support the entity's mission, goals, and objectives. Minimize the cost and maximize the utility of the assets acquired. Fixed asset management is a complex matter, involving governing laws, operating rules and regulations, administrative law rulings, recommended practices, designated procedures, and specific conflict-of-interest provisions. The entity must also ensure that "enough but not too much" capital equipment is available. Management controls over the recording, reporting, and safeguarding of assets are also necessary. At the entity level, the nature and scope of the fixed asset management function depends upon the needs of the entity. A small entity with one location that has few fixed assets other than office furniture will have a different fixed asset management structure than an entity with multiple field offices and heavy equipment. The degree of coordination and communication between these various levels of fixed assets management can have a material effect on the efficiency, economy, and effectiveness of any specific entity and on the state as a whole. Fixed asset management is a part of the materials management process, which also includes procurement, inventories, maintenance, and transportation.

f. Inventory. Acquire, maintain, safeguard, distribute, and administer the inventory needed to support the entity's mission, goals, and objectives. Minimize the cost and maximize the utility of the items acquired. Inventories include goods purchased for resale, internal usage, or consumption. Inventory management is a complex matter, involving governing laws, operating rules and regulations, administrative law rulings, recommended practices, designated procedures, and specific conflict-of- interest provisions. In addition to all of these compliance issues, the entity must also ensure that "enough but not too much" inventory is available. Management controls over the recording, reporting, and safeguarding of inventory items are also necessary. At the entity level, the nature and scope of the inventory management function depends upon the needs of the entity. A small entity with one location that has few inventory items other than office supplies will have a different structure than an entity with multiple field offices and varied supply needs. The degree of coordination and communication between these various levels of inventory management can have a material effect on the efficiency, economy, and effectiveness of individual entities and on the corporate as a whole. Inventory management is a part of the materials management process, which includes procurement, fixed assets, maintenance, and transportation as well.

g. Investment. Ensure that investments are properly managed so that returns from funds are maximized while capital is safeguarded and investments are in compliance with laws, regulations and other contractual obligations. Investments allow entities to use idle funds to generate additional revenue. These additional revenues may allow governments to reduce tax burdens while increasing the resources available to provide goods and services to the general community. The management of investments is an important part of ensuring that public funds are used effectively and efficiently. Investments must be protected against theft and fraud as well as non-systematic decision-making. The process of investment management should be linked to strategic planning. Returns should be used as specified by law or organizational policy.

h. Procurement. Buy the right quantity and the right quality at the right time at the right price from capable suppliers. Purchasing and contracting is a complex process subject to governing laws, operating rules and regulations, court decisions, administrative law rulings, recommendations, recommended practices, designated procedures, specific conflict-of-interest provisions, and the overall proprieties that attach to public service. The fundamentals of successful purchasing are competition, impartiality, conservation of funds, and openness. Procurement is a part of the materials management process, which includes inventory, fixed assets, maintenance, and transportation as well.

i. Receivables. Ensure that reported receivables accurately reflect all bona fide receivables and provide the data necessary to forecast cash availability and analyze efficiency of the collection process while safeguarding assets. Receivables reflect money, goods, or services which have been earned but not received. Receivables encounter accounts receivable, accrued interest receivable, notes receivable, bond proceeds, taxes and/or fees, and inter-fund transfers. It is shown as assets on the balance sheet, allowing the asset to be recognized during the period in which the revenue is earned.

j.   Revenue: to collect all revenues due in a timely and efficient manner. Revenue management is one of the most important functions of corporation. There could also be large amounts of cash receipts that do not represent revenue to the entity, such as taxes collected for and distributed to local governments. The principles of revenue management should also apply to these receipts.

PROCUREMENT MANAGEMENT

Procurement management is management of contracting activities from formation, such as product and contract definition, market analysis, through the tendering process up to contract formation, to contract performance, management and administration after contract award.

The Management should set out the policy and procedures to be followed by authorized delegates, managers and staff involved in purchasing and contracting, to ensure that ethical and sound purchasing practices underpin the achievement of value for money outcomes for the company.

The principle of procurement policy is that the procedures and methods adopted should be beyond reproach. This can only be achieved if (1). Give the suppliers the opportunity to compete for its business in an open and transparent manner; (2). Maintain a reputation for fair dealing in its arrangements with suppliers; (3). Best value for money is the outcome sought in all transactions. Balance of price, quality, and performance achieved through competitive procurement methods in accordance with stated selection criteria; (4). Make the use of emerging technologies to achieve economies in its purchasing processes; (5). Analysis necessary to achieve best value should not be confined to the actual procurement process; it should begin in the planning and appraisal of alternatives and continue through the definition of requirements which would include assessment and award criteria, evaluation of sources, selection of contractor, preparation, negotiation, execution and award of contract, contract administration and post-contract evaluation;

(6). Regard to skill, ability and integrity to do faithful, conscientious work, and promptly fulfill the contract according to its letter and spirit

Procurement aims to contribute to the overall corporate and financial aims of the corporate; become more effective in driving down the total cost of acquisition and achieving value for money; increase our negotiation strength by closely managing expenditure and the supply base; develop and integrate sustainability into the procurement process by adopting sustainability into supplier selection criteria; eliminate or minimize non-added value procurement activities by the use of appropriate technology; secure commitment for effective procurement; create a platform from which procurement staff can be trained and developed to continuously improve the corporate procurement activity.

Procurement strategy, which orders the right quantity and the right quality at the right time at the right price from capable suppliers, includes:

a. Determine requirements. Procurement requirements are identified, with input from stakeholders and guidance of higher project authorities, as the basis for procurement planning and the contract; agreed procurement management plans and strategies are implemented and maintained to ensure clarity of understanding between stakeholders and achievement of project objectives

b. Establish agreed processes. Information is obtained from established sources capable of fulfilling procurement requirements to determine the extent to which project objectives can be met; established selection processes and selection criteria are implemented and communicated to stakeholders and prospective contractors to ensure fair competition; approvals are obtained from higher project authority to enable formal discussions to be conducted

c. Conduct process activities. Agreed proposals are communicated to prospective contractors to ensure clarity of understanding of project objectives; responses are evaluated and preferred contractors are selected in accordance with current legal requirements and agreed selection processes; negotiations are conducted with preferred contractor, with guidance of higher project authority if necessary, to agree contract terms and conditions, establish common goals and minimize uncertainty

d. Implement contract. Established procurement plans are implemented, and modified with higher project authority approval, to ensure common approach to achievement of objectives; progress is reviewed and agreed changes are managed to ensure timely completion of tasks, resolution of conflicts and achievement of project objectives within the legal framework of the contract; procurement management problems are identified, reported to higher project authorities, and agreed remedial actions are implemented to ensure project objectives are met

e.   Manage contract finalization procedures. Finalization activities are conducted to ensure contract deliverables meet contractual requirements; project outcomes are reviewed to determine the effectiveness of procurement processes and procedures; lessons learned and recommended improvements are identified, documented and passed on to higher project authority for application in future projects

AUDIT MANAGEMENT

Audit Management provides independent assessments as to the economy, efficiency, effectiveness, compliance and financial regularity of the corporate operations and evaluates the adequacy of the corporate risk management framework, i.e.:

a.   Control, system and procedure: appraising the adequacy of controls in the corporate administrative systems, computing and communications systems; reviewing systems and procedures and recommending improvements to existing processes and procedures, where appropriate;

b.   Corporate risk: reviewing corporate risk management strategies, guidelines, policies and procedures; and reporting significant risk exposures and serious incidents of non-compliance to management; ensuring that appropriate resources are directed towards areas of high risk;

c.   Compliance: overseeing the implementation of the corporate compliance framework; assessing the extent of compliance with relevant legislation, regulations and industry codes; assessing the extent of compliance with corporate and/or other relevant policies, guidelines and procedures;

d.   Resource: appraising the economy, efficiency and effectiveness with which corporate resources are employed; assessing the accuracy and adequacy of management information;

e.   Independence: providing an on-going audit of the income and expenditure of the corporate; providing audit certifications and audit opinions as required by various granting bodies; providing advice on a range of administrative and financial matters; maintaining contact and liaising with the corporate external auditors to ensure an effective use of resources and to avoid possible duplication of effort; and

f.   Follow up: conducting ad hoc and confidential investigations at the request of senior management of the corporate

Effective audit management requires a combination of people, processes, and technology to achieve maximum results. Technology-based audit programs are in and of themselves, insufficient. The best practices summarized below highlight the essential requirements for automated audit management systems and the required processes and human resource requirements to ensure sustained compliance and reduce regulatory risk, e.g. (1). Obtain top-down management support and commitment. A fundamental requirement of any compliance initiative that impacts the entire organization is support from senior management. Top-down support ensures that compliance is treated as a corporate mandate versus a departmental challenge. It also ensures that resources will be available as needed to ensure success; (2). Establish clear policies, procedures, and metrics. Audit management programs should incorporate defined policies, procedures, and metrics as performance benchmarks. These elements should be reviewed periodically for continuous improvement; (3). Integrate essential quality management processes. To ensure success, an effective audit management system should automate the entire audit process and include integration of the following processes: corrective and preventive actions; change control; non-conformance tracking and management; regulatory document/content management; custom reporting, analysis, and analytics; training; compliance intelligence dashboard; (4). Ensure closed-loop processes. For automated audit management systems, ensure that they are designed to successfully close out all audit processes in a timely manner. As obvious as this sound, the number one reason for regulatory citations in this area is due to ineffective process closure; (5). Avoid "stand-alone" audit management systems. Audit management is an integrated process that requires a blend of several process and compliance technologies to achieve real compliance; (6). Establish proactive internal audit schedule. Continuous improvement demands that organizations periodically review internal policies and procedures and apply the necessary corrective and preventive actions to ensure quality. One fundamental preventive action is to perform periodic audits to ensure compliance and operational performance. Corrective action should be applied to all process or production issues revealed during audits to ensure sustained compliance; (7). Automate enforcement of audit checks and balances. Automated systems should segregate duties so that the responsibility for the audit is distributed among the organizations; (8). Ensure online and offline access and control. Automated audit management systems must be accessible to across the extended enterprise. Most point solutions that address audit management are only accessible in the office while the auditor is online. This is impractical and promotes process inefficiencies and redundancies; (9). Leverage integrated document/content management technologies. Audit processes inevitably require documented evidence supporting the entire audit event. During the progression of the audit process, auditors may reference controlled documents as well as generate new documentation in support of the audit. To ensure ready access to production documentation and the management and control of audit documentation, a good audit management system should include integrated document management/content management technologies; (10). Built-in audit alerts and notification. One of the key reasons for non-compliance is the lack of follow up. Day-to-day challenges and other business issues change priorities in a very dynamic manner. These alerts should be coupled with corrective action plan items to ensure follow up and subsequent closure in a timely manner.

Responsibilities

It describes the roles and responsibilities of the board of directors, executive, and internal or external auditor, i.e.:

a. Executive Board: are responsible for ensuring that the institution's system of internal controls operates effectively. To meet its responsibility of providing an independent audit function with sufficient resources, the board of directors should: provide an internal audit function capable of evaluating internal controls; engage outside consultants or auditors to perform the internal audit function, or use a combination of both methods to ensure that the institution has received adequate internal controls audit coverage.

b. Audit executive: responsible for implementing board-approved audit directives. The executive oversees the audit function and provides leadership and direction in communicating and monitoring audit policies, practices, programs, and processes. The internal audit executive should establish clear lines of authority and reporting responsibility for all levels of audit personnel and activities. The internal audit executive also should ensure that members of the audit staff possess the necessary independence, experience, education, training, and skills to properly conduct assigned activities. The internal audit executive should be responsible for internal control risk assessments, audit plans, audit programs, and audit reports. Audit management should oversee the staff assigned to perform the internal audit work, should establish policies and procedures to guide the audit staff, and should ensure the staff has the expertise and resources to identify inherent risks and assess the effectiveness of internal controls in the corporate operations.

c.   Internal audit staff: to assess independently and objectively the controls, reliability, and integrity of the corporate environment. Evaluate internal control plans, strategies, policies, and procedures to ensure adequate management oversight. Additionally, they should assess the day-to-day internal controls to ensure that transactions are recorded and processed in compliance with acceptable accounting methods and standards and are in compliance with policies set forth by the board of directors. Auditors also perform operational audits, including system development audits, to ensure that internal controls are in place, that policies and procedures are effective, and that employees operate in compliance with approved policies. Auditors should identify weaknesses, review management's plans for addressing those weaknesses, monitor their resolution, and report to the board as necessary on material weaknesses.

d.   Operating executives: responsible for correcting the root causes of the audit or control exceptions, not just treating the exceptions themselves. Response times for correcting noted deficiencies should be reasonable and may vary depending on the complexity of the corrective action and the risk of inaction.

e.   External auditor: review internal control procedures as part of their overall evaluation of internal controls when providing an opinion on the adequacy of an institution's financial statements; review the general and application controls affecting the recording and safeguarding of assets and the integrity of controls over financial statement preparation and reporting; control procedures as part of an outsourcing arrangement

Audited Subjects

Effective audit programs are risk-focused, promote sound internal controls, ensure the timely resolution of audit deficiencies, and inform the board of directors of the effectiveness of risk management practices, i.e.:

a. Construction and Facility Management: cover construction project management, property management and facility planning, operations, maintenance, and support services. To ensure that construction projects achieve a specified level of quality at a minimum of cost, and in compliance with state laws and rules.

b. Data Analysis: discuss the basic steps in the analytical process and the various approaches/methods auditors can use to gather and analyze the evidence needed to support audit findings. This section of the Manual has four parts: choosing a method, designing the evaluation, methods, and analysis tools.

c. Financial: provide information about various financial practices and processes, including accounts payable, budgeting, cash management, debt management, fixed assets, inventory, investments, procurement, receivables, and revenue.

d. Human Resources: cover the major components of a human resources management control system, including planning, recruitment/selection, performance appraisals, compensation/rewards, training/development, and employee relations.

e. Management: cover the management processes necessary to achieve entity mission, goals, and objectives. Topics include: governance, internal auditing, mission, organization structure, performance measurement, policies and procedures, policy environment, problem-solving and decision-making, risk assessment, and strategic planning.

f. Managing Information Systems (MIS): discuss how to manage information to support good decision-making and how to ensure that automated information systems are developed, managed, and controlled effectively and efficiently.

Management Review

Investors may lose confidence in a company's management and financial statements if sudden changes in its financial condition and results occur. To minimize such a loss of confidence, corporate should consider following conditions:

a. Each company's management and auditor should bring particular focus to the evaluation of the critical accounting policies used in the financial statements. As part of the normal audit process, auditors must obtain an understanding of management's judgments in selecting and applying accounting principles and methods. Special attention to the most critical accounting policies will enhance the effectiveness of this process. Management should be able to defend the quality and reasonableness of the most critical policies, and auditors should satisfy themselves thoroughly regarding their selection, application and disclosure.

b. Management should ensure that disclosure in MD&A is balanced and fully responsive. To enhance investor understanding of the financial statements, companies are encouraged to explain in MD&A the effects of the critical accounting policies applied, the judgments made in their application, and the likelihood of materially different reported results if different assumptions or conditions were to prevail.

c. Prior to finalizing and filing annual reports, audit committees should review the selection, application and disclosure of critical accounting policies. Consistent with auditing standards, audit committees should be apprised of the evaluative criteria used by management in their selection of the accounting principles and methods. Proactive discussions between the audit committee and the company's senior management and auditor about critical accounting policies are appropriate.

d. If companies, management, audit committees or auditors are uncertain about the application of specific accounting principles, they should consult with our accounting staff. We encourage all those whose responsibility it is to report fairly and accurately on a company's financial condition and results to seek out our staff's assistance. We are committed to providing that assistance in a timely fashion; our goal is to address problems before they happen.

CUSTOMER COMPLAINT MANAGEMENT

Complaint management can be defined as the planning, execution and control of all measures, which a company performs when dealing with complaints. It is a system of procedural instructions, structures and instruments to stabilize fragile business relationships by solving the problems that have happened. The complaint management concept is strongly linked to the service policy (after-sales marketing) of a company and can also be regarded as an important part of a quality management system. In addition, current research indicates the impact of complaint management not only on customer satisfaction and loyalty but also on employee satisfaction.

Customer complaint management has become an integral part of business, both from a regulatory perspective and a customer service standpoint. Regulatory bodies have established specific requirements for capturing, investigating, resolving and reporting customer complaints. Simply stated, complaints management is the formal process of recording and resolving a customer complaint. Complaints are expensive, both in direct and indirect costs. But for this price, companies can extract priceless knowledge, because complaints contain the direct voice of the customer. If complaints are transformed into knowledge about customers, they can provide a valuable amount of capital for enterprises. To exploit this capital, companies must design, build, operate and continuously upgrade systems for managing complaints. These systems are called Customer Complaint Management Systems (CCMS). Complaints management is just one initiative under a broader compliance management strategy.

Customer compliant management processes, i.e.:

a. Classify Customer Complaints—As individual complaints are recorded, the nature of the complaint, along with the product or service the complaint is about, requires classification. In the banking sector, complaints that violate federal laws, or internal bank policies and procedures, should be classified separately from other customer service issues.

b. Analyze & Report Trends—Once complaints are classified, the data should be analyzed and reported on a regular basis. The goal of analysis is to identify themes or trends that occur with front-line service delivery. This is done with an eye toward both regulatory matters, and those that help improve customer experiences. Given that many bank Ombudsmen report to their chief executive and board of directors on a semi-annual basis, this ensures complaints management activities receive senior executive attention and accountability.

c.   Take Management Action—With issues identified, actions must be taken to improve front-line service delivery. This may include updating customer service standards, improving communications, or providing additional training to staff on products/services. Actions should remedy systemic issues. Changes should be monitored closely to ensure actions result in fewer customer complaints.

d.   Continuous Improvement of the Complaint Process—Although a complaints management process may exist, it is important to know how well it is working. Ask key questions of customers who use the system, including whether or not they view the process as accessible, easy to use, and fair. This will identify areas for improvement. Since research indicates that complaints handled professionally and in a timely manner result in customers continuing to do business with a company, it is essential that customers who complain are satisfied with the complaint management process. This will not only help to retain business, but will also reduce the damage that negative 'word of mouth' has with existing or potential customers.

PRODUCTION MANAGEMENT

Production management concerns with the production of goods and services, and involves the responsibility of ensuring that business operations are efficient and effective. It also is the management of resources and the distribution of goods and services to customers; focuses on the effective planning, and scheduling.

The philosophy is to keep improving the quality of an organization. It is defined by four keys: plan: design or revise business process components to improve results; do: implement the plan and measure its performance; check: assess the measurements and report the results to decision makers; act: decide on changes needed to improve the process. The consolidation phase enables the organization to take stock of what has been taking place and to ensure made to processes that require documentation (both to allow processes to be repeatable and to facilitate recognition of the achievement of some form of quality standard). There are two key methodologies—DMAIC and DMADV. DMAIC is used to improve an existing business process. DMADV is used to create new product designs or process designs in such a way that it results in a more predictable, mature and defect free performance.

DMAIC

DMAIC basic methodology consists of the following five phases: define: formally define the process improvement goals that are consistent with customer demands and enterprise strategy; measure: to define baseline measurements on current process for future comparison. Map and measure process in question and collect required process data; analyze: to verify relationship and causality of factors; improve: optimize the process based upon the analysis using techniques like design of experiments; control: setup pilot runs to establish process capability, transition to production and thereafter continuously measure the process and institute control mechanisms to ensure that variances are corrected before they result in defects

DMADV

DMADV basic methodology consists of the following five phases: define: formally define the goals of the design activity that are consistent with customer demands and enterprise strategy; measure: identify product capabilities, production process capability, risk assessment, etc. analyze: develop design alternatives, create high-level design and evaluate design capability to select the best design; design: develop detail design, optimize design, and plan for design verification. This phase may require simulations; verify: to verify design, setup pilot runs, implement production process and handover to process owners. This phase may also require simulations.

QUALITY MANAGEMENT

Quality management is a systematic way of ensuring that all the activities necessary to design, develop and implement a product or service which satisfy the requirements of the organization and of users take place as planned and that the activities are carried out cost effectively. In engineering and manufacturing, quality control and quality engineering are involved in developing systems to ensure products or services are designed and produced to meet or exceed customer requirements and expectations

Quality Assurance covers all activities from design, development, production, installation, servicing and documentation, this introduced the rules: "fit for purpose" and "do it right the first time". It includes the regulation of the quality of raw materials, assemblies, products and components; services related to production; and management, production, and inspection processes. One of the most widely used paradigms for Quality Assurance management is the PDCA (Plan-Do-Check-Act) approach. The main goal of Quality Assurance is to ensure that the product fulfills or exceeds customer expectations.

Quality Assurance involves failure testing that is process to perform a product until it fails, i.e. under stresses such as increasing vibration, temperature and humidity. This exposes many unanticipated weaknesses in a product, and the data is used to drive engineering and manufacturing process improvements.

Company quality with the focus on management and people came to the forefront. It was realized that, if all departments approached quality with an open mind, success was possible if the management led the quality improvement process. The company-wide quality approach places an emphasis on three aspects : elements such as controls, job management, adequate processes, performance and integrity criteria and identification of records; competence such as knowledge, skills, experience, qualifications; soft elements, such as personnel integrity, confidence, organizational culture, motivation, team spirit and quality relationships. The quality of the outputs is at risk if any of these three aspects are deficient in any way

Total Quality Control

Total Quality Control is the most necessary inspection control of all in cases where despite statistical quality control techniques or quality improvements implemented, sales decrease. Total Quality Management (TQM) is a management strategy aimed at embedding awareness of quality in all organizational processes. TQM is a set of systematic activities carried out by the entire organization to effectively and efficiently achieve company objectives so as to provide products and services with a level of quality that satisfies customers, at the appropriate time and price. TQM comprises of four process steps: focuses on continuous process improvement, to make processes visible, repeatable and measurable; focuses on intangible effects on processes and ways to optimize and reduce their effects; examining the way the user applies the product leads to improvement in the product itself; broadens management concern beyond the immediate product.

The major problem which leads to a decrease in sales was that the specifications did not include the most important factor, "What the customer required". The major characteristics, ignored during the search to improve manufacture and overall business performance are: reliability, maintainability, and safety

As the most important factor had been ignored, a few refinements had to be introduced: marketing had to carry out their work properly and define the customer's specifications; specifications had to be defined to conform to these requirements; conformance to specifications i.e. drawings, standards and other relevant documents, were introduced during manufacturing, planning and control; management had to confirm all operators are equal to the work imposed on them and holidays, celebrations and disputes did not affect any of the quality levels; inspections and tests were carried out, and all components and materials, bought in or otherwise, conformed to the specifications, and the measuring equipment was accurate, this is the responsibility of the QA/QC department; any complaints received from the customers were timorously and satisfactorily dealt with; feedback from the user/customer is used to review designs; if the original specification does not reflect the correct quality requirements, quality cannot be inspected or manufactured into the product. For instance, all parameters for a pressure vessel should include not only the material and dimensions but operating, environmental, safety, reliability and maintainability requirements. To conclude, the above forms the basis from which the philosophy of Quality Assurance has evolved, and the achievement of quality or the "fitness-for-purpose" is "Quality Awareness" throughout the company

Quality improvement: break down barriers between departments; management should learn their responsibilities, and take on leadership; improve constantly; institute a program of education and self-improvement

Quality Standard

ISO Compliance is no longer a matter of choice for competitive companies. ISO accredited companies have a distinct edge while competing for international business and ensuring customer confidence. ISO compliance is perceived by many as an important value-addition by quality conscious buyers around the world. In particular, the ISO 9000 Series of Standards is the most widely accepted quality assurance model in the world, as well as ISO 14001. The goal of these standards is to reduce waste and variation in product

characteristics and process parameters, address traceability issues and to promote continual improvement of the effectiveness of quality management systems.

Adherence to ISO 9001 standards can be one of the most effective risk management tools organizations can use to prevent, or detect and control, nonconforming product and services and increase sustained compliance.

ISO standards are categorized into several distinct "families" of standards. The quality management family is defined by ISO 9000. This body of standards addresses all quality management and continuous improvement standards to ensure compliance with regulatory standards and guidelines that ultimately help enhance customer satisfaction. Environmental management is address through the ISO 14000 family. The goal of this body of standards is to help minimize harmful effects on the environment caused by its activities, and to achieve continual improvement of its environmental performance.

To achieve compliance with ISO guidelines organizations must establish an effective management system to facilitate the management of its core processes. Processes such as customer satisfaction, product quality, compliance, or environmental all require effective controls to meet ISO standards. Most forward-thinking companies have automated critical procedures to help increase operational efficiency and reduce error using the latest technology solutions available on the market.

To achieve compliance with ISO guidelines, the following best practices should form the basis of all ISO programs:

a.   Establish clearly defined business processes. Clearly define business processes that are essential to quality control. Once these processes have been identified and documented, steps can be taken to optimize processes for maximum efficiency.

b.   Conduct detailed internal audits and identify gaps. An internal audit of all quality and business processes is a good first step towards ISO compliance. The audit will reveal quality gaps and identify process inefficiencies. It is important to take corrective action to ensure that all audit issues are addressed in a timely manner after this proactive step is taken.

c.   Conduct external quality audits. An external audit serves as independent validation and verification of the processes and is an essential requirement for ISO compliance.

d.   Establish effective closed loop corrective and preventive action processes. Once processes have been established, an effective closed-loop corrective and preventive action process should be implemented for optimal results. The closed-loop nature of the process ensures that all issues will be addressed and closed as is appropriate.

e.   Define and publish quality control procedures. ISO mandates written quality control procedures. These procedures should be written, approved, and distributed throughout the organization to ensure compliance.

f.   Define quality monitoring processes. No ISO process is complete without an effective way to monitor processes. Monitoring is an essential requirement for ISO because it ensures that guidelines are consistently being followed.

g.   Establish continuous improvement guidelines and procedures. The monitoring process will reveal the need for continuous improvement of the product or process governed. Continuous improvement guidelines should be established to ensure that these issues are addressed in the most appropriate manner. These guidelines should be published and distributed to ensure consistency and completeness.

h.   Establish and maintain an effective training program. ISO compliance also mandates that all affected persons within an organization receive proper training. This is essential to quality assurance and risk mitigation. It is current best practice to automate the training and tracking process to ensure compliance with stated training requirements. Most organizations use training tracking technology to address these requirements.

i.   Implement quality process automation. As organizations mature in their approach towards ISO compliance, they are seeking to automate ISO-related processes. More importantly, they seek to do this without expensive software customization and professional services which are the bane of the industry.

j.   Drive quality from the top-down. Quality impacts every aspect of business and ultimately affects the client or end user. Thus, it is current best practice to drive ISO initiatives from the very top of the organizations to ensure adequate resource allocation where appropriate and enforcement of ISO policies.

TECHNICAL MANAGEMENT

Technical management is usually within the scope of the product and the engineering area, but often these key people rely on their engineering staff for this critical function. It provides an efficient, effective, and economical solution and control of the concept, definition, design, test, manufacture, and support of a projected technical system.

Engineering management is management of the engineering and technical effort to transform a conceptual requirement into an operational system. It includes the system performance parameters and preferred system configuration to satisfy the requirement, the planning and control of technical program tasks, integration of the engineering specialties, and the management of a totally integrated effort of design engineering, computer software engineering, test engineering, safety engineering, security engineering, logistics engineering, production engineering, and specialty engineering (environmental, etc) to meet cost, technical performance and schedule objectives.

To support high achievement of technical availability, following efforts are required: (1). To provide systems engineering process, in order to satisfy customer needs with effective products and processes at an optimized expenditure of life cycle resources; (2). Defining and overseeing the life cycle engineering processes to acquire, design, develop, test, install, and support complex real-time processing systems; (3). To apply the system engineering process throughout a system's life cycle as a comprehensive, iterative process to translate an operational need into a configured system meeting that need through a systematic, concurrent approach to integrated design of the product and its processes; (4). To integrate all technical disciplines and inputs (development, configuration management, integration and testing, production, installation, and logistics) into a coordinated effort that meets established cost, schedule, and performance objectives; (5). To ensure the compatibility of all functional and physical interfaces and ensures that system definition and design reflect the requirements for all system elements (hardware, software, facilities, personnel, data, material, services and techniques); (6). To characterize technical risks, develops risk abatement approaches and reduces technical risk through market surveys, trade-off analyses, and early test and demonstration of system elements; (7). To provide engineering support for planning, scheduling, cost estimation, configuration management, risk analysis, contractor performance measurement, contractor work specifications, proposal evaluations, contract negotiations, defining and management system requirements, and developing system architectures; (8). Support other parts of the organization by performing benchmarking/sizing analyses, data and other system modeling activities and prototype development; (9). To identify process improvement opportunities, analyze application requirements, conduct system testing, performs site installations, and defining system performance and availability reporting procedures, and task specialized contractor support; (10). Provide specific expertise in maintenance, logistics, and full-scale production; (11). Control all activities necessary for software acquisition and software life cycle management via a contractual vehicle; (12). Manage the software requirements and their traceability to the design, documentation, testing, training, and standards; (13). Provide software project tracking and oversight for the entire life cycle; (14). To perform software technology assessment; estimate software costs; perform software risk analysis; and evaluate technical, cost, and schedule impact of all software decisions; (15). Take technical decisions on software quality assurance, verification, and validation; (16). Evaluate and apply software, and other tools to develop and manage the project; (17). To evaluate the design, engineering, implementation, and support of communication systems; the implementation and standards compliance of system and network monitoring provisions; the implementation of system hardware architecture; and the integrated performance and capability assessment of computer platforms and other hardware platforms, network components, and telecommunications circuits; (18). Complying the standard data communication protocol and hardware interface definitions and serves as the technical lead for the hardware, network/communications, and monitoring and control system configuration item areas; (19). To provide technical expertise and oversight in the areas of hardware configuration item testing and telecommunications circuit testing.

ENVIRONMENTAL MANAGEMENT

Environmental Management is a commitment to ensuring advanced protection of the environment, compliance with governmental regulations and implementation of state-of-the-art technology. The Environmental Management reflects the corporate emphasis on continuous improvement in operations by measuring and evaluating its environmental performance; including: policy, planning, implementation, assessment and corrective action, management review processes. These components work in a continuous improvement cycle in order to achieve superior environmental performance:

a. Policy: commitment to the care of the environment and the control and prevention of pollution arising from its waste collection activities. Comply with all applicable regulatory requirements and the international standards; establish processes and procedures for meeting the commitments in our environmental policy; managing environmental program and encouraging continuous improvement; develop skills, knowledge and values that promote behavior in support of a sustainable environment

b. Planning: establish the objectives and processes necessary to deliver results following the organization's environmental policy; providing balanced solutions that add value and meet the corporate goals; improve corporate environmental performance; minimize waste, promote recycling initiatives, reduce energy consumption, reduce harmful emissions and where possible, to work with contractors/suppliers who also have and maintain an environmental policy. If possible, operate a zero landfill policy.

c. Implementation: monitor and measure processes against environmental policy, objectives and targets, legal and other requirements, and report the results; pollutant prevention; environmental training; engineering and emission controls; communication; environmental bench marking; develop an appropriate reporting mechanism

d. Assessment: risk assessment: qualitative or quantitative characterization of the nature and magnitude of human health or ecological risks, i.e. hazardous-waste-site evaluations, superfund sites, air toxics reviews, landfill permitting, environmental impact statements, and brown-fields sites; process evaluation; audit the compliance with international standard; investigations

e. Corrective action: take actions to continually improve the performance of the environmental management system

f. Management Review process: process to identify opportunities for greater efficiency and economy, or to improve effectiveness in carrying out procedures of operations. The objective is improvement in relation to the goals of the organization: involve people with right information/knowledge and people with authority to decide; schedule the meetings; record/document the meeting outcome; use management review to assess hoe changing circumstances might influence the suitability, effectiveness, adequacy of environmental management system, i.e. materials, customers, regulatory requirement etc; ensure that people follow up the actions plan arising from management reviews; consider other organizational plans and goals that may affects to environmental management system; integrate environmental decision making into overall management and strategy

INVESTMENT MANAGEMENT

Investments allow entities to use idle funds to generate additional revenue. These additional revenues may allow governments to reduce tax burdens while increasing the resources available to provide goods and services. Investment management purposes to ensure that public investments are properly managed so that returns from funds are maximized while capital is safeguarded and investments are in compliance with laws, regulations and other contractual obligations. The management of investments is an important part of ensuring that public funds are used effectively and efficiently. Investments must be protected against theft and fraud as well as non-systematic decision-making. The process of investment management should be linked to strategic planning.

The basic phases of investment management process are:

a. Identify investment constraints and preferences. Investment activities are often limited by state statutes and other contractual obligations. The preferences of boards, legislators, customers, and the public should be considered. Preferences may indicate investment strategies to be pursued, or risk levels, or added constraints over future investments.

b.   Establish objectives and investment policies, i.e. the board's expectations for portfolio diversification; allowable investments; acceptable risk levels; expected rates of return

c.   Develop and document administrative systems and internal controls. Transaction documentation creates a mechanism for monitoring and facilitates the training of personnel for assigned tasks. Internal controls should be used to reduce or prevent errors (i.e. technical and judgment errors) and irregularities (i.e. fraud and embezzlement)

d.   Select an investment outlook and strategy. An investment outlook refers to an entity's expectations about future opportunities based on existing information. The outlook should be broad enough to encompass stock and bond markets and financial instruments, as well as general economic conditions, both domestic and abroad. It may need forming an investment advisory committee; hiring investment consultants

e.   Select investment instruments, i.e. Corporate bonds; Domestic stocks; International stocks; Mortgage-Backed Securities (MBS); Collateralized Mortgage Obligations (CMO); etc

f.   Record and report investment transactions. The entity must record investment transactions in accordance with generally accepted accounting principles. The entity must have a process in place to report investment activity and balances in accordance with reporting standards.

g.   Monitor the portfolio and the environment. communicate issues or events that could affect the entity's portfolio; evaluate performance of the investment advisors; identifying new or changing laws and regulations that govern the financial markets; evaluating the risk level of the portfolio

h.   Reevaluate the investment management process. Investment performance is the return on invested capital over a specific period of time (monthly, quarterly, year to date, annual, etc.). It is the total return of the fund or segment of the fund (including income, capital gains and losses, and unrealized gains and losses) and is calculated on the basis of the market value at the end of each time interval. The main point in evaluating the performance of an investment portfolio is that the evaluator cannot ignore the entity's goals, risk parameters, and investment philosophies during the evaluation process.

There are four primary causes of less than optimal investment results, i.e. speculation, abrogation of responsibility, lack of internal controls and lack of supervision.

SAFETY MANAGEMENT

Company should establish Safety Management System in order to exploit synergies inside the organization. Among the key tasks in this area is the assurance of compliance both with external legal provisions as well as internal company standards. Supporting continuous improvement is another important task. The system should be based on international standards such as OHSAS 18001 (Safety). The management system's check is within the scope of the regular Corporate EHS audits and external certification. Key elements of the system report are:

a. Define annual target. The goal is to have a safe working environment in which everyone that comes into contact with the corporate operations. Safety target will be zero accidents all the years.

b. Identifying and minimizing risk: (1). A comprehensive risk assessment includes steps, i.e.: identify all key compliance requirements; identify those that apply to your staff, processes and systems; for each area of potential compliance risk, identify the nature of that risk of non-compliance as it applies to the firm; using a risk rating scale, score the risk and record it; for each identified risk, prescribe a mitigating, controlling or corrective action and timescale for completion, (including assigning it to a person or function). (2). Risk management that is achieving continuous control over the incidence and impact of risk which requires: comprehensive understanding of the business and operations environment; detailed risk assessment process founded on quality principles; experienced resources to identify risks and assess their importance and implications; creative minds to develop cost-effective risk mitigation strategies that control and neutralize unacceptable risks; top-down management commitment to implement protective strategies and monitor progress; continuous management vigilance to control new risks.

c. Establish audits: (1). Organization (people and their duties): individual job descriptions having a safety content; details of specific safety responsibilities; the role and function of safety committee(s); the role and function of safety representatives; and a management chart clearly showing the lines of responsibility and accountability in terms of health and safety management; Making adequate resources available to implement the policy; setting health and safety objectives; developing suitable procedures and safe systems; delegating specific responsibilities to others; monitoring the effectiveness of others in carrying out their responsibilities; monitoring standards within the workplace; and feeding concerns up through the organization; (2). Arrangement (systems and procedures): safety training; safe systems of work; environmental control; safe place of work; machine/area guarding; housekeeping; safe plant and equipment; noise control; radiation safety; dust control; use of toxic materials; internal communication/participation; utilization of safety committee(s) and safety representatives; fire safety and prevention; medical facilities and welfare; maintenance of records; accident reporting and investigation; emergency procedures; workplace monitoring, first aid; occupational health; control of contractors and visitors; consultation with employees; audits of health and safety arrangements; (3). Plant Equipment and substances: maintenance of equipment such as tools, ladders, etc.; maintenance and proper use of safety equipment such as helmets, boots, goggles, respirators, etc; maintenance and proper use of plant, machinery and guards; regular testing and maintenance of lifts, hoists, cranes, pressure systems, boilers and other dangerous machinery, emergency repair work, and safe methods of doing it; maintenance of electrical installations and equipment; safe storage, handling and, where applicable, packaging, labeling and transport of dangerous substances; controls on work involving harmful substances, such as acid, caustic, CS_2, H_2S, etc; the introduction of new plant, equipment or substances into the workplace—by examination, testing and consultation with the workforce; procedures ensure safe operation of the plant as well as the integrity of the staff and all persons working in the plant; maintain and develop operational readiness for emergencies; maintains awareness of any risks threatening the company, the personnel and the operating environment; (4). Environmental protection and safety at the production plants should be organized with management systems established according to international standards. Minimum requirements for various factors are developed in close collaboration with the executives and the operating units. Regular audits form is an important part of the comprehensive system. It serves not only to check the status of environmental protection and safety, but also provide an opportunity to exchange views. Audit that are conducted, include production sites, stand-alone R&D sites, and warehouses.

Continuous improvement process has resulted in a significant decrease in the number of audit findings and an ever-growing awareness of environmental protection and safety.

d. Perform Report: (1). Accident report: an accident is an unplanned occurrence that may result in damage to people, property, equipment, or the environment. When accidents are reported promptly, injured employees, and visitors receive timely medical care and unsafe conditions receive prompt corrective action. The Environmental Health & Safety Executive/staff should investigate accidents to identify accident trends, determine the effectiveness of current safety programs, and prevent future accidents. Report unsafe conditions or potentially hazardous situation is also mandatory, so that the Environmental Health & Safety Executive/staff as quickly as possible will then contact other departments and outside agencies as appropriate; (2). Safety training report: The training required by each employee is dependent upon the job assignment and the nature of the hazards to which that individual may be exposed. Resources must be provided to ensure that each employee is trained to the minimum requirements of the corporate; (3). Employee's involvement: employees should be directly involved in environmental protection, health and safety activities. Of those, they are to be volunteers in the company's fire brigades, emergency response and spill teams, and as safety representatives; (4). Audit report: The EHS Executive will annually monitor the overall EHS performance by observing accident/incident trends, compliance trends, EHS program implementation, and employee behaviors over the year. This information will be combined with information obtained during inspections and audits to develop an annual report EHS performance. Performance related to specific EHS objectives that may have been established in the operations plan, the corporate EHS tactical plans, contract, and other applicable institutional plans; (5). Accreditation: providing accreditation to ensure accountability and minimum compliance international standards; analysis of corporate safety and loss control program that measures its overall effectiveness; promote safety and loss control, preserve lives, prevent injury and help reduce the escalating costs associated with preventable injuries and/or death; (6). Management review follow up: violations of hazardous material-related acute, critical and severe regulations and violations of safety management-related acute and critical regulations, respectively, that were discovered during a compliance review

EHS policy insists the commitment to corporate social responsibility includes the well-being of the workers and the environment, as well as people living and working in communities near company's facilities; immediately control and report all spills and releases as required by local regulations, facility rules and company standards; safety and remediation measures must be promptly initiated to minimize any adverse environmental impacts from such incidents.

Corporate to take all possible steps to ensure the health, safety and welfare of all employees and other persons engaged in work for the organization and any third parties who come into contact with the business, i.e.: set priorities for and manage EHS activities, resources, and corrective actions in their area of responsibility; enforce all EHS policies; analyze operations to identify hazards and EHS concerns and implement measures to control the hazards, prevent occurrences, and minimize the risk of the operations to humans, facilities, and the environment; ensure that employees, affiliates, subcontractors, and visitors are properly trained and equipped for the programs, procedures, hazards, and control measures associated with their tasks; evaluate EHS performance in each employee's performance evaluation; invite reporting of EHS issues by all employees and ensure that no intimidation, harassment, or retaliation results; ensure that all EHS concerns raised by employees are adequately addressed.

BEST VALUE MANAGEMENT

Best value enables management to deliver continuous improvement in all services and to meet the needs and expectations of service users. Under the best value management is a principal means by which executives are held accountable for the quality and efficiency of their services. Best value management will need to include: objectives in respect of its functions; current performance; comparison with performance in previous financial years; approach to efficiency improvement; key results; targets set for future years; plan of action; response to audit and inspection reports; financial statement. Resources and policy implications:

a. Financial: implementation of best value will require additional direct funding. Best value will deliver financial benefits to corporate, either in terms of reduced costs or in terms of securing improved service delivery from existing resources.

b.   Staffing: best value will affect all staff within the corporate. The importance of the staffs in delivering best value can never be understated.

c.   Equalities: equalities issues are an integral part of moving towards best value.

d.   Economic: best value focuses heavily on corporate interaction with the community, and specific interests with it.

e.   Environment: Environmental issues are an integral part of moving towards best value.

f.   Corporate Wide Impacts: best value will change the way corporate works. Its fundamental and challenging nature will result n a level of scrutiny of service purpose and delivery not seen before. Over time, all staff and customers are likely to see the impact. The imperative for corporate is to remain focused on securing continuous improvements for its customers

Process of producing best value management should provide an opportunity for (1). Illustrate corporate strategy across their range of responsibilities and foster greater transparency and accountability; (2). Demonstrating how entity plans link with those of other stakeholders with a shared responsibility to meet entity needs; (3). Engaging the staffs in determining the priorities of management and measuring the extent to which best value has been achieved; (4). Providing appropriate information to enable staffs to judge their performance, there is a need to ensure that the plan is readable and accessible; (5). Subject to audit and inspection

Best value management is about delivering performance and doing the right thing, quality management is about assessing performance and doing the thing right. Both can be achieved by: empowering staff to make their full contribution, investing in people and being a 'learning' organization, creatively challenges the status quo, change-welcome to improve performance

RISK MANAGEMENT

Risk Management is the process of measuring, or assessing risk and then developing strategies to manage the risk. Corporate has to encounter a range of risks that threatens its' ability to meet business objectives and deliver cost effective and quality services. These risks can originate from many different sources, i.e.:

1. Market Risk refers to the risk that the market value of an investment, collateral protecting a deposit, or securities underlying a repurchase agreement will decline. This type of risk is affected by the length to maturity of a security, the need to liquidate a security before maturity, the extent that collateral exceeds the amount invested, and the frequency at which the amount of collateral is adjusted for changing market values.

2. Price risk is associated with dramatic price fluctuation of product. Especially product futures market provides a means for all sectors of the product trade to manage or hedge their exposure to the risk of unexpected price fluctuation. By hedging the price of product they must buy and sell, they can avoid the potentially devastating effects of unexpected price fluctuation. It also involves basis risk, a risk that is associated with widening or narrowing the basis between the time a hedge is established and the time it is liquidated. Basis itself is the difference between the specific futures contract for product at a local delivery point. Future price may consider present cash price, cost of storage, insurance and interest charges, and location of delivery.

3. Interest Rate Risk: sensitivity to a decline in interest rates

4. Customer Risk: associated with failure to meet the current and changing needs and expectations of customers

5. Currency Risk: performance relative to currency markets, i.e. spot contracts, forward transactions, window forwards, options, currency swaps, non-deliverable forwards.

6. Energy Risk: financial risks posed by volatile energy prices (electricity, oil, natural gas, and fuel)

7. Equity Risk: related to depreciation because of stock market dynamics causing one to lose money

8. Competitiveness Risk: affecting the competitiveness of the service (in terms of cost or quality)

9. Commodity (Raw Material) Risk: affecting state budgets and company cash flows and makes future revenues less predictable as commodity (raw material) price uncertainty

10. Reinvestment Risk: uncertainty in the interest rate at which future cash flows may be invested

11. Earnings/liquidity Risk: due to uncertainty in future reported earnings

12. Social risk: relating to the effects of changes in demographic, socio-economic trends, environmental demands, health demands, political change

13. Environmental Risk: relating to the environmental consequences of pollution, recycling, landfill requirements, emissions etc. environmental and green supply assurance, commit to conserving energy, water and other resources, reducing waste, phasing out the use of ozone-depleting substances and minimizing the release of greenhouse gases and substances damaging to health and the environment.

14. Employee Risk: associated with sickness absence, turnover, work related illness and injury, medical and long term disability, employment practice, insurance

15. Community Risk: associated to public health and environmental quality

16. Political Risk: associated with failure to deliver either local or central government policy, or meet the local administrations manifesto commitments

17. Model Risk: risk that models are applied to tasks for which they are inappropriate or are otherwise implemented incorrectly

18. Operational Risk: loss resulting from inadequate or failed internal processes, people and systems, or from external events, e.g. Employee errors, systems failures, fire, floods or other losses to physical assets, fraud or other criminal activity.

19. Technological Risk: associated with the capacity of corporate to deal with the pace/scale of technological change, or its ability to use technology to address changing demands. They may also include the consequences of internal technological failures to deliver its objectives.

20. Legal Risk: uncertainty due to legal actions or uncertainty in the applicability or interpretation of contracts, laws or regulations

21. Liquidity Risk/Cash Flow Risk: due to uncertainty in future reported cash flows

22. Economical Macro Risk: affecting the ability of corporate to meet its financial commitments because of macro level economic changes

23. Contractual Risk: associated with the failure of contractors to deliver services or products to the agreed cost and specification or failure of corporate to ensure that contracts are properly specified. It must be appropriately managed; achieves value for money by procuring against pre-determined standards not only for the goods, services and works but also for the suppliers that are used; legal, ethical and transparent.

24. Professional Risk: associated with failure to meet the particular nature of each position.

25. Credit Risk: refers to the likelihood that a party involved in an investment transaction will not fulfill its obligations. This type of risk is often associated with the issuer of the investment security and is affected by the concentration of deposits or investments in a single instrument or with a single institution. Custodial credit risk is the risk that a government will not be able (a) to recover deposits if the depository financial institution fails or (b) to recover the value of investment or collateral securities that are in the possession of an outside party if the counterparty to the investment or deposit transaction fails.

26. Extension Risk is the risk that a security will lengthen in average life due to slower prepayment speeds. This type of risk is generally associated with mortgage securities.

27. Contraction Risk is the risk that a security will shorten in average life due to faster than expected prepayments. This type of risk is normally associated with mortgage securities.

28. Capital Risk refers to the risk that an investor may not recover all or a portion of his or her original capital at the time an investment has been liquidated

Risk management should be a proactive part of all activities to minimize potential risks that occurs because of uncertainty or exposure. It includes:

a. Strategy: ensure risk management is appropriately considered as part of the corporate strategic planning; demonstrate high level support for embedding risk management throughout the corporate; promote risk awareness, instead of risk avoidance, to empower frontline staff; establish a corporate approach to identify and prioritize key services and key risks across the corporate; establish a corporate mechanism to evaluate key risks and determine if they are being adequately managed and financed; establish procedures which will help allocate limited resources, on a fair and objective basis, to help reduce significant risks; establish a clear reporting system which will provide assurance on how well the corporate is managing its key risks including the creation of key performance indicators; ensure responsibility for risk management is clearly and appropriately allocated.

b. Step of action: establish the context (planning the remainder of the process and mapping out the scope of the exercise, the identity and objectives of stakeholders, the basis upon which risks will be evaluated and defining a framework for the process, and agenda for identification and analysis, identify the risks (source analysis: may be internal or external, problem analysis: related to loss, privacy information, accident); analyze the risks (the likelihood of any risk arising needs to be assessed. Also the consequences or impact it may have if it does arise); profile the risks (once analyzed the risks need to be profiled according to their likelihood and severity); prioritize the risks (the risks need to be ranked based on the corporate ability, or not, to deal with the consequences and the funding available); decide on action (whether the risk should be avoided, reduced, transferred (to an insurance company in return for a premium, or to a contractor) or accepted); control the risks (this involves taking action to minimize the likelihood of a risk occurring and/or reducing the severity of the consequences should it occur); monitor and report progress (progress in managing risks should be monitored and reported so that losses are minimized and intended actions are achieved. Risk management is an on-going process that should be constantly revisited and reviewed)

COMPENSATION MANAGEMENT

Developing the right philosophy, then implementing the best, most supportive compensation programs, requires thoughtful planning that involves the right,

bright people from throughout the organization. An effective compensation philosophy must be as relevant to employees in the mail room as it is to the officers;
fit the organization's decision making and managerial style, and become part of
the corporate culture. The philosophy or strategy should provide guidance for a
wide range of issues, such as: alignment of compensation and corporate objectives; compensation program objectives (more than attract, retain and motivate;
role of different pay components); desired competitive posture (relevant competitors; base salary/total compensation); internal equity considerations (relevant dif-
ferentiating factors; performance, seniority, skills, responsibilities, interpersonal
abilities; individual vs. team vs. organization roles); regulatory compliance objectives; economic factors (sharing of risks; limits of ability to pay); responsibility for
program design, administration; differences by function, levels. Following type of
compensation systems are commonly used, i.e.:

1. Salary: wage received on a regular basis, usually weekly, bi-weekly, or
    monthly. Salary will have variation within a level that depends on working
    time service, skill/expertise; responsibility diversity; cost of living adjust-
    ments for different markets; educational adjustments; superstar adjustments
    (acknowledged and recognized by their peer)

2. Profit-sharing: is a compensation plan which allows the employee and the
    employer to share profits in the company. It helps the employee to gain trust
    in the company that when profits are above a certain percentage, they will
    receive a bonus depending upon the policy of the company.

3. Incentive Systems: employee incentive systems are an increasingly popular
    way of rewarding employees based on their performance, rather than hours
    worked or years of service. Individual incentives and gain-sharing are the
    "fastest growing trend in compensation management." Performance-based
    compensation is a key to the future success of firms which operate in highly
    competitive markets. Employee stock ownership plans (ESOP) are another
    way of compensating workers. They provide employees with an actual stake
    in the corporation. Companies must continually find new ways to cut costs
    and increase worker productivity. By implementing programs which include
    the employees, they feel as though they are working toward a common goal,
    which in turn leads to increases in performance, quality and productivity.

4. Piecework: a type of incentive program where the employee is paid based on
    each unit of output. Employees are paid a certain rate per unit times the

number of units produced. This is a system that works for only a limited number of jobs such as assembly line or agricultural. Piecework incentive programs are declining in popularity due to the fact that it does not always lead to higher productivity. It is also difficult to measure a person benefit based solely on the units they can produce in a given period of time.

5. Production Bonuses: are incentives that reward extra effort in the work place. When an employee either saves time on a given production run, or they produce more units in a given time period, they are given a per unit monetary reward. Production bonuses are very similar to piecework, except that the employee still earns a good base salary.

6. Commission: is a percentage of the selling price which is given to the seller as a form of incentive. Most commission related jobs have a minimal base salary, and commission is a way to make the employee a more aggressive seller.

7. Pay-for-Knowledge and Pay-for-Skills compensation systems: give employees higher pay as an incentive for each new skill or job they learn". Since "pay-for-knowledge" is a new concept, The Management should use the PFK Compensation System as an enhancement to their current compensation programs. Companies and organizations should encourage their employees to learn as much as they can about their career by compensating them for learning new skills about their job and the company. Paying employees based on job knowledge is not necessarily for the task he is assigned to, but it is based on what he learns to enhance more skills and knowledge of additional tasks. When an employee learns all he can about his job and the company, he becomes a part of the organization. This will help to hire, maintain, and retain employees who will be a contributing factor to the mission and goals of the organization. Paying employees for knowledge and job skills will benefit not only the employee, but the employer as well. The more organizations encourage their employees to enhance their skills as an employee, the greater morale, turnover, absenteeism, and productivity will improve. It will be interesting to see how the future for Pay-for-Knowledge will be as more research is done to determine the reliability and validity of the PFK compensation plan.

8. Indirect Compensation: compensation not related to wages and salaries or incentives and gain-sharing, but employee fringe benefits that are given to employees as an incentive for becoming a part of the organization. Some

benefits of direct compensation are insurance benefits, life and disability insurances, mandated leave and benefits, retirement plans, vacation and personal days, holiday pay, leave of absence, employee services, and special programs.

9.   Maturity Curves: are a way rewarding higher level employees by making adjustments to their income level based on productivity and experience. There are several different degrees of performance ranging from outstanding to marginal. Maturity curves are valuable because they enable high level high productivity employees the opportunity to make more money without have to seek a higher position.

10. Merit Raise: are increases in pay based on an evaluation of an employee performance. Immediate supervisors are the ones responsible for the evaluation and subsequent raise. The main problem of this system is that it is subject to bias, and therefore many merit deserving employees do not receive fair compensation

11. ESOP: employee stock ownership plans are the ultimate form of gain-sharing. Instead of receiving a raise or other forms of incentive compensation, an employee is issued company stock. Overall, employees now control about 6% of corporate equity. An ESOP is a kind of employee benefit plan, similar in some ways to a profit-sharing plan. In an ESOP, a company sets up a trust fund, into which it contributes new shares of its own stock or cash to buy existing shares. Alternatively, the ESOP can borrow money to buy new or existing shares, with the company making cash contributions to the plan to enable it to repay the loan. Regardless of how the plan acquires stock, company contributions to the trust are tax-deductible, within certain limits. Shares in the trust are allocated to individual employee accounts. Although there are some exceptions, generally all full-time employees over 21 participate in the plan. Allocations are made either on the basis of relative pay or some more equal formula. As employees accumulate seniority with the company, they acquire an increasing right to the shares in their account, a process known as vesting. Employees must be 100% vested within five to seven years. When employees leave the company, they receive their stock, which the company must buy back from them at its fair market value (unless there is a public market for the shares). Private companies must have an annual outside valuation to determine the price of their shares. In private companies, employees must be able to vote their allocated shares on major issues,

such as closing or relocating, but the company can choose whether to pass through voting rights (such as for the board of directors) on other issues. In public companies, employees must be able to vote all issues

12. Golden Parachute: Golden handshake or golden parachute is a clause in an executive employment contract that provides the executive with a significant severance package in the case that the executive loses their job through firing, restructuring, or even scheduled retirement. This can be in the form of cash, equity, and other benefits, and is often accompanied by an accelerated vesting of stock options. Typically, "golden handshakes" are offered only to high-ranking executives by major corporations and may entail a value measured in millions of dollars. Golden handshakes are given to offset the risk inherent in taking the new job, since high-ranking executives have a high likelihood of being fired and since a company requiring an outsider to come in at such a high level may be in a precarious financial position. In more general usage, "golden parachute" has come to signify any deal that—be it through money, another job (usually well-paid but more ceremonial, a sinecure)—makes it easier for an organization to get rid of a high-ranking member without fuss, trouble, protests, or bad press. This may be, for example, the offer of an ambassadorship (which is considered prestigious and socially desirable) to a minister not wanted anymore in the cabinet, or the promotion of a manager to chairman of the board of an affiliate. In other case, golden handshake schemes are called Voluntary retirement schemes, where employees are offered benefits in return for early retirement.

Compensation is what employees receive in exchange for their contribution to the organization. Direct Compensation—compensation directly related to wages and salaries, incentives and gain-sharing. Direct compensation is based on performance, not a condition of employment, unlike indirect compensation. Benefits of Effective Compensation Management, includes: recruit qualified employees; maintain employee satisfaction; retain current workforce; strive toward internal and external equity; reward desired employee behavior; control costs; comply with state and federal regulations; easy to understand compensation system; manageable compensation system

ANTI FRAUD AND CORRUPTION MANAGEMENT

Corporate must commit to making sure that the opportunity for fraud and corruption is reduced to the lowest possible risk. Where the possibility of fraud, corruption and other problems occur, the corporate will deal with it in a firm and controlled manner.

Prevention

a. Policies and Procedures: procedures and rules to make sure that the corporate financial, working and organizational procedures are properly controlled. It consists of: (1). Financial regulation; (2). Code of Conduct for employees; (3). Employees conditions of service; (4). Procurement policy and strategy; (5). Accounting procedures and records; (6). Internal control systems and internal audit; (7). Fraud response plan; (8). Recruitment and selection procedures; (9). Disciplinary procedure and criminal acts procedure; (10). Confidential reporting (Whistle Blowing) Code; (11). Investigatory procedure

b. Define examples: (1). Theft is defined as the dishonest taking of property belonging to another with the intention of permanently depriving the owner of its possession; (2). Fraud is defined as the intentional distortion of financial statements or other records by persons internal or external to the authority which is carried out to conceal the misappropriation of assets or otherwise for gain; (3). Corruption is defined as the offering, giving, soliciting or acceptance of an inducement or reward, which may influence the action of any person; (4). Fraudulent or corrupt acts may include systems issues i.e. where a process/system exists which is prone to abuse by employees; financial issues i.e., where individuals or companies have fraudulently obtained money, (e.g. invalid invoices/work not done, housing benefit fraud); equipment issues i.e., where company's equipment is used for personal use, (e.g. personal use of company's telephones); resource issues i.e., where there is a misuse of resources, (e.g. theft of cash/assets); other issues i.e., activities undertaken by executives which may be: unlawful; against the procedures or policies, falls below established standards or practices; or amounts to improper conduct, (e.g. receiving unapproved hospitality)

c. Bring to expected levels of behavior: (1). Corporate should encourage all people and organizations that are in any way associated with it to be honest and fair in their dealings with Management, and customers. Board members and employees are expected to lead by example in these matters; (2). Employees must act in line with the code of conduct and ethics all the time; (3). Set out the expected level and guide line; (4). committed to working and co-operating with other organizations to prevent organized fraud and corruption

d. Develop Anti-Fraud culture: (1). Selflessness. Take decisions in terms of the corporate interest. Employees should not do so in order to gain financial or other material benefits for themselves, their family, or their friends; (2). Integrity. Not place themselves under any financial or other obligation to outside individuals or organization that might influence them in their performance of the official duties; (3). Objectivity. Not make any choice, in carrying out public business, including making public appointments, awarding contracts, or recommending individuals for rewards and benefits; (4). Accountability. Accountable for any decision or action and must submit themselves to whatever scrutiny is appropriate to the corporate; (5). Openness. Be as open as possible about all the decisions and actions that are taken; (6). Honesty. Declare any private interests relating to their duties and to take steps to resolve any conflicts; (7). Leadership. Promote and support these principles by leadership and example.

e. Audit: (1). Plan internal audit; (2). Internal check: no one person can carry out a complete transaction without some form of checking process being built into the system; 3). External audit

Tackling

a. Raising a concern: (1). Staff should normally raise concerns with their immediate manager or their superior. In general, however, the whistle-blowing procedure is expected to be used for potentially more serious and sensitive issues (e.g. corruption, fraud); 2). Investigative process should not be misused and, therefore, any abuse, such as raising unfounded malicious allegations, will be dealt with as a separate disciplinary matter.

b. Establish Committee: (1). Review on an annual basis to reflect any amendments to the corporate rules, or changes in legislation and working practices;

(2). Action: Take appropriate action against those who commit or seek to commit some sort of fraud or corruption; (3). Deal firmly and quickly with anyone who is involved in fraud or corruption Detecting and Investigating; (4). Employees must report any instances of fraud and corruption; (5). Decide on the type and course of the investigation; (6). Check the previous employment records of anyone considered for appointment

c. Taking forward a complaint: (1). Provide staff with an avenue to raise concerns with the Authority; (2). All information will be dealt with fairly and confidentially

d. Safeguard Whistle-blowing: (1). Not tolerate harassment or victimization for staff when they raise a concern in good faith; (2). Protect an individual's identity when s/he raises a concern and does not want their name to be disclosed; (3). Encourages staff to put their names to allegations; (4). If staff make an allegation in good faith, but it is not confirmed by the investigation, no action will be taken against them

e. Training: (1). Communicate the Anti-Fraud and Corruption Policy to staff and to promote a greater awareness of fraud within their departments; (2). Included on induction program for new employees

MANAGEMENT INFORMATION SYSTEM

Management Information Systems (MIS) is typically computer-based, that are used within an organization. It is commonly referred to as information technology management. The study of information systems is usually a commerce and business administration discipline, and frequently involves software engineering, but also distinguishes itself by concentrating on the integration of computer systems with the aims of the organization. Management information system can be defined as a system that collects and processes data (information) and provides it to managers at all levels that use it for decision making, planning, program implementation, and control. An information system is comprised of all the components that collect, manipulate, and disseminate data or information. It usually includes hardware, software, people, communications systems such as telephone lines, and the data itself. The activities involved include inputting data, processing of data into information, storage of data and information, and the production of outputs such as management reports. MIS are not just statistics and data analysis, it supports: to establish relevant and measurable objectives—to monitor results and performances (reach ratios)—to send alerts, in some cases daily, to managers at each level of the organization, on all deviations between results and pre-established objectives and budgets.

Information technology management is a combination of two branches: Information technology and Management. This aims at achieving the goals and objectives of an organization through computers. Also called IT management, this name is a common business function within corporations. It involves two aspects. One implies the management of a collection of systems, infrastructure, and information that resides on them. Another implies the management of Information Technologies as a business function. In business, information systems support business processes and operations, decision-making, and competitive strategies. Information systems support business processes and operations by: recording and storing sales data, purchase data, investment data, payroll data and other accounting records—processing these accounting records into income statements, balance sheets, ledgers, management reports, and other forms of financial information—recording and storing inventory data, work in process data, equipment repair and maintenance data, supply chain data, and other production/operations records—processing these operations records into production schedules, production controllers, inventory systems, and production monitoring systems—recording and storing personnel data, salary data, employment histories, and other human resources records—processing these human resources records into employee expense reports, and performance based reports—recording and storing market data, customer profiles, customer purchase histories, marketing research data, advertising data, and other marketing records—processing these marketing records into advertising elasticity reports, marketing plans, and sales activity reports—recording and storing business intelligence data, competitor analysis data, industry data, corporate objectives, and other strategic management records—processing these strategic management records into industry trends reports, market share reports, mission statements, and portfolio models—use of all the above to implement, control, and monitor plans, strategies, tactics, new products, new business models or new business ventures.

Information systems can support a company's competitive positioning. Here are three levels of analysis:

a. Help in piloting the chain of internal value. It is the most recent and the most pragmatic systems within the reach of the manager. They are the solutions to reductions of costs and management of performance. Tool networks, they ensure control over piloting the set functions of a company. The real-time mastery in the costs of dysfunctions cause distances from accounts, evaluation and accounting that are presented in the evaluation and qualitative reports.

b. Focus on core competencies. If a company's core competency gives it a long term advantage in the marketplace, it is referred to as a sustainable competitive advantage. For a core competency to become a sustainable competitive advantage it must be difficult to mimic, unique, sustainable, superior to the competition, and applicable to multiple situations. Company characteristics that could constitute a sustainable competitive advantage include: superior product quality, extensive distribution contracts, accumulated brand equity and positive company reputation, low cost production techniques, patents and copyrights, government protected monopoly, and superior employees and management team. The list of potential sustainable competitive advantage characteristics is very long. However, some experts hold that in today's changing and competitive world, no advantage can be sustained in the long run. They argue that the only truly sustainable competitive advantage is to build an organization that is so alert and so agile that it will always be able to find an advantage, no matter what changes occur.

c. Constitute the competitive advantages. The rapid change has made access to timely and current information critical in a competitive environment. Information systems, like business environmental scanning systems, support almost all sustainable competitive advantages.

Management Information Systems deploys in regulated systems environments deliver document/content lifecycle management, collaboration, search and navigation, web access, workflow, knowledge management and business process automation. It is a collaborative repository for capturing, managing and storing information such as workgroups, folders, documents, discussions, memos, links and other objects. Content lifecycle management includes check-in/check-out, version control, audit trails and document-level security for all kinds of document file types, including word processing documents, Web pages, images. Information must be easily accessible so end users can browse, search, manage tasks and view content and electronic documents quickly. These systems must also manage document content and all associated metadata (properties) that further describes the document to facilitate content-based searches. Companies often store information in a structured way, enhance information retrieval by intranet, extranet or Web site and automatically find and index new or modified documents. Increased operational efficiencies can be achieved by the comprehensive management of all electronic documents. Any documents, that are a part of a version/revision lifecycle, are maintained for iteration electronically, securely stored for future management or rollback. They are available for sharing and group collaboration based on specified employee security levels. System operational efficiency and compliance involves: (1). Ensure system has integrated document process lifecycle capability; (2). Built-in compliance regulation; (3). Predicate rule requirements that govern the type of documents stored and validate the system accordingly. It is important to establish a set of user requirements for the system so that all validation activities can be performed in accordance with intended use; (4). Establish ubiquitous web portal interface to ensure rapid adoption. To ensure rapid system adoption, it is current best practice to design the system using a ubiquitous web portal interface. The global familiarity with web technology will ensure that users adopt the system for its intended use; (5). Adapt extensible architectural framework. Regulatory content management systems must operate in an integrated systems environment; (6). Integrate records management technology. Regulatory requirements mandate security, records control, and retention policies; (7). Establish effective policies and procedures upfront. Compliance cannot be met with technology alone. It requires the establishment of effective policies and procedures to ensure compliance; (8). Develop comprehensive strategy for migration. Migration is often an afterthought for many content management systems; (9). Use federated systems approach for global/large deployments; (10). Define cabinet/folder hierarchy prior to deployment; (11). Establish security/access policies and procedures up front; (12). Leverage integrated off-the-shelf tools for: document rendering; document watermarking; controlled printing; regulatory publishing; scanning and input/capture; (13). Avoid over-customization; (14). Train all authorized users.

Once documents are available in electronic form, it can be instantly viewed by anyone through the document management system, a web browser, or any other integrated application system. Electronic records management in most companies has historically been a very manual process delegated to a group of well respected professionals in the back office. Electronic records management includes four basic aspects: indexing—the process of establishing access points to facilitate retrieval of records; classification—systematic identification and arrangement of business activities or records into categories according to logically structured conventions, methods, and procedural rules represented in a classification scheme; long term archival—the process of creating a backup copy of computer files for long-term storage; storage—the function of storing records for future retrieval and use. The characteristics of trustworthy electronic records are:

a. Reliable—electronic records whose content can be trusted as a full and accurate representation of the transactions, activities, or facts to which it attests and can be depended upon in the course of subsequent transactions or activities.

b. Authentic—records proven to be what they purport to be and were sent or created by the person who purports to have created and sent them

c. Integrity—refers to the complete and unaltered characteristic of a record. Another aspect of integrity is structural integrity. The structure of a record, that is its physical and logical format and the relationships between the data elements comprising the record, should remain physically and logically intact. Failure to do so may hinder the records' reliability and authenticity.

d. Usability—a record which can be located, retrieved, presented and interpreted.

PROJECT MANAGEMENT

Project management is application of knowledge, skills, tools and techniques to a broad range of activities to meet the requirements of the particular project. Project management should cover:

a. Project Organizations: to establish organizational guidelines and reporting relationships for project teams.

b. Project Initiation: to specify steps for project selection, initiation and prioritization.

c. Project Planning: to define project planning methods and procedures.

d. Roles & Responsibilities: to establish resource roles and responsibilities for project management, planning and execution.

e. Risk Management: to establish risk management guidelines and procedures.

f. Change Management: establish change management guidelines and procedures.

g. Communications: structure communications and status reporting requirements.

h. Vendor Relationships: to establish outsourcing guidelines.

i. Purchasing Guidelines: to establish purchasing and cost control strategies.

j. Project Evaluation: to establish evaluation criteria and exit strategies for failing projects.

k. Project Closure/Transition: to create guidelines for project completion, transition and post project activities.

l. Project Tools: to specify requirements and standards for the selection and utilization of project planning, reporting and tracking software.

In essence, a project can be captured on paper with a few simple elements: a start date, an end date, the tasks that have to be carried out, and when they should be finished, and some idea of the resources (people, machines etc) that will be needed during the course of the project. Project management is a carefully planned and organized effort to accomplish a specific target, includes: developing a project plan, which includes defining project goals and objectives, specifying tasks or how goals will be achieved, what resources are need, and associating budgets and timelines for completion; implementing the project plan, along with careful controls to stay on the "critical path", that is, to ensure the plan is being managed according to plan; follow major phases (with various titles for these phases), including feasibility study, project planning, implementation, evaluation and support/maintenance

The success of a project will depend critically upon the effort, care and skill that are applied in its initial planning, i.e.: project specification: written definition of what is required, by when; and this must be agreed by all involved. It should fulfill clarity (reveal misunderstandings), completeness (avoid contradictory assumptions), rigor of the analysis (expose technical and practical details); structuring: decide what actually need to do, and how to do it, includes: work break down structure (set of simpler separate activities), task allocation (allocate the tasks to different people and at the same time), guesstimation (realistic estimate of the time involved in the project); controlling: establish at the start (within the plan) the means to monitor and to influence the project's progress (milestones and communication)

Defining Goals

Project management can range from calendars and to-do lists to work breakdown structures. However these practices may vary, the goals are usually the same: to produce the desired project results within the boundaries of time, costs and available resources.

Defining Requirement

Every project should be based on a sound specification of requirements (functional, technical, business and process). Projects must be designed to deliver effective business and technical solutions. To meet that goal, every project must also begin with an approved requirements specification. But, before project requirements can be selected and approved, they must be collected, culled and defined. Considering the complex nature of technology projects, requirements are typically multi-faceted and often elusive, subject to opinion and bias. As such, the requirements collection process must reflect these realities to identify requirements at all levels and perceptions.

Estimate and Track Project Cost

The management of project costs can be the most complicated, political, (and tedious) element of the project management process. Costs have to be controlled by identifying project cost factors, estimating cost values and create a budget, tracking costs and monitor variances.

a.   Cost Factor. While cost factors will vary based on project characteristics and business circumstances, in general, project costs can be viewed from four basic perspectives:

(i).   Resource Costs: the costs involved in staffing a project, which can include: salary, benefits, outsourcing contracts, temporary staffing, overtime—(1). Asset Costs: the costs of asset acquisition, usually involving tangible assets that are used to create or implement project deliverables, which can include: hardware, software, peripherals, infrastructure, telecommunications equipment, installation tools; (2). Overhead Costs: the costs involved in maintaining the project environment, enabling project completion, which can include: office supplies, premises (rent, utilities), support services; (3). Project Specific Costs: costs of project execution, consumed in the completion of the project, which can include: travel, meals, meeting costs, print production & photocopying

- Cost estimate and budget. Project budgets quantify the expected costs associated with a project, and these budgets must be based on a reasonable, realistic estimate of likely project costs and expenses. The estimation of project costs is part science, and part logic, common sense and experience. In fact, past projects can be the most valuable indicator of current project expenses. As project costs are estimated, the following factors should be considered: The specific cost factors involved depending on the needs of the project, the costs of similar projects in the past, the opinions and feedback of project participants. When estimating costs, it is important to get a broad spectrum of information, experience and opinion. Depending on the degree of internal experience with a given type of project, contingency reserves may or may not be necessary. In addition, there is a philosophy that says that contingency reserves are dangerous, leading to unwarranted project spending.

- Tracking Costs and Cost Variances. Once the project budget is created and approved, and the project is underway, costs and expenses must be tracked to ensure that budget utilization matches project progress. Budget variances can be tracked on a monthly basis, for a targeted project picture, as well as on the basis of the project as a whole, for a global perspective. A positive variance: indicates that you are under budget, but appearances to the contrary not withstanding, this is not necessarily a good thing. When project expenses are less than expected, this may be a sign that the project is not proceeding according to plan, and may be behind schedule. In addition, a positive variance may be a sign of ineffective estimating. A negative variance: indicates that the project is over budget. Depending upon whether the negative variance is at a monthly or overall project level, this variance may be the result of serious project problems, such as excessive changes, schedule delays or ineffective budgeting.

As the project budget is tracked, the results of the tracking process can be used to monitor project success, and to highlight potential problem areas for further analysis and possible corrective action.

Project Tracking

Project tracking needs processes, i.e.: understand goals & capabilities (project efficiencies, availability of skills and resources), examine the project schedule (identify dependencies and concurrent tasks), re-work the project timeline (create a schedule that allows tasks to be completed in the shortest time possible, removing dependencies), examine alternatives (additional resources be added, additional work hours, scope of the project be changed, deliverables functionality be reduced, project be outsourced); seek consensus (all points of view are considered); monitor progress and track problems (track multiple tasks, manage issues and problems)

Project Closure

Projects are designed to produce a specific unique outcome, and when that outcome is delivered, the project should end. Depending on the nature and complexity of the project, closure can consist of any or all of the following elements: final testing, acceptance, production turnover, end-user training, deliverables documentation, resource re-allocation, post project performance reviews.

5

CODE OF CONDUCT AND ETHICS

Integrity is one of the fundamental values to which corporate is committed in carrying out its mission. Truth, objectivity, and independence are the foundation of corporate business. They are the standards that every employee, executive and director should meet in all business conduct. The Code of Conduct and Ethics is intended to help ensure compliance with the highest legal and ethical standards. It is the responsibility of every employee, executive and director of the company to understand and adhere to the code. Code of conduct is a set of principles and expectations that are considered binding on any person who is a member of a particular group or company. Any employee who knowingly violates any provision of this code will be subject to disciplinary action, including reprimand, suspension and/or termination. It is also the responsibility of executive of the company to ensure that employees reporting to them understand and comply with the code. Employees who have questions concerning the code or become aware of a possible violation of the code should promptly contact their superior or human resources.

Cause to the effective running of the company is that all staffs are clear about the functions of the organization, their own role and the roles of others and that decision is made in a clear and accountable way. The Management, in compliance with legal requirements and good practice, is to establish formal guidelines for how staff should work setting standards of personal behavior, which everyone should adhere to. Also includes the formal process by which decisions are made in the organization, scheme of delegation and standing orders which govern how we operate. Corporate should implement and enforce the code; review and update the code as appropriate; disseminate copies of the code to employees; obtain from each employee a certification that he or she has read, understands and agrees to abide by the requirements of the code; create and maintain a work environment that promotes ethical conduct, integrity, trustworthiness, accuracy and compliance with the code as the prevailing principle in all business activity

157

and relationships; provide employee training concerning the meaning and application of the code; enable employees to obtain advice and guidance concerning the meaning and application of the code; provide employees with the procedures and mechanisms to respond, in confidence and without fear of retaliation or retribution, to actual or possible code violations; investigate promptly any allegations or indications of illegal or unethical conduct, and promptly correct the conditions causing or contributing to such conduct; regularly audit and monitor company-wide compliance with the Code; provide appropriate disciplinary action for code violations or for the failure of any employee to take appropriate steps to detect, report or correct such conduct

CORPORATE CODES

Ownership

(1). Shareholders own the business. All employees must maintain their respect and trust, (2). The rights of company owners need to be clearly recognized and upheld

Transaction and Accounting

(1). Expenditures of company funds should be made only as properly authorized; (2). Accounting should comply with accepted accounting rules and controls; (3). All expenditures and payments should be properly recorded and documented.

Payment

(1). Not permit or condone any illegal or improper payments, transfers or receipts; (2). Employees should not offer, give, solicit or accept any money or anything else of value for the purpose of obtaining or bestowing business or preferential treatment; (3). No outside consultant, attorney, accountant, contractor, vendor, or agent of any kind should be used in any manner that would be contrary to this prohibition against illegal or improper payments; (4). Fees, commissions and expenses that are paid to such outside agents should be based upon proper billings and reasonable standards for services rendered.

Corporate Opportunities

(1). Prohibit to taking for themselves personally opportunities, that are discovered through the use of corporate property, information or position; (2). If employees become aware of a business opportunity that corporate would have an interest in pursuing, they cannot divert that opportunity for personal gain. Employees must make this opportunity available to company.

Corporate Properties

(1). Not to use corporate property for personal benefit, only for legitimate business purposes. Unauthorized use or distribution of this information would violate Company policy. It could also be illegal and result in civil or even criminal penalties; (2). Endeavor to protect the corporate property and ensure their efficient use. Theft, carelessness and waste have a direct impact on the company's profitability. The obligation of employees to protect the corporate property includes its proprietary information. Proprietary information includes intellectual property such as trade secrets, patents, trademarks and copyrights, as well as business, marketing and service plans, engineering and manufacturing ideas, designs, databases, records, salary information, processes, computer passwords and software, product formulations, business forecasts, plans and strategies, and information concerning our operations, customers and vendors and any unpublished financial data and reports. Confidential information may also be received from other companies or individual employees must not disclose confidential information to anyone outside of company without specific authorization; (3). Electronic and/or computer technology, including email, voice mail, cellular telephones, personal computers, computer networks, software, access to the Internet or other electronic services are the property of corporate. Limited, occasional personal use of the phone system, e-mail, internet, and voice mail is acceptable provided that the use is appropriate and lawful. However, information created, received or disseminated through these systems is not private. Authorized company representatives may, without advance notice, monitor these systems. These systems are not to be used to create, store or transmit information that is hostile, malicious, unlawful, sexually explicit, discriminatory, profane, or abusive. Employees should not send or receive messages that are derogatory toward others. Web sites, which contain illegal, sexually explicit, adult oriented or discriminatory content, are not to be accessed. It should be used in accordance with applicable software agreements, copyright, trademark, patent and other laws. These services, including Internet chat rooms, should never be used to communicate company confidential, non-public or proprietary information, copyrighted information, or information which may be harmful to the company, its employees or customers.

Record

(1). Accurate record keeping is critical. Employees have a responsibility to accurately report all business information such as reporting of hours worked, business and travel expenses, shipping and receiving data and financial figures in a timely and accurate manner; (2). No employee may falsify company information whether stored in writing or electronically; (3). All transactions must be properly authorized, completely and accurately recorded on the company's books, and recorded in accordance with generally accepted accounting principles. No secret, undisclosed, or unrecorded funds or assets may be established or maintained for any purpose; (4). Business records and documents should be retained and destroyed in accordance with the company's retention policy as well as department's policies and regulatory requirements.

Quality

Quality services and products that meet or exceed the customers' expectations will set the corporate apart from the competition and assure corporate future success. It is employees' responsibility to understand the customer's requirements and to satisfy those requirements with quality products and services.

Report

(1). Ensuring that information is reported fully, accurately and in accordance with company policies. Employees are responsible for ensuring full, fair, accurate, timely and understandable disclosure in reports and documents filed; (2). Employees involved in the company's reporting regarding operations, are responsible for ensuring full, accurate and timely disclosure, adherence to the company's policies and compliance with the rules.

Finance

(1). Act with honesty and integrity. Avoid actual or apparent conflicts of interest; (2). Information that is accurate, complete, objective, fair, relevant, timely, and understandable; (3). Comply with rules and regulations; (4). Act with good faith, responsibly, due care, competence and diligence; (5). Respect the confidentiality of information; (6). Not coerce, manipulate, mislead, or unduly influence any authorized audit

Audit

(1). Inspire trust and confidence and possess credibility—honestly and sensitively with respect to acceptance; (2). Open to good cooperative working relations; (3). Integrity—shall not apply for, receive or accept from any source any advantage, direct or indirect, which is in any way connected with his mandate in the corporate; (4). Independence, objectivity and impartiality—shall not neither seek nor accept instructions from any government, any other organization or any person within or outside the corporate; (5). Confidentiality—shall not divulge any information or data coming to their knowledge during the performance of their duties to persons or bodies outside the corporate; (6). Competence—should incorporate into the term professionalism and its duty to meet standards of quality. This is also closely connected with due care; (7). Open for good faith complaint regarding accounting or auditing matters to the management of the company without fear of dismissal or retaliation of any kind; (8). Commit to achieving compliance with all applicable securities laws and regulations, accounting standards, accounting controls and audit practices

Employment

(1). Not employ child labor; (2). Not employ forced labor; (3). Freedom of: labor association and collective bargaining; (4). Providing employees with a safe and healthy work environment; (5). Ensure that overtime is voluntary and paid in accordance with local laws and regulations; (6). Workers shall be provided with clear, written information about their employment conditions with respect to wages; (7). Keep employee records in accordance to local and/or national regulations

Tax

(1). Complying with tax law; (2). No tax-planning advice must rely in any way on less than full disclosure; (3). Tax-planning advice must be given in the knowledge of the actual facts; (4). Involve discussion of the wider consideration of all risks involved

Corporate Citizenship

(1). Strive to improve the well being of our communities by providing quality products and services; (2). Get involved in the life of our communities by being good citizens, volunteering, and working to support local charities.

PERSONALITY CODES

Conflicts Of Interest

(1). Employees should avoid any personal or business relationships, dealings or investments that might create a personal interest that conflicts with the best interests of the company. A conflict situation can arise when an employee, officer or director takes actions or has interests that may make it difficult to perform his or her company work objectively and effectively. It is not possible to foresee or define with precision every situation that may constitute a conflict of interest. Conflicts may be actual, potential and even matters of perception. Conflicts may occur in, but are not limited to, situations where an employee, officer or director, or a closely-related family member; (2). Personal Business Relationships: Employees must take care that personal business relationships never influence the decisions made for the company. Employees must disclose any financial interests that they or their immediate family have in company's suppliers, customers, or competitors; (2). Outside Employment: Before employees accept employment outside of company, they consider whether this job could create a conflict of interest. Employees should not accept outside employment, part-time or otherwise, by a competitor, supplier or customer of the company (in the case of a family member, as a supervisor or manager), or sells products to company employees or recruits company employees to sell or distribute products; (3). Organizational Relationships: Not allowed to serve on the board of directors of, or acts as a consultant or advisor to, a competitor, supplier or customer of the company (other than at the request of the company), even if they receive no money for their services. Relationships with prospective or existing suppliers, contractors, customers, competitors or regulators should be structured so that they could not reasonably appear to affect your independent and sound judgment on behalf of corporate. Employee is prohibited from doing directly should not be done indirectly through relatives, friends or others; (4). Transact business with the company, including buying from or selling to the company any goods or services (other than transactions in the ordinary course of the company's businesses, e.g., newspaper subscriptions); (5). Not allowed to use equipment, computer software and services, materials, supplies, content (including outtakes), data and other information or business relationships obtained in the course of employment with the company to advance personal interests; (6). Receive improper personal benefits as a result of his or her position in the company; (7). All employees should conduct themselves with high standards of integrity, honesty and fair dealing and should avoid any conflicts of interest with corporate. A conflict of interest occurs when an individual's personal interests either interfere or could reasonably appear to interfere with the interests of corporate; (8). Competing: Employees should not compete with corporate, take advantage of a corporate opportunity or misuse confidential or proprietary information for personal gain. Employees should not: (a) take for personal gain opportunities that are discovered through the use of corporate property, information or position or (b) accept discounts on personal purchases of a supplier's or customer's products or services unless such discounts are offered to all employees in general. Employees should not have a personal business interest that is similar or related to work the employee, the company, or any of its business units performs or produces; (9). Accept Gift. Employees should never accept gifts that would appear to undermine or influence good business judgment. Employees should never solicit gifts or favors from the people with who corporate does business; (10). All funds expended for business entertainment and gifts must be fully and accurately documented and reflected in the books and records of the company; (11). Offering bribes, kickbacks, payoffs or other unusual or improper payments to obtain or keep business, gifts and entertainment extended to governmental officials is unacceptable; (12). Accept tip and compensation. Employees should never ask for a tip for extra services or pick-ups. Employees should not accept compensation for services performed for the corporate outside of their regular job; (13). Each employee should base business decisions on the needs and interests of corporate rather than their own personal interests. Employees should not participate in any activity that could conflict with their responsibilities to the corporate; (14). Accept Entertainment. Employees should not accept an occasional invitation to entertainment or meals from the people with who corporate does business that would appear to undermine or influence good business judgment. Contractors or suppliers do generally not pay for air travel and accommodations related to entertainment events; employee should not accept business entertainment at company facilities; (15). Accept loan. Personal loans by corporate to employees, or guarantees of such obligations, are prohibited. Employees should not accept loan from a current or potential customer, supplier or competitor; owning a financial interest in, or serving in a business capacity with, an outside enterprise that does or wishes to do business with, or is a competitor of, the company; serving as an intermediary for the benefit of a third party in transactions involving the company, using confidential company information or other corporate assets for personal profit, conducting business for another enterprise during our normal working hours or using company property to conduct business for another enterprise.

Integrity

(1). Provide impartial, professional service and advice, that is frank and apolitical; (2). Act with honestly; (2). Appropriately manage interests. A conflict of interest may come in many forms and must be managed at the earliest possible opportunity; (3). Not accept gifts, benefits or favors that may influence or be reasonably seen to influence decision making; (4). Prevent nepotism and patronage. It is unacceptable to favor relatives (nepotism) or people they know (patronage) in the decision making and provision of service; (5). Ensure all selection decisions are based on a proper assessment of merit. They must not improperly bypass the principle of merit in a selection process. They must ensure selection processes apply merit principles in order to select the most suitable applicants with abilities, aptitudes, skills, qualifications, knowledge, experience (including community experience) and personal qualities relevant to the position. This can include the need to assess applicants' employment backgrounds or duties and their potential for development; (6). Ensure employment or remunerative work within the company is appropriate; (7). Conduct his/her self in the corporate by creating an environment of trust and respect for each other

Respect

(1). Treat other employees with respect and courtesy, having regard for the dignity of the people with whom he/she interact. Employees can reasonably expect to work in an environment that promotes their ability to work with one another and shows regard to the sensitivities of people within the workplace; (2). Promote equity, and value and utilize diversity in the work environment; (3). Prevent unlawful discrimination against employees or persons seeking employment in the public sector. Employees must ensure that no form of unjustifiable discrimination is exercised against employees or persons seeking employment in corporate; (4). Take reasonable care to ensure employees own health and safety at work and avoid adversely affecting the health and safety of others; (5). The importance of people shall be recognized and fostered through the provision of career assistance such as mobility options, mentoring, and training and development opportunities appropriate to the work they are undertaking or may be reasonably expected to undertake; (6). Diversity: An important part of respecting others is valuing their diversity. By valuing the differences that all employees bring to the workplace, employees can better meet the objectives of corporate.

Accountability

(1). Utilize and manage people and the resources, information and authority at his/her disposal in an efficient, responsible and justifiable manner through implementation of risk management standards and practices; (2). Ensure decisions have regard for the well-being of people and the environment, both now and for the future; (3). Ensure all decisions are fair and made without excessive formality; (4). Ensure all decisions are transparent and in keeping with confidentiality requirements; (5). Provide responsive, timely, effective and efficient services to the community and the government; (6). Deal with information gained through your work in accordance with legal requirements; (7). Observe all regulatory requirements, policies, procedures, and lawful and reasonable instructions from people with authority to give such instructions; (8). Endeavour to ensure employees, and those for whom the employees are responsible, perform well in order to meet or exceed performance standards and other organizational requirements; (9). Ensure accountability throughout the corporate by reporting inappropriate conduct to the appropriate authority.

Decision Making

(1). Effective decision making takes into account the needs of people both now and into the future, integrating social, environmental and economic factors; (2). Decisions may affect other employees, customers and, therefore, must be fair and consistent. This means that all the decisions are honest, based on the relevant information, justifiable and understandable both by those who are affected by the decisions and those who may need to review the decision. He/she should also ensure that decisions are made without excessive formality; (3). Ensure no personal interests conflict, or reasonably appear to conflict, with the corporate interest; (4). Apply risk management principles to identify the impact on different stakeholders; (5). Get a second opinion from an independent, trusted person.

Leadership

(1). Care, show empathy toward others and act as good friend would; (2). Courtesy, use manners and basic good grace; (3). Respect, treat others fairly, honestly and keep their dignity in tact; (4). Have self-discipline, self-control of feelings and actions; (5). Register of interests and of gifts and hospitality; (6). Avoid all conflicts of interest between work and personal affairs; (7). Obey the applicable laws and regulations; (8). Sustain a culture where ethical conduct is recognized, valued, and exemplified; (9). Provide a work environment supportive of flexible work practices and adaptable to staff needs both in and outside the workplace; (10). Ensure equal access to training and development for all staff; (11). Develop comprehensive and realistic goal agreements with staff, monitoring progress against agreements and ensuring that performance problems are highlighted and dealt with; (12). Behave in ways consistent with corporate values; (13). Ensure that personal information of customer and staff is protected

Equality

(1). Equity is about being fair and just the all people, but does not necessarily mean treating everyone in the same way. He/she may need to treat a person differently according to their circumstances and needs, in order to give them an equal chance in comparison with others. The policy and services that you are involved in developing and delivering must be made inclusive and responsive to all groups; (2). Discrimination, i.e. to treat an individual less favorably because of an attribute or to impose unreasonable terms or conditions with which individuals with a particular attribute are unable to comply. Attributes are: parental status, pregnancy, religion, political belief or activity, marital status, sex, lawful sexual activity, age, race, impairment, trade union activity, or association with an individual having these attributes; (3). Building a work environment where all employees are treated with dignity and respect. Provide a positive working environment in which all individuals may grow, contribute, and participate free from discrimination; (4). Providing equal opportunity to all qualified individuals in lawful human resource policies and practices in all aspects of employment, including recruiting, hiring, evaluation, training, discipline, work and service assignments, career development, compensation, promotion, and termination. Not tolerate unlawful discrimination of any kind; (5). Prohibit discrimination against any employee or applicant for employment because of race, color, religion, ethnic or national origin, gender, sexual orientation, age, disability or veteran status; (6). It is corporate responsibility to treat employees fairly without regard to race, color, religion, gender, age, national origin, marital status, or whether an individual is disabled, a veteran, or holds other protected status as defined by laws; (7). Employees must not discriminate, directly or indirectly, in their treatment of individuals or groups on the grounds of age, gender, race, disability, sexuality, marital status, pregnancy, or any other ground covered by equal opportunity or other anti-discrimination legislation. Discrimination includes treating a candidate in a job selection process less favorably because of a characteristic or circumstance that has no bearing on their capacity to perform the job for which they are competing.

Harassment

Harassment, i.e. workplace harassment, is repeated behavior, other than behavior that is sexual harassment that is (1) directed at an individual or group, and (2) offensive, intimidating, humiliating or threatening, and (3) unwelcome and unsolicited, and (4) a reasonable person would consider being offensive, intimidating, humiliating or threatening for the individual or group. Harassment includes: verbal harassment, such as derogatory comments, jokes or slurs; physical harassment, such as unnecessary or offensive touching, or impeding or blocking movement; and visual harassment, such as derogatory or offensive posters, cards, calendars, cartoons, graffiti, drawings, messages, notes or gestures.

Sexual harassment consists of unwelcome sexual advances, requests for sexual favors, or other verbal or physical conduct of a sexual nature when:

(1). Submission to such conduct is made a term or condition of an individual's employment; (2). Submission to or rejection of such conduct is used as the basis for employment decisions; (3) Such conduct has the purpose or effect of unreasonably interfering with an individual's work performance or creating an intimidating, hostile or offensive work environment; (4). Provide employees with a work environment free of any type of harassment; (5). Prohibit any deliberate harassment, in word or action, against a fellow employee or applicant for employment; (6). Provide guidance for addressing harassment situations; (7). Preventing Harassment: Behavior that targets an employee because of his or her race, color, religion, gender, age, national origin, marital status, disability, or veteran status or any other protected status as defined by federal, provincial, state, or local laws is prohibited. Such verbal or physical conduct that unreasonably disrupts another employee in his or her work is harassment. Each employee has the right to be free from improper or offensive conduct at work. Employees, customers, vendors, and visitors should be treated with respect, courtesy, and dignity. Unwelcome, insulting, or offensive remarks or actions have no place at corporate. To maintain a work atmosphere free from harassment, each employee should exercise good judgment in our relationships with coworkers. If an employee experiences/observes workplace harassment, they should report the incident for immediate resolution of the problem; (8). Workplace bullying/harassment: Employees must not bully or otherwise harass other employees or members of the public. Behaviors that characterize bullying may include victimization and unwelcome, offensive, abusive, belittling or threatening behavior directed at another person or a group of people. Bullying may lead to the person or group of people subjected to the behavior feeling victimized, offended, demeaned, humiliated, intimidated, or suffering detriment or disadvantage; (9). Executives and employees must take action to address and prevent bullying and harassment. Behavior that amounts to bullying or harassment can also be the subject of criminal and/or disciplinary proceedings.

Confidentiality

(1). Being scrupulous in using information gained through the employment appropriately, that is, for the purpose for which it was gathered. Employees should comply with the organization's directions and guidelines on the use of information; (2). Ensure that the privacy of individuals is maintained and release personal information only in accordance with privacy requirements, organizational guidelines or as otherwise lawfully permitted; (3). Seek and obtain authorization from the appropriate officer, before commenting to the media. Confidential Company information and proprietary information is a valuable corporate asset. This includes among other things pricing and cost data, merger, acquisitions and divestiture information, business processes and procedures, financial data, trade secrets and know-how, computer programs, wage and salary information, marketing and sales programs, customer/supplier/subcontractor information and other information and developments which have not been released to the general public; (4). Continue to respect the confidentiality of information gained during the employment, when employees leave the employment; (5). Employees must maintain the confidentiality of confidential information entrusted to them by the company or its customers, except when disclosure is authorized by company or required by laws or regulations. Confidential information includes all information that might be of use to competitors, or harmful to the company or its customers, if disclosed. It also includes information that suppliers and customers have entrusted to company; (6). Employee information and data are confidential and are used only for valid business purposes. This includes information in an employee's personnel file such as Social Security number, home address, telephone number, medical information, and other confidential information; (7). Prohibit to disclose, use or record any messages or conversations, intercept, interfere with, or intrude on any transmission, listen to, or monitor, conversations or non-voice communications or divulge any details, permit any unauthorized person access to information concerning a communication transmitted over the network, allow the installation, connection or modification of telecommunications equipment which would enable a conversation to be listened to, recorded or monitored; (8). While corporate respects employee privacy, employees should not expect privacy when using company provided services and equipment. Corporate reserve the right to inspect our facilities and property, such as computers, telephone records, lockers, e-mail, Internet usage, business documents, offices, and other workplaces; (9). All of this information must be used solely for company purposes and never for personal gain. Confidential information must not be shared with anyone outside of corporate unless they have a legitimate need to know in order to do business with us. Inappropriate disclosure of confidential information may damage our business and the business of our customers, suppliers, and subcontractors; (10). Employees who have access to company confidential information must protect that information from disclosure.

Violence

(1). Prohibit for any kind of violence. Report of violence or a threat of violence must be investigated and appropriate action should be taken; (2). Employees who engage in violence or threaten violence are subject to disciplinary action, up to and including termination of employment, as well as criminal prosecution; (3). Workplace Violence: Corporate provides a safe working environment for everyone. Corporate should have a zero tolerance policy on acts of violence and verbal or physical behavior that could lead to or cause workplace violence. Corporate should not tolerate violent behavior at corporate workplaces, whether committed by or against the employees. These behaviors are prohibited: making threatening remarks, causing physical injury to someone else; (4). Employees should use good judgment and inform their superior, if they observe behavior that could be dangerous.

Drugs and Alcohol

(1). Drug and alcohol abuse can have serious safety and job performance consequences and can involve criminal conduct; (2). Require a drug and alcohol impairment-free working environment; (30. Subject to disciplinary action are employees who, while on duty or on company property, distribute, sell, buy, manufacture, dispense, possess or use illegal drugs; (4). Employees who report for duty with illegal drugs in their system or report with levels of alcohol or other chemical substances that could impair performance are subject to disciplinary action; (5). Employees should maintain a workplace that is free from the effects of drug and alcohol abuse. Alcohol abuse and illegal drug use threatens corporate ability to serve our customers. It compromises the safety of the products and services; (6). Not tolerate any use or abuse of drugs or alcohol while employees are engaged in company business or while working at a company location: (7). All employees are subject to pre-employment screening, reasonable suspicion, periodic, and/or random drug and alcohol testing; (8). Employees, who are taking a prescription drug which may interfere with the ability to perform their job, must discuss the situation with an immediate superior; (9). Employees should contact the 'Employee Assistance Program' for help with drug and alcohol related problems before these problems affect job performance.

Research

(1). Ensure that research conducted by persons associated with the corporate embodies: the highest standards of intellectual honesty, adherence to ethical principles of justice and veracity, respect for people and their privacy, avoidance of harm to people, respect for non-human subjects of research; (2). Contribute to knowledge, the pursuit and protection of truth, the researcher's skill and experience, the objectives of the proposal being likely to be achieved owing to: reliance on research methods appropriate to the discipline, including: being based on thorough study of current literature thorough prior observation, approved previous studies, previous laboratory and animal studies

BUSINESS CODES

Customer

(1). Advertising. Present clear and accurate information about pricing, services, and products. Not exaggerate, mislead, omit, or lie. Never resort to deceptive advertising to gain an advantage over our competitors. Not criticize or misrepresent the services or qualifications of our competitors; (2). Never offer, give, ask for, or take any form of bribe or kickback. Customers justify for using corporate services and products because of their value, not because they have received "something extra" on the side. A bribe or kickback is the giving or accepting of money, fees, commissions, credits, gifts, favors, or anything of value, which is either directly or indirectly provided in return for favorable treatment. Bribes or kickbacks in any form should not be tolerated; (3). Develop and provide services and products that meet or exceed the requirements of the customers and do so at a fair price. Negotiate in good faith, adhere to the contracts, and resolve disputes promptly. Perform all contracts in a fair and ethical manner, without discrimination or deception, and in strict compliance with applicable laws, regulations and the terms of the contract; (4). Compete solely on the merits of the products and services. Not persuade customers to purchase by offering gifts, meals, or entertainment; (5). He/she may provide advertising novelties, promotional items of a nominal value, or modest gifts if: the gift does not conflict with the standards of the recipient, this happens only occasionally, the gift was not solicited; (6). Entertainment. Employees may offer business meals or entertainment to a customer when entertaining. The activity should be of reasonable value and occur infrequently; (7). Focus on integrity for customers, i.e.: provide quality and reliable products and services, meet or exceed their expectations, communicate honestly and fairly

Supplier

(1). Corporate should select suppliers and vendors who best meet corporate needs using objective criteria such as price, quality, performance, and technical excellence. At times it may require competitive bids. Executive should evaluate all proposals fairly; (2). Follow all applicable laws and regulations and uphold good business practices; (3). Not share with a third party confidential; (4). Deal honestly, lawfully, and ethically in contractual negotiations; (5). Honor contractual obligations and commitments; (6). Compliance with the applicable laws, comply with all applicable trade control, compliance with antitrust and fair competition laws, comply with all applicable environmental laws, be honest, direct, and truthful in discussions with government officials, not participate in international boycotts that are not sanctioned by government, comply with the anti-corruption laws

Competitor

(1). Seek to outperform our competition fairly and honestly. We seek competitive advantages through superior performance, never through unethical or illegal business practices. Employees should endeavor to deal fairly with the company's customers, suppliers, competitors and employees. With respect to the competitors, none should take unfair advantage of anyone through manipulation, concealment, abuse of privileged information, misrepresentation of material facts, or any other intentional unfair-dealing practice; (2). Practice fair, open and honest competition. Obtain information about them fairly, honestly, and legally; treat them with respect; promote open and honest competition; (3). Gathering Competitive Information: Obtain information about other companies, including those with whom corporate competes; through public, ethical, and legal means such as public conferences and documents, magazines, trade journals, and other published and written information; never seek information through improper means such as inducing a competitor to disclose confidential information, burglary, spying, or wire-tapping. Employees should not misrepresent themselves, either directly or indirectly through a representative or agent, to obtain such information; do not use our customers as a funnel for price information about our competitors; always respect the proprietary information and trade secrets of others, including former employers; if employees are aware of a confidentiality agreement, they never solicit or accept information which would violate that agreement; never disclose any client or vendor proprietary information unless the individual or organization owning the information properly authorizes release or disclosure; newly hired employees should not divulge proprietary information about their former employers; (4). Antitrust: Business should independently pursue its activities in a competitive and free marketplace, not one that has been limited by restrictive agreements among competitors; promote honest, fair, and vigorous competition in open markets; (5). Price Fixing: Never enter into any general understanding or agreement with a competitor concerning prices that will be charged to customers; includes price levels, pricing methods or policies, timing of price changes, bid information, intent to bid or not bid on a contract, profits or profit margins, terms or conditions of sale, and/or supply of a product or service; prices and bid amounts are to be arrived at independently without consultation of any kind with a competitor; (6). Territorial Allocation: Not agree with competitors to divide or allocate markets or territories nor discuss market information with our competitors; (6). Not discuss the antitrust topics (competitive information, antitrust, price fixing, territorial allocation) with a competitor even though the discussion may fall short of an agreement; (7). Not allow abusive or unfair acts intended to acquire or maintain a monopoly or injure competitors (Monopolization); (8). Not agree with or have any discussion with our competitors regarding which vendors or customers with whom we will or will not conduct business; (9). Decisions not to do business with a vendor or customer must be arrived at independently of any decision or action by our competitors; (10). Insider Information and Securities Trading: We may learn of material, inside information about our company or about other companies before such information is known publicly. It is illegal to buy or sell stock based on inside information or to pass this information on to someone else who then buys or sells stocks.

REGULATORY CODES

Corporate should comply with all laws and government regulations applicable to corporate business. Commit to cooperating with government inquiries and takes seriously any investigation or review. Notwithstanding this commitment, the company may reserve the right to protect the newsgathering and editorial process from inappropriate intrusion. Employees should consult their superior about instances where there is doubt or ambiguity concerning legal requirements or appropriate practices. Employees should also consult with company legal counsel regarding any request for information, other than in the ordinary course of business; from any government official or agency before any information is furnished and before there is any agreement or understanding to furnish such information.

Patent and Intellectual Property

(1). Intellectual Property is proprietary business or technical information of value protected by patent, trademark, copyright or trade secret laws; respect the valid IP rights of other companies and persons; when corporate desires to receive, use, or purchase the IP of another party, the legitimate bounds of such property should be identified and appropriate legal counsel obtained; (2). Create an equitable balance between the rights of the originators of intellectual property and the rights and interests of the corporate; (3). Intellectual property is a valuable asset. This includes copyrights, patents, and trademarks. Corporate respects and protects intellectual property, whether it belongs to corporate or to others. And prohibit from making unauthorized copies of copyrighted written documents or computer software; (4). Corporate may claim ownership of all intellectual property created by a staffs in the course of fulfilling his or her contract of employment. Corporate may claim ownership of all inventions, discoveries, ideas, and trade secrets created by employees on the job or produced using company resources; (5). Originators retain copyright in any materials, other than course materials, created by the originators in the course of fulfilling their contract of employment with the corporate except where an agreement to the contrary has been negotiated between the corporate and the staffs; (6). Grant to the originator a royalty-free, non-exclusive and irrevocable license to use the intellectual property in those materials for teaching, research and professional purposes.

Securities Laws

(1). Insider Trading Is Prohibited. Employees of the company are prohibited from buying or selling company securities while they are in possession of material inside information concerning the company. "Inside information" is any information that has not been publicly disclosed. "Material information" is any information that would be of significance to an investor in deciding whether to buy, sell or hold a security or if it would have a substantial effect on the market price of a security if it were disclosed; (2). Employees who learn material inside information about other companies through their work at the company are prohibited from trading securities of that company while they are in possession of material inside information about that company; (3). Prohibit providing other people (friends, financial advisors, business associates, etc.) with any material inside information. This is known as "tipping" and it can result in liability to the employee as well as the other person, even if the employee did not receive monetary profit from the other person's illegal trading. Accordingly, all employees should exercise extreme care when they are in possession of material inside information to ensure that such information is not disclosed, either on purpose or by accident, to any other person other than those to whom the information is essential for company-related business, and even in that situation, the employee should make it known that such information has not been publicly disclosed. Some examples of information about a company that might be material are: a proposed acquisition or divestiture; a stock split or a change in the dividend rate; a significant expansion or curtailment of operations; a significant change in revenues or earnings from those from a prior period or from those publicly projected; a significant product development or significant information regarding a product.; the institution of a stock repurchase program; extraordinary management or business developments; (4). If this type of information is known to an employee and has not been publicly disclosed by the company to which it relates, that employee is prohibited from trading in the securities of that company or encouraging others to trade in those securities.

Compliance with Procedures

(1). It is difficult to know right from wrong, in some situation. Since he/she cannot anticipate every situation that will arise, it is important that we have a way to approach a new question or problem. These are the steps to keep in mind: make sure you have all the facts. In order to reach the right solutions, we must be as fully informed as possible; focus on the specific question we are faced with, and the alternatives we have; use our judgment and common sense—if something seems unethical or improper, it probably is; (2). Clarify responsibility and role. In most situations, there is shared responsibility; (3). Discuss the problem with superior. This is the basic guidance for all situations. In many cases, his/her superior should be more knowledgeable about the question, and will appreciate being brought into the decision-making process. It is superior's responsibility to help solve problems; (4). Seek help from company resources. In the rare case where it may not be appropriate to discuss an issue with superior, or where he/she does not feel comfortable approaching superior with the question, discuss it with higher level person or human resources department; (5). Always ask first, act later: If he/she are unsure of what to do in any situation, seek guidance before acting; (6). Taking active role by being knowledgeable about all laws and regulations, attending training and requesting information.

CORPORATE RELATED POLITICAL CODES

(1). Being a partner with the government and regulators who oversee corporate business so that our operations and business practices are lawful; (2). Lobbying: Obtain prior approval from the authorized senior executive to hire outside counsel or a public affairs firm to contact government officials about legislation, regulatory policy, or rule making. This includes grassroots lobbying contacts; (2). Political Activities: Encourages employees to participate in political activities on their own time and at their own expense. Such activities must not cause a conflict of interest. Employees should never put pressure on fellow employees to support or contribute time or money to a candidate or a political cause. When employees participate in political activities, they do so as individual citizens. Employees are to never give the impression that they are speaking on behalf of corporate. Not allow their own personal or political opinions to interfere with their work. Ensure that the individual rights are respected; (3). Political Contributions: No Company funds or assets may be contributed to any political candidate or political party, unless such contribution is expressly permitted by law. Avoid a political contribution on behalf of corporate. Political contributions are made only in compliance with company policy. A "contribution" is any direct or indirect payment, distribution, subscription, loan, advance, deposit, or gift of money, services or anything of value in connection with an election or to an organization or group formed to support or defeat a referendum or ballot issue. Not directly or indirectly reimburse an employee or other person for political contributions he or she has made; it's not intended to discourage employees from making personal contributions to political candidates or parties of their choice. Employees shall not be reimbursed by the company in any way for personal contributions; (4). Neutrality: Prohibit an expression of company support for any particular candidate, political party or governmental entity; (5). Regulatory Agency Investigations, Inspections, and Requests for Information. Cooperate courteously with all government inspectors and provide information they are entitled to during an inspection, investigation, or in response to a request for information. Notify corporate senior executive immediately of any inspection, investigation, or request for information. During a government inspection employees never: conceal, destroy, or alter any company documents; lie or make misleading statements to a government investigator; obstruct the collection of information, data, or records; attempt to cause another employee to fail to provide accurate information; (6). Hiring Former Government Employees. Employment with a current or former government employee should be done according to corporate policy; (7). When corporate focuses on integrity for the government and regulatory agencies, the organization should comply with both the spirit and letter of the law; conduct out interactions with honesty and integrity

REPORTING ILLEGAL OR UNETHICAL BEHAVIOR

(1). Employees are required to immediately report regulatory violations, suspected regulatory violations, or potentially harmful/dangerous conditions; (2). Employees should talk to superiors, executives or other appropriate personnel about observed illegal or unethical behavior and when in doubt about the best course of action in a particular situation; (3). It is not to allow retaliation for reports of misconduct by others made in good faith by employees. Employees are expected to cooperate in internal investigations of misconduct; (4). Responsibility to report does not apply to inappropriate conduct of a trivial nature that does not result in significant detriment to the corporate interest; (5). If he/she does make a report of misconduct, he/she must have a reasonable belief. He/she must not knowingly make a false disclosure; (6). If he/she is unsure to whom, or how, to report, he/she should refer to the existing policies within his/her organization in the first instance; (7). He/she may report ethical violations in confidence and without fear of retaliation. If his/her situation requires that the identity be kept secret, his/her anonymity must be protected; (8). Employees are required to immediately report regulatory violations, suspected regulatory violations, or potentially harmful/dangerous conditions.

6

GOVERNANCE AND ORGANIZATIONAL STRUCTURE

GOVERNANCE

Governance is a leadership process through which Directors set and oversee policies designed to achieve the corporate mission and ensure accountability. Effective governance requires establishing and promoting vision of corporate current and future outcomes. This vision must be based on clearly stated, values and philosophies. Corporate then develops mission that reflects the agreed-upon values and guides the implementation of the vision. Governance process will include: establishment of committees and their responsibilities; regular review and revision of mission, as necessary; annual review and revision of strategic plan; adoption of a model or process for identifying, implementing, and managing change; schedule for periodic board self-assessment and training. It ensures accountability for: ethical practices, statutory compliance, risk assessment and risk management, efficient use of resources, fiduciary and performance accountability, progress toward achievement of mission, effective change management

AUTHORITY AND DELEGATION

In accordance with corporate governance, the Board of Directors is authorized to:

a. Monitor the performance of the corporation, establish and approve the corporate beliefs and values, determine the strategic direction of the corporation, assess relevant risks, approve the investment principles and policy, approve the funding policy, review and approve audited financial statements, approve policies taking into consideration the corporate principle, legislation, and the fairness to customers.

b. Establish succession policy: (a) identify and make recommendations regarding new director candidates; (b) review and recommend the re-nomination of incumbent directors; (c) review and recommend committee appointments; (d) review and recommend changes to the Board of Director Governance Guidelines; (e) in conjunction with the presiding non-management director, lead the Board in its annual review of the Board's performance; and (f) perform other related tasks, including studying the size, committee structure or meeting frequency of the Board

c. Recommend CEO, Directors, and executive compensation, retirement or welfare benefit plans

d. Establish committees in governing the corporate

e. Recommend corporate engagement with government or political party as far as permitted by law

Some authorities may need to be delegated to a person or group of persons with intent of: best interests of customer, cost-effectiveness, opportunities to develop experience, having explicit—lawful authority, ensure the efficiency and effectiveness, ensure Internal Controls are effective, support the responsibilities (entrust), formally designated the person—not everyone nor no one. Delegation should include the following elements: (1). Identify the tasks to be performed; (2). Specify the responsibilities associated with the tasks. Provide authority over resources required to perform the tasks and discharge the responsibilities.

Two key concepts are involved in delegation of authority: unity of command and chain of command. Unity of command implies that no one has more than one supervisor. This eliminates conflict and confusion about implementing tasks. Chain of command refers to the hierarchy of authority linking those at the top of the organization to those at the bottom. Chain of command provides authority to issue commands to those lower in the hierarchy. Decision making should be delegated to the lowest point at which employees are capable of making a decision that is consistent with the objectives of the organization and its related units.

Roles and reporting relationships should be well-defined and understood.

Accountability, authority, and responsibility, especially for supervisory personnel, should be clearly aligned and understood.

Scheme of Delegation

The functions of Board of Director (or Director), which need to be delegated:

a. Contract: ensure that all agreements, memorandum of understanding, and other contracts which are binding on the corporate, are signed by persons having explicit, lawful authority to do so and to describe the procedures to be followed in delegating such authority.

b. Financial: ensure the efficiency and effectiveness of the corporate administrative processes; ensure that the appropriate officers have been provided with the level of financial authority necessary to discharge their responsibilities; and ensure Internal Controls are effective.

c. Controlled Act: ensure the best quality, in order to most effectively meet customer needs. When controlled acts are delegated in appropriate circumstances, this process can result in more timely delivery of quality product and service, and can make optimal use of resources and personnel.

d. Human Resources Delegations: delegations are categorized by position or committee, i.e. responsibilities and requirements for approval of the company's human resource functions.

STAKEHOLDERS MEETING

Various matters of corporation have to be discussed and decided upon. This discussion takes place at the various meetings which take place between members and between the directors. Needless to say, the importance of meetings cannot be under-emphasized in case of companies. Meeting will definitely help people to review and take decision on related matters, i.e. budget development, legal considerations, strategic planning, business plan development, marketing, human resource management, policies, guide lines, etc. In the meeting, members do not only listen, comment but also gather information that affects organization or the company as a whole.

Shareholders Meeting

Annual shareholder meeting is the meeting of shareholders each year called to elect officers and directors, to ratify actions of officers and directors and to vote on corporate matters which come before it; presentation of the parent company and consolidated financial statements, as well as the auditors' reports; approval of the parent company and consolidated financial statements; measures occasioned by the profit or loss according to the approved consolidated financial statements; granting of discharge from liability to the members of the Board of Directors and the CEO; the number of members of the Board of Directors and their remuneration, etc. Special meetings of the stockholders can be called by the Chief Executive Officer or the Board of Directors, if it's necessary. Meetings of stockholders shall be held at location as is designated by the Board of Directors or the CEO.

Shareholders Meeting includes:

a. Statutory Meeting. A public company limited by shares or a guarantee company having share capital is required to hold a statutory meeting. Such a statutory meeting is held only once in the lifetime of the company. Such a meeting must be held within a period of not less than one month or within a period not more than six months from the date on which it is entitled to commence business i.e. it obtains certificate of commencement of business. In a statutory meeting, the following matters only can be discussed: floatation of shares/debentures by the company; modification to contracts mentioned in the prospectus

b. Annual General Meeting. Must be held by every type of company, public or private, limited by shares or by guarantee, with or without share capital or unlimited company, once a year. Every company must in each year hold an annual general meeting. Not more than 15 months must elapse between two annual general meetings. However, a company may hold its first annual general meeting within 18 months from the date of its incorporation. In such a case, it need not hold any annual general meeting in the year of its incorporation as well as in the following year only.

c. Extraordinary General Meeting. Every general meeting (i.e. meeting of members of the company) other than the statutory meeting and the annual general meeting or any adjournment thereof, is an extraordinary general meeting. Such meeting is usually called by the Supervisory Board (CEO) for some urgent business which cannot wait to be decided till the next Annual General Meeting. Every business transacted at such a meeting is special business. An explanatory statement of the special business must also accompany the notice calling the meeting. The notice should give the nature and extent of the interest of the directors or manager in the special business, as also the extent of the shareholding interest in the company of every such person.

Supervisory Board Meeting

Supervisory Board (CEO) is under increasing pressure to improve the governance processes of the corporate. As a result, Executive Officers are being held more accountable for the actions of the corporate, and they must increasingly prioritize communication and work harder to improve governance processes. The agenda for a board meeting, if there is a non-executive chairman of the board, or if the board has appointed a CEO, that person should seek recommendations from other board members and work with the Executive Board (Board of Director) to develop the meeting agenda. If the board does not have a CEO, the board should designate an Executive Officer to perform this function. A similar procedure should be followed for producing committee agendas, with the committee chair, the Executive Board, and senior management collaborating to develop appropriate agendas. The packages delivered to board members before the meeting should provide important data regarding the corporation's past and projected performance (including charts, graphs, memos, reports, recommendations, and analyses) to assist the Executive Officers in evaluating management's proposals.

The Supervisory Board should believe that their primary responsibility is to provide effective governance over corporate affairs for the benefit of its stockholders. That responsibility includes: evaluating the performance of the Executive Board and taking appropriate action, including removal, when warranted; fixing the Executive Board's compensation for the next year; reviewing succession plans and management development programs for members of executive management; reviewing and approving periodically long-term strategic and business plans and monitoring corporate performance against such plans; adopting policies of corporate conduct, including compliance with applicable laws and regulations and maintenance of accounting, financial, disclosure and other controls, and reviewing the adequacy of compliance systems and controls; evaluating annually the overall effectiveness of the Board; and reviewing matters of corporate governance.

Executive Board Meeting

The Executive Board needs to decide its remit and some essential points about how it wishes to perform its business, i.e. report on the performance of shared services; financial reports, covering outturns and forecasts; preparation for Supervisory Board strategic discussion; drafts of papers to Supervisory Board on corporate issues. The remit of the Executive Board would be to decide on management issues, share good practice, and discuss particularly important corporate policy issues. The priority will be to take decisions on policy relating to a wide range of high level corporate issues:

a. Providing leadership and setting direction for the corporate as an organization; setting the corporate policy on corporate matters, in particular personnel, training, information technology, information management, finance, risk management, corporate identity, health and safety, procurement and security. Managing performance in these areas by monitoring delivery against desired outcomes.

b. Ensuring the effective operation of the corporate, in particular by: monitoring the performance of corporate; approving work programs and; resolving difficulties which arise.

c. Providing a forum for the formulation of advice on corporate policy issues

d. Providing a forum for the sharing of best practice.

Executive Board is to manage the day-to-day activities of the company reasonably, in good faith and solely in the interests of the company, and ensure Executive Board report to Supervisory Board and the shareholders. To provide for the efficient operation of the company, Executive Board should take into account the interests of third persons, including creditors of the company and state and municipal bodies of the territory where the company or its structural subdivisions are located. As The management of the company, they should encourage employees' to be concerned about the efficient operation of the company; provide for the efficient control over the financial and business operations of the company in order to protect the rights and legal interests of shareholders; create an efficiently functioning system of daily supervision of their financial and business operations. For this purpose it is recommended that the company operate on the basis of a financial and business plan, which should be annually approved by the Supervisory Board of the company.

Executive Board need to distinguish between the roles of those bodies and persons included in the system of supervision of financial and business operations of the company and those persons involved in the development, approval, application and evaluation of the internal control system. It is advisable that development of internal control procedures should be assigned to an internal control service (hereinafter referred to as the "control and audit service"), which should be independent of the executive bodies of the company, while approval of internal control procedures should be assigned to the board of directors of the company. Decisions connected with the ongoing management of the company's current operations are made by the Executive Board of the company. The responsibilities of the Chairman and the other members of the Executive Board are laid down in the by-laws of the Executive Board. These regulate which key matters pertaining to the Company and its subsidiaries require a decision to be made by the Executive Board. The Executive Board is the managing body for the corporate. Its work is guided by the principle of a sustainable increase in enterprise value. The tasks performed by the Executive Board include defining the company's strategic orientation, planning and adopting the company's budget and allocating resources. The Executive Board is responsible for preparing the quarterly, annual and consolidated financial statements, as well as appointing key personnel within the company. The Executive Board cooperates closely with the Supervisory Board. They should report regularly, promptly, and extensively to the Supervisory Board on all questions relating to business planning, strategic further development, business developments, and the position of the corporation, including its risk position and risk management. Any business developments that depart from the plans and objectives are discussed in detail. The company's strategic orientation is agreed with the Supervisory Board.

Customers Meeting

Meeting with valuable customers' purpose is to gather general ideas about customer requirements for corporate services and products. In which, corporate may have tried to understand customer's expectations. Corporate should also assist customer in the area of activity they need, effective and economical service, and offer what they need; giving important to development, following the latest technology, and sharing knowledge; convince customers that company does not disturb the environment with its services, be equal in its services, and integrated with the society; ensure applying the idea of total quality management in all departments, pays attention at the top level for customer satisfaction; presenting corporate quality policy that minimizing the mistakes, increasing efficiency, obtaining standardization, doing processes according to their needs; do customer survey; encourage customers to inspect worksite.

Contractors and Vendors Meeting

Vendor meeting is hosted to encourage vendors to participate in the evaluation process, technical assistance, and commercial and regulatory issues. Corporate should dedicate to working with vendors closely to build strong and productive business partnerships together. It needs to articulate their issues and concerns with corporate procurement policies and procedures that may impede their interest in seeking to do business with the corporate. Vendor meeting is a medium to inform suggestions, recommendations or best practices regarding possible changes to corporate procurement policies to procedures and increase the odds of vendors to win corporate business opportunities. Corporate need also an access for vendor information; and importance of assessing vendor performance time to time. The meeting will provide information regarding a procurement posting opportunity to showcase their products and services; provide an opportunity for vendors to ask contracting, and technical staff questions about a solicitation; vendor can take advantage for prompt payment; able to fulfill requirement to adhere to corporate standard terms and conditions; improvement for future procurements reviewing the contract

Marketing Group Meeting

Marketing group meeting will provide an update of the regional marketing progress, includes a review of existing research, a review of past marketing initiatives, new research on attitudes and behavior, and a proposed integrated marketing plan. Marketing group meeting should summarize activities, marketing campaigns and budgets of the regional agencies and jurisdictions that will aid in the effective promotion. It will include: branding, consumer behavior, promotion, distribution, pricing, and sales; assessment of supply, demand and consumption. Marketing group meeting may redefine marketing development strategy, i.e.:

a. Identifying the policy framework (increasing the type and number of market intermediaries, producing and marketing higher value product, reduce post-bagging losses and to improve handling)

b. Improving access to market facilities (increasing the density of markets/reduce distance to market and networking the wholesale markets), encouraging the export, effective market information service to promote the product, increasing the availability of fresh produce, enhancing the revenue and capacity)

c. Reviewing the existing marketing system (improvement program to remove marketing constraints, policy guidelines for marketing, mechanisms for the establishment of a sustainable market information service, encouragement to potential investors in marketing activities, extension, publicity programs and promotion, financial and physical monitoring of the market development program's performance, operational marketing procedures, reflecting the impact of changes occurring in the type of sales method (i.e. by direct negotiation, auction or commission sales), training schemes, investment programs for further marketing infrastructure development, mechanisms for coordinating external assistance of helps involved with the planning, financing, construction, management or training aspects of market development);

d. Defining the basic purpose and function of the development (actions to develop project (and any related marketing activities) on an effective and sustainable long-term basis—making production more responsive to market demand rather than in constructing markets);

e. Deciding what are main elements or functions to be included (identify the demand, identify what standards are required, establishing a market committee);

f. Reviewing the available financial resources and expertise (define capital and operating cost limits, time limits completing the development, appropriate technical resources)

Company's Lawyers Meeting

Meeting with company's lawyer will improve communication and provide legal advice with full knowledge of all relevant facts; provide opinion on law;

strengthen legal services; assist in some legal proceeding; and prevent committing a crime or tort. The meeting shall review business document (due diligence) which is a process of reviewing existing legal and business contracts of a business (including corporate documents, agreements and financial statements) for potential problems and issues prior to a proposed transaction, such as a merger or acquisition. The goal is to make sure that there is nothing in any of the contracts that would prohibit the sale of the company (or require a third party's consent) and to make sure that the contract will not terminate as a result of the sale. The meeting should able to guide the management writing memoranda—looking up applicable laws and figuring out what practical impact they have on corporate decisions and actions. Company's lawyer may help contract drafting and review—preparing the contract, so that there are no ambiguities in the future when the same parties or others read those documents. Review of a contract is simply reading the contract to determine what the parties' rights are under its terms and whether any of the terms may be detrimental to the corporate. Company's lawyer needs to read so many agreements that identify what's standard and what could be disadvantageous to the corporate. Company's lawyer will also assist legal aspect for the entity of organization structure—i.e. determining what the rights of the owners are in relation to each other and making sure that all of this is reflected in the company's documents. In short, company's lawyer is to drafting contracts, house keeping the corporate documents, and advising management on all matters of legal significance.

Mother/Sister Company Representative Meeting

Based on the assumption of the sister company may operate as separate profit centre with independent management, there are several ways to take the control of the same corporate umbrella. It enables centrally coordinate and manage several common processes, including procurement, warehousing and distribution. The sister company meeting purposes to:

(1). Ensure that appropriate criteria and systems are in place to evaluate the performance and continuing capability of the sister company to supply the required products in accordance with the organization's requirements; (2). Meet the criteria established for selection, evaluation and re-evaluation, as this will affect the organization's ability to maintain the effectiveness of its product realization processes; (3). Maintain the same degree of control and diligence over all suppliers; (4). Purchase from sister facilities for cost-reduction, and considering the sister company as an internal preferred supplier;

(5). Evaluate capability and performance of sister company; (6). Operator exchange visits to understand products and services, as well as technical exchange; (7). Position the organization, the supplier and the parent corporation to obtain the maximum benefits of creating value, flexibility, speed of joint responses and optimization of costs and resources; (8). Have common understanding current and future customer needs and expectations; (9). Promote purchasing policies and objectives to increase awareness, motivation and involvement of cross-functional teams within the organization; (10). Establish continual improvement as an objective for purchasing processes of the organization; (11). Plan for the future of the organization and manage change; (12). Set and communicating a framework for achieving the satisfaction of its customers and other interested parties; (13). Evaluate relevant experience; (14). Evaluate performance of internal supply chains against competitors; (15). Review of purchased product quality, price, delivery performance and response to problems; (16). Audit supplier (internal/external) managements systems, and evaluate their potential capability to provide the required products effectively and within schedule; (17). Check available data on customer satisfaction; (18). Financial assessment: to assure the viability of the supplier throughout the intended period of supply and cooperation; (19). Supplier response: to make inquiries, quotations and tendering; (20). Supplier service, installation and support capability and history of performance to requirements; (21). Supplier awareness: compliance with relevant statutory and regulatory requirements; (22). The supplier's logistic capability includes locations and resources; (23). The supplier's standing in the community and its roles, as well as perception in society.

Labor Union Meeting

Labor-Management meetings shall be for the purpose of maintaining communications in order to cooperatively discuss and resolve problems of mutual concern to the parties. Labor-Management meeting's agendas are (1). Maintain administration of the Agreement; (2). Communicate interest; (3). Express employee's views or suggestions on subjects of interest to employees of the Bargaining Unit; (4). Criteria for staffing ratios and production standards—a proper relationship of work load to staff is a desirable goal to obtain; (5). Examine and attempt to resolve issues of interdepartmental impact and/or statewide concerns; (6). Litigate unfair labor practice complaints; (7). Avoid conflict and misunderstanding; (8). Jointly decide how the results of discussion are implemented and followed up;

(9). Develop a protocol, so that disputes about the degree, timing and character of the union's participation do not become an issue for disagreement, conflict and litigation, overshadowing the importance of the subject matter of the meeting.

Investor Meeting

Unless the Management addresses the needs of investors, they may not be interested in investing in corporate business. Investor meeting will be: (1). Effective way to communicate with the investor and provide an opportunity to build trusting, open relationships; (2). Providing a chance to clarify and explain points that are not immediately clear through written documentation, such as investment proposal; (3). Persuading the investor to give corporate the financing it needs; (4). Communicate investment strategy, i.e. rate of return; acceptable risk balances with the rate of return; a viable avenue for liquidity or exit strategy; strong management team capable of executing the plan; and the ability to monitor, influence or control actively the investment.

Creditor Meeting

Sometimes, a company, either as a running concern or in the event of winding up, has to make certain arrangements with its creditors. Meetings of creditors may be called for this purpose. In case of winding up of a company, a meeting of creditors and of contributories is held to ascertain the total amount due by the company and also to appoint a liquidator to wind up the affairs of the company. Meetings should not be limited to the above mentioned. Executives can decide kinds of meeting that is needed now or in future.

COMMITTEES

Need of establishing committees depends on corporate policy and strategy. It may not be similar one to other corporate. Following considerations may guide the requirement to establish a committee:

a.   Ensure that corporate mission statement continues to describe accurately the corporate and its characteristics, which needs periodically studied its mission and goals statements, taking into account internal changes as well as the changing responsibilities of the corporate and its stakeholders.

b. Monitor and control expenditure, performance or effectiveness of department and corporate; matter in annual report of department and corporate

c. Bring employees and management together in a non-adversarial, cooperative effort to promote safety and security in the workplace;

d. Assist the board of directors in fulfilling its oversight responsibilities for the integrity of the company's financial statements, the company's compliance with legal and regulatory requirements, the independent auditor's qualifications and independence, and the performance of the company's internal audit function and independent auditors.

e. Make recommendations to improve human relations

f. Assessment and dissemination of research results

g. Identifying qualified individuals to become board members and recommending to the Board a group of director nominees; determining the composition of the Board; developing and implementing a set of effective corporate governance policies and procedures; monitoring a process to assess the effectiveness of the Board.

h. Review moral soundness of certain policies, practices, initiatives; to help maintain highest ethical standards; establish through a code of conduct a value foundation in relation to misconduct & discipline, complaints, and unsatisfactory performance

i. Foster an awareness of, and sensitivity to, environmental concerns that affect the corporate community

j. Recommend goals and objectives, performance; reviewing and approving the human resources philosophies, policies, succession plans and compensation and benefits plans.

k. Oversees the Company's lending programs, investment portfolio, asset/liability mix, and funding sources.

Corporate Governance Committee

Committee may review the membership, responsibilities and charters of the various committees of the Board of Directors. They identify the standards for integrity and ethics that will be maintained by employees, Board members and anyone else acting on behalf of the company. Committee authorizes to:

a.   Identify and recommend individuals qualified to become a director, CEO or shareholder nominee

b.   Provide performance assessment and recommend for improvements of the Board's operations.

c.   Review and recommend qualification, size, election and structure of directors and CEO

d.   Review and assess the adequacy of the corporate governance guidelines and recommend changes.

e.   Review corporate mission (business philosophy); corporate strategy (courses of action to achieve corporate mission and purpose); corporate governance (who determines the corporate mission and regulates the activities of the corporation); corporate culture; corporate communication; organization of the corporation; decision processes and system; performance management process and system; reward process and system

Compensation Committee

The Compensation Committee is a committee to assist the Board of Director in relating to compensation and benefits programs for Board of Director, CEO, or senior executive. The Compensation Committee may form and delegate authority to subcommittees or employ a consultant. Committee will: (1). Evaluate on a periodic basis the competitiveness of the compensation; (2). Make recommendations to the Board regarding functional improvements or changes to the Plans or adoption of new plans when appropriate; (3). Review, and make recommendations for the compensation for Supervisory Board, Executive Board and other Senior Executive of the corporation, including base salary, bonus, incentive and equity compensation, and other compensation, perquisites, and special or supplemental benefits; (4). Review corporate goals and objectives relevant to the Chief

Executive Officer (CEO), Board of Director and Senior Executives compensation; (5). Evaluate the CEO, Board of Director, and Senior Executive performance in light of those goals and objectives

The responsibility of Compensation Committee can also be extended to determine compensation, bonus, incentive and other benefits for lower level employees.

Committee for Operation and Technical

Important aspects of operation and technical are lower development cost, shorter time to market, robust products with lower maintenance or warranty cost. Committee for operation and technical will: (1). Ensure un-interrupted, predictable operation and technical. Review deviations and monitor action plans, i.e. balanced scorecards, key performance indicators; (2). Ensure high quality—low cost product; (3). Use strict controls to insure that the content of the materials is not compromised or disclosed to unauthorized individuals; (4). Ensure changes and modernization carried out are implemented in compliance with plans approved in advance to enable maintaining the plant in operating condition for as long as possible; (5). Regular tests and inspections are performed to the appropriate extent in order to ensure safe and reliable operation of the plant. All plant maintenance activities are carried out according to plans to foresee and prevent any failures and disturbances with appropriate procedures; (6). Increase as possible by always utilizing state-of-the-art technology; (7). The best and most viable technology that will minimize the environmental impact is applied to the design throughout its life cycle; (8). Maintain operating conditions that allow effective procedures, which display a high degree of safety, quality and cost awareness; (9). Ensure that the work practices employed in the Company are of high quality, as they form the basis for safe and economical operation; (10). Competence and operation is developed according to the principle of continuous improvement. The staff is encouraged to introduce; (11). Introduce development initiatives and report any detected deficiencies, nonconformities and errors; (12). Ensure work tasks are performed in an appropriate and timely manner to high standards; (13). Elimination of the environmental impact; operation shall not harm people, the environment or property

Audit Committee

The Audit Committee shall assist the Board of Directors in its oversight of the integrity of the Company's financial statements, the Company's compliance with legal and regulatory requirements, the Independent Auditor's qualifications and independence, and the performance of the Company's internal audit function and Independent Auditors and procedures. The Committee will: (1). Evaluate the adequacy and effectiveness of the corporate system of internal accounting and operating controls; (2). Review the reliability and integrity of financial and operational information; (3). Monitor compliance with the policies, plans, procedures, laws and regulations that have an impact on corporate operations; (4). Review the means of safeguarding assets and verifying their existence when appropriate; (5). Appraise the economy and efficiency with which resources are employed; (6). Review financial and operational activities and programs to determine if results are consistent with established goals, objectives and authorized plans; (7). Serve as liaison for coordination of all external audit activities; (8). Assisting in fraud and theft assessment at the request of legal counsel and executive management; (9). Provide staff guidance to staff and managers on matters relating to audits and internal control functions; (10). Provide reviews to assure that the organization's plans are carried out, policies and procedures are observed, assets are accounted for, and records and reports are reliable.

Risk Management Committee

Committee provides risk management process, enabling people to identify, assess, manage, control and communicate risk across Board of Director up to operational. The protection of company reputation and operations and resources is a fundamental element in the medium-long term business strategy. Therefore, it is essential that the company has a high quality risk management framework to ensure risks are identified and appropriately managed to ensure the further development and protection of this reputation. Committee will focus on risks to the corporate, i.e.: (1). Coordination of a risk management framework; (2). Facilitate the development, ratification and adoption of a risk management policy and implementation plan; (3). Development and implementation of a risk management plan; (4). Link the policy and delegations framework with the risk management framework; (5). Assist in the development and application of risk management procedures across the organization; (6). Coordinate, monitor and report on progress in managing business/operational, enterprise-wide and specialist risks; (7). Report on progress of managing strategic risks to Board of Director; (8). Provide advice to the executives on risk management issues affecting their area; (9). Risk management training; (10). Raise the profile of risk management within the company and ensure a culture of risk management is developed; (11). Policy, strategy and toolkit: for managing company risks; (12). Risk Registers and associated action plans—details on risks and how they are managed; (13). Annual Corporate Risk Review and Report

Cooperative Development Committee

Cooperative are voluntary, independent business enterprises formed to meet specific needs of their members through a common venture. As private sector organization, their development effectiveness is measured by the same standards as other private organizations. In order for the members to realize the benefits from a cooperative it must first be a viable business enterprise. Appropriate policy and legislation is a key to enabling the formation, growth and effectiveness of cooperatives. Corporate and its members have been active in identifying areas which continue to hinder the viability of democratic cooperative organizations and have taken concrete actions to improve the policy and legislative environment for cooperatives.

The purpose of committee is: (1). To support the development of cooperative organizations because cooperatives embody aspects of the principles of voluntarism, democratic choice and the economic effectiveness of private enterprise that historically have shaped our own nation's development. Cooperatives are able to reach and benefit sectors of the population that would not normally be served by other private sector institutions, provide an institutional framework through which other resources and programs can be channeled. The high premium placed on member participation in the operations and decision making of the cooperative promotes independence and self-reliance encouraging members to take an active role in their own development. Cooperatives offer an attractive alternative to public sector programs. The paternalistic approach of governments and absence of competition provide little incentive to seek efficient methods of product or service delivery. A cooperative, because it is recipient owned, has an automatic incentive to maximize benefits to the members; (2). Provide environment need: to judge whether the cooperative will be successful, the local environment must be assessed to determine if it is supportive to the creation of a viable cooperative business enterprise; (3). Give assistance: to encourage the development and use of cooperatives where they can be effective instruments for program and project implementation, i.e. community development projects

Community Development Committee

Community development is about building active and sustainable communities based on social justice and mutual respect. It is about removing the barriers that prevent people from participating in the issues that affect their lives. Corporate should support individuals, groups and organizations in this process on the basis of the values: (1). Social Justice: enabling people to claim their human rights, meet their needs and have greater control over the decision-making processes which affect their lives; (2). Participation: facilitating democratic involvement by people in the issues which affect their lives based on full citizenship, autonomy, and shared power, skills, knowledge and experience; (3). Equality: challenging the attitudes of individuals, and the practices of institutions and society, which discriminate against and marginalize people; (4). Learning: recognizing the skills, knowledge and expertise that people contribute and develop by taking action to tackle social, economic, political and environmental problems; (5). Co-operation: working together to identify and implement action, based on mutual respect of diverse cultures and contributions); (6). Commitment: engage to action and financial obligation; (7). Challenge discrimination and oppressive practices within organizations, institutions and communities; (8). Develop practice and policy that protects the environment; Encouraging networking and connections between communities and organizations; (9). Ensure access and choice for all groups and individuals within society; Influencing policy and programs from the perspective of communities; (10). Prioritize the issues of concern to people experiencing poverty and social exclusion; (11). Promoting social change that is long-term and sustainable; (12). Reverse inequality and the imbalance of power relationships in society; (13). Supporting community led collective action

Committee is to establish work program and implementation by (1). Strengthening communities through the development projects which reflects on the relationship between company and community empowerment. A process, which joins up environmental, economic, social, demographic, technological, political and other issues by empowering communities to work on their own agendas to improve the quality of life; (2). Provide strategy and development in partnership with local authority and informal leaders; (3). Provide development policy that defines the roles of the company in supporting an integrated approach to education, social, economic, environmental and cultural development in communities; (4). Act on the basis of the values and commitments of community development; (5). Support action by community groups and organizations, community businesses and neighborhood councils, have clear processes which enable communities to influence their policies, programs and priorities, recognize the right of communities to propose alternative courses of action, value different types and levels of participation, build strategy through dialogue with people and organization active in communities, recognize the function of community development and allocate resources to it in their strategies, recognize the resources, information and support required by community representatives and organizations when working in partnerships

Suggestion System Committee

Suggestion System is a meritorious service award program which provides for equitable compensation and/or recognition to employees who develop and submit valid suggestions that are implemented. As a productivity initiative in the company, it promotes efficiency and economy in the operations and services by increasing productivity, improving working conditions, improving services, identifying safety hazards, conserving energy resources, eliminating all forms of waste and unnecessary expenditures, and increasing employee morale. This program, carefully considered and implemented, is an easy and inexpensive way to enhance employee productivity and morale. Worker participation draws on the employee's firsthand familiarity with the job and allows the employee to become involved in the work process. Committee will focus in promotion, acknowledgement, evaluation, rejection, awarding, publicizing, implementation and documentation of suggestions; calculating, and audit cost saving; monitor and follow up back log alerts, investigation and implementation; organize award

Housing Colony Committee

Work program is to be set up by Committee and reviewed to achieve comfortable residency, includes: (1). Set out the objectives and actions necessary to meet the aims of the strategy, identifies the lead agencies responsible for implementation and the timescale in which the actions will be delivered; (2). Report highlight the issue of empty homes and carry out an analysis to estimate the numbers of people in housing need; (3). Guidance on maintenance, repair and development; (4). Guidance of neighborhood, safety and security

Security Committee

A security policy is the cornerstone of an effective security program. The security policy defines objectives, assigns responsibilities, and provides direction to protect your organization's critical information. Corporate security policy must be tailored to directly address the specific security issues that affect the organization. Security committee needs: (1). Strategy set out a vision for effectively addressing the issue of domestic violence and details the specific steps that will be taken to achieve this; (2). Guide lines for standards of protection required on particular crime; (3). Framework for deciding what action to take in particular circumstances; (4). Provides guidelines for the development of procedures applied to the plant; (5). Aspect of law; (6). Commitment to security-awareness culture, to customers, shareholders and employees to prevent security breaches; (7). Ensure each department is responsible for creating its own security policy. This policy should lay down rules for protection of business data and processes corresponding to the threats/risks involved and the value of those assets. (8). Define practices, procedures, and guidelines for configuring and managing security in the environment; (9). Minimize risks, demonstrate due diligence to customers and shareholders, and provide excellent baselines from which to work from; (10). Heighten security awareness among institution personnel; (11). Demonstrate the organizations commitment to protecting vital information assets from existing and new threats; (12). Appropriate, effective, and updated security policy exists and is implemented throughout the organization; (13). Conduct a series of in-depth vulnerability assessments, detailed audits of current policies and procedures, and by formulating the results into a new or revised security policy; (14). Identify sensitive information, critical systems, and security requirements; (15). Incorporate local, state, and federal laws, and relevant ethical standards; (16). Define institutional security goals and objectives based on vulnerability assessments, audits, interviews, and the analysis of results; (17). Setting a course for accomplishing these goals and objectives in an agreed upon time periods; (18). Ensure that necessary mechanisms for accomplishing the goals and objectives are in place; (19). Data security procedures are adapted to the criticality of the functions and to the associated risks; (20). Secure financial interests and personal privacy protection and to ensure availability of reliable information and to prevent damages caused by processing of data; (21). Data security procedure covers the availability, authenticity and confidentiality of information and data systems, as well as the management of access rights; (22). Information received from outside sources shall be treated pursuant to at least the data security procedures used or defined by the outside source in question

Safety Committee

Safety committee is to evaluate, recommend and assure implementation of safety policies, practices and procedures that prevent human injuries, property damage and loss to process arising from accidental causes. This will be accomplished by working as a team to resolve these issues in the spirit of sustainability and continuous performance. Their mission is to promote zero accidents by developing positive safety attitudes throughout the workplace with the support and involvement of management and employees through communication, inspections and training. This committee and its individual members are dedicated to promote the health, safety and welfare of the employees, with the support of management, to create a safe and healthful work environment for our employees, their families and the community. Safety committee will review: (1). General statement of good intent, usually linked to a commitment to comply with relevant legislation, policies so as to relate also to the health and safety of others affected by their activities, demonstrate clearly that there is commitment at a high level; (2). Safety policy covers the safety of production and operation as well as the safety of persons and work places, rescue and emergency operations and data security.

Standards Committee

(1). Set meeting to evaluate the progress of implementation for Policies and Procedures of Corporate Standardization (ISO, OSHAS etc) and standard work procedure in the plant; (2). Provide rules governing corporate standardization; (3). Establish formation of committees and the development, preparation, interpretation, revision, reaffirmation, withdrawal—and submittal to the Board of Directors for approval; (4). Ensure that approved procedures have been followed; (5). To promote effective and consistent standards policies in furtherance of company goals, to foster cooperative participation by the authority and other private organizations in standards activities, including the related activities of product testing, quality system registration, certification, and accreditation; (6). Ensure compliance to the standard; (7). Consistent approach to government in standards preparation matters and in particular respect of dealings with standard auditor; (8). Assign duties and responsibilities with respect to a standard. It is expected to provide addenda as needed, generate revision on a regular basis, and render interpretations; (9). Continuous maintenance of a standard by establishing a documented schedule for publication of addenda or revision includes procedures for timely, documented consensus action on requests for change to any part of the guideline.

MEP (Margin Enhancement Program) Committee

Corporate should highlight the need to establish robust margin enhancement unction in order to effectively manage critical business risks across key revenue generation processes. In order to assess the health of such processes, a comprehensive set of key performance indicators (KPI) should be implemented across an organization, to include all functions—senior management, revenue assurance, billing, networks and so on—and all elements of an effective margin enhancement program (revenues, costs, capital and profitability). These indicators will be critical in enabling communications companies to monitor, in real time, the revenues and costs associated with individual functions, products/services, suppliers and customer relationships and take the appropriate action to address weaknesses and issues continually throughout the year. As the industry moves into a new business environment—with organizations having to manage numerous products and services throughout their life cycles—effective margin enhancement is likely to emerge as one of the critical determinants of success. Work program should be developed and evaluated by Committee to achieve company competitiveness level.

a. Marketing (marketing and selling processes to systematically profitably grow the business, commercial sales and marketing system and plan, pricing policy and procedures); finance (financial capabilities, pricing procedures, and financing, management system to reach profit and growth objectives); product/service delivery (product/service delivery, customer care/retention processes, and market capabilities, company operating objectives); organizational (organizational structure, job tasking, roles and responsibilities), technical (work quality, shut down, break down, machine reliability, procedure, modification, preventive maintenance, training), production (quality, material loss, capacity increasing, energy saving, procedure), logistic (material management, pricing, outsourcing), Information technology (communication technology, computer program/software)

b. Revenue enhancement (pricing of products and services, tracking and recon-
    ciling service orders through the pre-ordering, ordering, provisioning, bill-
    ing, and maintenance and repair processes); and revenue enhancement
    strategies (customer activation, change management, billing and invoicing,
    product development, financial processing; efficiency and effectiveness of
    policies and procedures, accountability and reporting, organizational influ-
    ence)

c. Cost management (analyze and evaluate key cost management processes,
    including contracts and negotiations, service ordering and provisioning,
    invoice reconciliation, dispute management, cost monitoring, and financial
    processing), and cost management strategies (contracts and agreement,
    ordering and provisioning, Invoice reconciliation, dispute management, cost
    management and processing, financial processing, efficiency and effective-
    ness of policies and procedures, span of control)

d. Profitability enhancement: ineffective processes to assess and report reve-
    nues, costs, and margins by business unit, product, service, customer, and
    geography; cost assignment and allocation methods that are either undefined
    or noncompliant with regulatory or management decision-making require-
    ments, minimize corporate tax; ineffective management of product;
    unknown individual product revenues and costs related; lack of appropriate
    performance measures linking sales efforts and revenue growth with profit-
    ability targets; and profitability enhancement strategies

e. Process-oriented approach: to review, evaluate, and increase overall profit-
    ability, include market entry assessment (assessing the potential for profitable
    introduction of products and services to a new market; product demand
    forecasting (assessing the potential product demand and profitability); cus-
    tomer value management (assessment of customer segment or individual
    customer profitability and retention processes); profitability assessment
    (assessment of profitability of specific products or services); sales force assess-
    ment (assessment of sales goals and sales force behavior in light of strategic
    objectives)

Human Resources Development Committee

Human resources development committee should ensure that the human
resources planning process analyzes, anticipates, and meets the entity's need for

sufficient and appropriate human resources and does so in a manner that supports the entity's mission, goals, and objectives. Human resources planning are the process of analyzing an organization's human resources needs under changing conditions and developing the activities necessary to meet these needs. Such planning helps entities anticipate the impact of change and respond to such change in a systematic and integrated way. Human resources planning and strategic planning are intimately related. On one hand, strategic planning provides the basis for the development of all human resources functions. On the other, human resources planning play a key role in the strategic planning process. Human resources committee should be involved in:

a. Organization structuring

b. Performance Improvement Plan: to facilitate constructive discussion between a staff and his or her supervisor, to clarify the work performance to be improved, to provide feedback to the employee regarding his or her performance, to take additional disciplinary action through the organization's

c. Discipline: a process for dealing with job-related behavior that does not meet expected and communicated performance standards; to assist the employee to understand that a performance problem or opportunity for improvement exists, to assist the employee to overcome performance problems and satisfy job expectations.

d. Absenteeism, overtime, health record

e. Human resources policies, procedures, guidelines, and forms;
    job descriptions, labor laws, motivation and retention,
    recruiting and staffing, manage performance/career, manage
    salary and benefits, training and education, communication, change management, team building/work teams, work relationships, coaching and mentoring

f. Remuneration: payments for services; travel and living expenses, expense reimbursement;

g. Benefits, i.e. housing, allowance, loan, transportation, bonus.

h. Succession planning: Planning undertaken for senior executives to ensure continuity of operations and the continued leadership and vitality of the corporation.

i. Define equality scheme that summarizes what the company intends to eliminate unlawful discrimination and promote equality. Make appropriate arrangements with regard to the principle that there should be equality of opportunity for all people irrespective of their race, sex, disability, age, sexual orientation or religion

j. Front Office/Public Relation

Project Management Committee

Project management is a carefully planned and organized effort to accomplish a specific (and usually) one-time effort, Project management includes developing a project plan, which includes defining project goals and objectives, specifying tasks or how goals will be achieved, what resources are need, and associating budgets and timelines for completion. It also includes implementing the project plan, along with careful controls to stay on the "critical path", that is, to ensure the plan is being managed according to plan. Project management usually follows major phases including feasibility study, project planning, implementation, evaluation and support/maintenance. Project management committee is needed to monitor:

a. Capital expenditure (capex) projects, project for technology improvement, and capacity increasing project, needs project management and controls (inconsistent construction processes and project or cost tracking, lack of continuous reassessment of construction-project feasibility, percentage of completion, remaining costs-to-complete, and cost/benefit, purchase of unnecessary materials and equipment while unused assets remain in warehouses, overpayment for assets and decreasing return on investment, receipt and acceptance of contractor bids and/or work performed that does not meet quality and cost standards, mismanagement of third-party contractors)

b. Project management strategies (planning and budgeting, regulatory requirements, construction design, benchmark, bid selection and contract management, procurement and logistics, cost recovery, post-construction review).

Shut Down Committee

A procedure is to be established to ensure the minimum requirements for lockout of plant that could cause production loss, injury to personnel. Executives will ensure all employees shall comply with the procedure. Duty of shut down committee is: (1). Reviewing shut down policy and guide line; (2). Scheduling and up dating shut down; (3). Organizing job planning and time/manpower/other requirement conflicts; (4). Reviewing safety and security needs; (5). Providing equipment release and hand over procedure; (6). Reviewing strategy to minimize unplanned jobs, delay, failure during start up, work procedure, time table, control and reporting; (7). Dealing with contractor and personnel issues

Environmental Committee

Corporate must have commitment to ensuring advanced protection of the environment, compliance with governmental regulations and implementation of state-of-the-art technology. These efforts will distinguish the corporate as the foremost leader in environmental protection and solid waste management excellence. The environmental management System reflects the Company's emphasis on continuous improvement in operations by measuring and evaluating its environmental performance, i.e. policy, planning, implementation, assessment and corrective action, management review processes. Environment committee shall be involved in: (1). Waste management strategy (solid, liquid, gas, and domestic waste), and progress made in implementing the strategy; include a strong emphasis on the environment and a legal requirement that each of the strategies be consistent with the principles of sustainable development; (2). Investigate environment complaint and action plan; (3). Waste management and disposal facilities to meet company future needs; (4). Establishing best practice guidance; (5). Raise Waste Awareness among the staffs; (6). Provide strategy for noise, and air quality monitoring; (7). Assess present relevant waste data to meet the standard; (8). Provide policy relating to Government interest in accreditation and certification; and social issues

Other kind of committee can be established. The requirement is different from one corporate to others.

ORGANIZATIONAL STRUCTURE

Organization development is a complex strategy intended to change the beliefs, attitudes, values, and structure of organizations so that they can better adapt to new technologies, markets, and challenges. Organization structure should consider: logical and chronological, establishment of goals and objectives; form should follow function, structure should follow strategy. Executives need to clearly define organizational structure in the plant, which aims to:

a. Ensure the roles and responsibilities of each position and staff are clearly defined and that individuals act in a way consistent with these roles.

b. Ensure that a senior officer is responsible for giving advice on financial matters, for keeping proper financial records and accounts and for maintaining an effective system of internal control.

c. Ensure that there is a senior officer who ensures that procedures are followed and that the company complies with relevant regulations and statements of good practice

d. Ensure the Chief Executive (Manager and above) is responsible for all aspects of operational management

Organization structure expresses managerial, administrative, and operational relationships within the entity. It also embodies authority, responsibility, and accountability. Organization structure groups activities for the purposes of administration and control and combines duties and responsibilities into jobs. Entity structure is the result of and a tool for implementing operational, financial, human resource, and strategic plans. It influences the entity's ability to communicate, coordinate its functions, and respond to environmental changes. The structure of an entity must simultaneously facilitate planning, problem solving, policy-making, communications, operations, resource allocation and use, and performance assessment in order to meet the demands placed upon it.

Organization structures are seldom, if ever, entirely rational. They reflect not only objective factors, such as the entity's environment, mission, size, resources, and technology, but also the knowledge and preferences of the entity's leaders and the compromises through which internal power struggles have been resolved.

Because of this, they can also be very difficult and costly to change. Process of structuring organization:

a. Define tasks required to accomplish entity's mission, goals, and objectives.

b. Group similar tasks into spheres of work (work units). Each work unit should contribute to overall entity goals and objectives. A hierarchy of objectives should exist, and members of a work group should share the same goals and objectives. Once an entity's work is divided, the jobs must be grouped together according to a plan (operations plan) that provides a system of coordination (departmentation): by function groups similar tasks within their own function, by product or services groups tasks according to the product or service the entity provides, by customer or location segments the entity by either the different customers served or the different geographical locations in which the entity operates.

c. Determine the extent to which entity activities will be centralized or decentralized.

d. Determine functional and authority relationships between advisory/support and line staff.

e. Document entity structure and communicate it in writing to entity staff. An organization chart should be created to show the chain of command and reflect relationships between different areas of the entity.

f. Monitor, evaluate, review, and, if necessary, adjust organization structure. At least annually, the entity should review lines of communication, chains of command, unity of command, and spans of control to determine whether the current structure facilitates or impedes decision-making and achievement of entity mission, goals, and objectives.

g. An organizational structure is effective, if facilitates the contribution of individuals to entity goals and objectives; efficient, if facilitates entity goals and objectives with minimum resources and fewest unsought consequences

ORGANIZATIONAL CHANGE

Budget cuts, departmental reorganizations, the introduction of new technology or other organizational changes may require the company to change or eliminate positions. The changes will require planning, communication, consultation with staff, retraining and relocation assistance. In order to ensure that staffs are treated fairly throughout the change process this policy sets out the principles for treatment of staff affected by organizational change and the requirements which must be met.

Changes should be in accordance with organizational mission and consider the following principles:

a. Develop an organizational change that enhances productivity and effectiveness in accomplishing both short-term goals and long-range strategic plans. Determine whether the change will be beneficial to the organization's mission. Determine the reorganization's objectives and the assignment of responsibilities.

b. Use tools such as streamlining and de-layering in order to use existing personnel and resources to their fullest potential, while minimizing any potentially adverse budgetary impact that change may have on the organization.

c. Analyze the potential impact. Determine if the result will be a flatter and simpler organization; a net decrease in organizational entities; and an improvement in supervisory ratios.

d. Determine whether personnel actions would eliminate the problem or issue, thus making reorganization unnecessary.

e. Clearly define organizational functions. Consider the nature and scope of the functions to be performed. Group similar functions to avoid overlapping responsibilities and fragmentation. Consider structural and functional alternatives.

f. Establish a separate organizational component only if the functions to be assigned are distinct from those of other established organizational components and cannot be performed by redistribution of tasks.

g.   Delegate decision-making authority to the appropriate level. Clearly state the lines of responsibility and maintain mechanisms of communication.

h.   Corporate may seek through its strategic and operational planning processes to respond to dynamic needs while upholding its mission and pursuing its organizational goals. As a result of planning, other management processes, and organizational assessment, the Management may determine that new or reorganized organizational entities are required to pursue the mission and goals. Or an organizational entity will be reorganized, reassigned, down-sized, made inactive, or permanently closed. An organizational entity might include, but would not be limited to, an operating unit, a department, or a division.

i.   The establishment of new organizational entities will arise out of planning processes and be based on the mission and institutional goals of the company. Appropriate sources of funds for establishing and maintaining the new entity must be identified, and all appropriate administrative approvals must be obtained before any new entity can be formally established.

j.   Determination to close an organizational entity is a management decision that will be reached through careful consideration of issues within established policies and procedures and will include participation from appropriate constituencies within the company before final decisions are made.

In situations in which organizational entity will be reorganized, reassigned, down-sized, made inactive, or permanently closed, institutional leadership will make every effort to continue to use the human talent that has contributed to the company through the program and will implement decisions in a compassionate and sensitive manner.

HIERARCHY

In the United States the CEO may also be the chairman of the board or the company president in small businesses, but these roles are often separated in larger organizations, to prevent the company from becoming dominated by a single personality, and to prevent a conflict of interest against the owners (the shareholders). Often, one person shares the chairman and CEO titles while another takes on the president and COO titles. Regardless, in virtually all cases where the CEO and president are not the same person, the CEO is of the higher rank.

In the European Union there are two separate boards, one executive board for the day-to-day business and one supervisory board for control purposes (elected by the shareholders). Thus, the chief executive and the chairman of the board will always be different people. This ensures a distinction between governance and management and allows for clear lines of authority. The aim is to prevent a conflict of interest and too much power being concentrated in the hands of one person

Shareholder

The shareholders (stockholders) are the owners of the corporation. As owners, shareholders hold ultimate power over the corporation and its activities. However, a shareholder does not hold any power over the management of the corporation. Shareholders possess the ultimate power in that they can appoint or remove Supervisory Board Member of the corporation. In the hierarchy, there are two-tier governance structure comprising a Board of Director with executive functions and a Supervisory Board with monitoring powers. A constant dialogue is maintained between the Board of Director and the Supervisory Board in the interest of good governance.

Supervisory Board

Supervisory Board is to oversee the work of the Board of Director and provide advice Supervisory Board is directly involved in decisions on matters of fundamental importance to the company and confers with the Board of Director on the company's strategic alignment. It also holds regular discussions with the Board of Director on the company's business strategy and the status of its implementation. While Executive officer literally refers to a person responsible for the performance of duties involved in running an organization, the exact meaning of the role is highly variable, depending on the organization. In business, the executive officers are the top officers of a corporation.

Chief Executive Officer (CEO) or Chief Executive is the highest-ranking corporate officer or executive officer of company. This position is separated from Board of Directors, in order to prevent the company from becoming dominated by a single personality, and to prevent a conflict of interest against the owners (the shareholders). Chief Operating Officer (COO) is a corporate officer responsible for managing the day-to-day activities of the corporation. COO is one of the highest ranking members of an organization, monitoring the daily operations of the company and reporting to the chief executive officer directly and responsible for operations management, i.e. design, operation, and improvement of the systems that create and deliver the firm's products/services. Chief Financial Officer (CFO) is a corporate officer responsible to direct the organization's financial goals, objectives, and budgets. They oversee the investment of funds and manage associated risks, supervise cash management activities, execute capital-raising strategies to support a firm's expansion, and deal with mergers and acquisitions. Chief Marketing Officer (CMO) is a corporate officer responsible for building a marketing strategy; build and implement brand awareness; develop online and offline advertising strategies and manage implementation; manage, oversee, and create strategies for the growth of traffic, visibility, and brand awareness; drive customer acquisition and member-base, using techniques such as co-branding and affiliate marketing; drive marketing to create keen awareness of the new service; provide direction regarding marketing programs and tactics; provide the leadership in defining and writing the marketing plan; develop marketing tactics, which provide for high visibility in a short time frame; identify, review, select and manage appropriate agency relationships; help design the PR strategy in conjunction with agency; and oversee merchandising efforts to maximize purchases, up-sells and cross-sells.

More corporate officers can be adopted into the organization; it depends on the large of organization/corporate, i.e. Chief Analytics Officer (CAO),
Chief Information Officer (CIO), Chief Networking Officer (CNO), Chief Information Security Officer (CISO), Chief Technical Officer (CTO), Chief Knowledge Officer (CKO), Chief Security Officer (CSO), Chief Strategy Officer (CSO), Chief Risk Officer (CRO), Chief Credit Officer (CCO), Chief Data Officer (CDO), Chief Investment Officer (CIO)

The primary responsibility of Supervisory Board is oversight—defining and enforcing standards of accountability that enable Management to manage well and in the interests of the Corporation and its stockholders. Consistent with that objective, the following are our primary responsibilities:

a. Attending Board meetings and evaluating the performance of the Corporation and its Management, which includes: (1) overseeing the conduct of the

Corporation's business to evaluate whether it is being effectively managed, (2) selecting and regularly evaluating the Chief Executive Officer, and (3) fixing the compensation of the Chief Executive Officer and other members of Management as deemed appropriate;

b.   Reviewing and, where appropriate, approving fundamental operating, financial and other corporate strategies, as well as major plans and objectives;

c.   Providing advice and counsel to the Chief Executive Officer and Management;

d.   Overseeing Management's efforts to ensure that the assets of the Corporation are safeguarded through the maintenance of appropriate accounting, financial and other controls, and that the business of the Corporation is conducted in compliance with applicable laws and regulations;

e.   Electing the Chairman of the Board; and

f.   Annually evaluating the overall effectiveness of the Board of Directors, as well as selecting and recommending to stockholders for election an appropriate slate of candidates for the Board of Directors.

Executive Board (Board of Directors)

The most important tasks of the Board of Director are defining corporate strategy, setting the budget, allocating corporate resources and developing management personnel.

The Board of Director also ensures that the Supervisory Board receives regular, timely and comprehensive information on all matters relating to corporate planning, business development, risk situation and risk management. Board of Directors (Director) is a high level official with a fiduciary responsibility of overseeing the operation of a corporation; nominally, Directors, other than the CEO are usually not considered to be employees of the company per se, although they generally receive compensation, often including benefits; in publicly-held companies, the Board of Directors is normally made up of members (Directors) who are comprised of a mixture of corporate officials who are also management employees of the company (inside directors) and members who are not employed by the company in any capacity (outside directors or non-executive directors), who can provide a perspective on a situation which is independent from management.

The three strata of directors are executive directors, non-executive/independent directors who are members or chairmen of Audit Committees, and other non-executive/independent directors. The actual power held by the board of directors varies widely from corporation to corporation. In some, the board of directors forms a powerful body to which senior management is subservient. Other times, the board is a formality which merely rubber stamps decisions of the CEO

Responsibility

The basic responsibility of Directors is to exercise their business judgment and act in what they reasonably believe to be in the best interests of the Company and its shareholders. In discharging that obligation, Directors should be entitled to rely on the honesty and integrity of the Company's senior executives and its outside advisors and auditors. The Directors shall also be entitled to have the Company purchase reasonable directors' and officers' liability insurance on their behalf, to the benefits of indemnification to the fullest extent permitted by law and the Company's charter, by-laws and any indemnification agreements, and to exculpation as provided by state law and the Company's charter.

Directors are expected to attend Board meetings and meetings of committees on which they serve, and to spend the time needed and meet as frequently as necessary to properly discharge their responsibilities. Directors are also expected to attend annual meetings of shareholders. Directors are expected to act ethically at all times and to adhere to the policies comprising the Company's Code of Business Conduct.

Authority

The Board of Director is accountable for the performance of company through corporate governance policy. For the purpose of governance, the Board of Directors directs and authorizes to: achieve results through the establishment of corporate objectives; provide and implement a development and succession plan annually; advise and inform on the operating, planning and development functions of the corporation; delegate authority, implement policy, establish procedures, make all decisions, take all actions, establish all practices, develop all activities to conduct the business of the corporation; enter into employment agreements with officers of the corporation setting out terms and conditions of employment, benefits, and salary, and advise of subsequent changes.

In exercising due diligence, the Board of Directors provides parameters for achieving results and will not allow assets to be unprotected, inadequately maintained, or unnecessarily risked; operate without strategies that adequately respond to the nature and level of risk, risk parameters, impairment, or loss of assets; endanger the corporation's public image or credibility, particularly in ways that would hinder the accomplishment of the mission; allow compensation and benefits to employees to jeopardize the corporation's public image; provide a budget that contains insufficient information to enable credible projection of revenues and expenses, separation of capital, operational and notes to the budget, cash flow and disclosure of planning assumptions ; provide a budget that does not support the achievement of the corporate objectives; expend more funds than those approved in the administrative budget, allowing for a five per cent variance, or neglect to report any variance to CEO as soon as practical; endanger the fiscal soundness of future years or ignore the building of organizational capability sufficient to achieve the corporate objectives in future years; operate inconsistently with the funding policy and/or investment policy; allow the corporation to operate without financial management control systems or financial records using generally accepted accounting principles; fail to advise the CEO of a change in accounting policy.

Senior Executive/Executive

Vice President is middle or upper manager in a corporation. Depending on the corporate structure Vice Presidents report to the President whom will in turn report to the Director. Manager is a person who has the ability to act independently and make decisions about supervising or directing employees or other resources. This may include: ensuring company policies are followed, authorizing overtime, time off or leaves of absence, calling employees in to work, altering work processes, establishing or altering work schedules, training employees, committing or authorizing the use of company resources, managing a budget. Manager reports to Vice President.

BOARDS QUALIFICATION

The role of Executive Officer or Director of a corporate in today's environment is more demanding, more complex and multi-dimensional than it has been in the past. There are also more risks, and potential liabilities are relatively heavy. Stakeholders expect and demand more from them, and consequently their role has become more onerous. Board members should fulfill following qualifications:

a.   Competencies: industry knowledge; accounting and finance; business judgment; management; leadership; market knowledge; business strategy; crisis management; corporate governance; and risk management

b.   Standard of conduct and ethics: confirm act in good faith, without any self-interest in their decision and with a reasonable basis for believing that their actions are in the lawful and legitimate furtherance of the corporation's and shareholders' best interests, and must exercise an honest business judgment after due consideration of what they reasonably believe to be the relevant facts

Assessment

The Board (Supervisory and Executive) is to be committed to assessing its performance as it relates to ongoing governance. Individual board members will be evaluated in terms of their contributions to the overall effectiveness and vitality of the Board. The effectiveness of the Board, as a whole, will be evaluated and will involve a discussion in Boards joint meeting at least once annually.

Boards can improve their performance through periodic assessment of their internal processes, group dynamics, and individual member contributions. Focused self-refection allows boards to identify strengths and areas for improvement, builds board unity, and provides an opportunity for members to reaffirm their commitment to board service. Self-assessments should result in the recommendation and implementation of performance goals. Goal progress can be evaluated during each self-assessment period. Boards may choose to design and conduct the self-assessment on their own, use existing evaluation tools, or hire an outside consultant or facilitator.

CEO will oversee and assess the performance of the Directors consistent with assessing the performance of the corporation by: regularly monitoring the performance of Directors against the beliefs and values, corporate governance policy, corporate objectives, and individual performance expectations. Monitoring will include: on going reports from the Directors; information and reports, as requested; regularly reviewing corporate performance; reports from external and internal audit and actuary. CEO will complete a formal evaluation of Directors and provide feedback. The CEO is responsible for having ongoing performance discussions with the Directors regarding performance expectations.

SUCCESSION

Organization's approach to succession management influences the perception of the system's effectiveness. It will need:

a. Organizational Support: The first step is for an organization's top management team and the public works' management group to agree to endorse succession management planning and then establish a process and specific steps to implement the program. Senior management/management involved in process of identifying competencies/key requirements for manager and above positions; involving line management in process design, implementation, and execution; Alignment with company strategy, competencies, and values.

b. Identifying Candidates: i.e. identifying needs for multiple candidates for each senior management position; using competencies to define readiness; identifying high potentials and high-performing candidates. Selecting those promising individuals can be the result of evaluating performance appraisals, consulting with other department management staff, and looking closely at productive division heads, creative key staff personnel and those who have shown an aptitude for doing very thorough work and going the extra mile on day-to-day tasks. And always, listening to be aware of those who want to move up, expand their job tasks and grow with the organization.

c. Development Process: expose employees to multiple situations, tasks, projects to build their competencies; coaching and mentoring; establishing on-the-job developmental assignments. One approach that has worked for many is to identify the rising stars first, then provide a formal management training and development program for each of those employees, followed by coaching, mentoring and making growth opportunities available to them. Concurrently with their training and development program it is good to make specific and challenging assignments that are within their grasp and capabilities, yet stretch them in their performance and critical thinking. Special assignments can include chairing a specific department task force, a short-term committee, or an assignment that does not involve others but that the person must develop solely on his or her own. An individualized work plan monitored with regularly scheduled weekly coaching and mentoring sessions between director and individual is critical to maximize the person's ability to recognize effective (as well as ineffective) actions, directions, critical thinking process and to see the "big picture" of the task and how it relates to the department or organization as a whole.

d. Other Practices: identify real needs in next three to five years; calibrating performance and potential assessment codes across departments for consistency; and stakeholders' assessment.

Succession management planning may be still debate-able, but it is truly essential to assure a continuity of philosophy, knowledge and direction for the department's or organization long-term success. And succession management planning can be a critical and helpful process to fill those ever-present management vacancies that public works departments are experiencing in today's mobile job setting.

7

HUMAN RESOURCES MANAGEMENT

It is important for organization to ensure that they employ the right people with the right organizations. The Management needs to therefore ensure that recruitment processes are fair and provide equality of opportunity thus encouraging a wide and diverse range of people to apply. In addition, the organization must ensure that it develops the capability of staff. Human Resources management should ensure that the roles and responsibilities of all staffs are defined in writing; ensure that all staff are trained and experienced; ensure that employees have access to advice and resources in order to carry out their roles effectively; ensure there is equality of opportunity in the recruitment process.

Human resources management needs to balance corporate mission with stakeholder and employee perspectives; i.e.:

a.   Establish a Results-Oriented Set of Measures. (1). Define what measures mean the most to stakeholder, and employee by having them work together; creating an easily recognized body of measures; and clearly identifying measures to address their concerns. (2). Commit to initial change by using expertise wherever the organization find it; involving everyone in the process; making the system non-punitive; bringing in the unions; and providing clear, concise guidance as to the establishment, monitoring, and reporting of measures. (3). Maintain flexibility by recognizing that performance management is a living process; limiting the number of performance measures; and maintaining a balance between financial and non-financial measures

b.   Establish Accountability at All Levels. (1). Lead by example. Cascade accountability: share it with the employee by creating a performance-based organization; encouraging sponsorship of measures at all levels; and involving the unions at all levels of performance management. (2). Keep the employee informed via intranet and/or internet; don't rule out alternative forms of communication. (3). Keep the customer informed via both the Internet and traditional paper reports. (4). Make accountability work: reward employees for success (supplement or replace monetary rewards with non-monetary means, reallocate discretionary funds, and base rewards in a team approach).

c. Data analysis. (1). Collect feedback data, which can be obtained from customers by providing easy access to your organization; remember too that "survey" is not a four-letter word. (2). Collect performance data by investing both the time and the money to make it right; making sure that your performance data mean something to those that use them; recognizing that everything is not on-line or in one place; and centralizing the data collection function at the highest possible level. (3). Analyze data: combine feedback and performance data for a more complete picture; conduct root-cause analyze; and make sure everyone sees the results of analyses.

d. Connect the Dots. If corporate performance management efforts are not connected to the entity's business plan (which defines day-to-day operations in a government agency) and to the budget (which is where the money is), then the executive will be doomed to failure because the entity's performance measurement approach will have no real meaning to the people running, or affected by, the program. Planning documents must connect to business plans, and data systems and the budget process must be integrated with all these other factors. By doing so, the executive can create a strategic management framework which serves to focus the entire organization on the same mission and goals

e. Share the Leadership Role. Leadership is a critical element marking successful organizations, both public and private. Cascaded throughout an organization, leadership gives the performance management process a depth and sustainability that survives changes at the top—even those driven by elections and changes in political party leadership

RECRUITMENT

The recruitment process for most organizations is designed along the same path, i.e.

a. Job Profiles. Identify job vacancy, job description, person specification, details for applicant, publicizing, processing applicant, selecting interview panel, monitoring, short-listing, arrangement for interview and interview, selection test, making decision after interview, references, criminal record check, appointment

b. Conditions of Service. Terms and conditions that form the contract/hire of employment.

Organizations are now starting to find that, with some skill, it is possible to assess the return on investment. It is possible to define the business benefits required, and track the results: (1). Start off with a clear analysis of the organizational and commercial outcomes required from recruitment. What is the business trying to achieve, and what part will successful candidates need to play; (2). Develop clear ways of tracking and measuring these outcomes; (3). Carry out an objective and open-minded analysis of the qualities people need to perform. Ruthlessly avoid a judgment being colored by past practice or "knowing what works from experience". If doing this well seems expensive in the short run, it's never as expensive as doing it badly in the long run; (3). Ensure for assessing the full range of qualities needed for success—include personality, motivation and aptitude as well as experience; (4). Ensure that everyone involved in recruitment is trained to the highest possible standards; (5). Carefully connect recruitment to induction, training, management and performance management—to ensure that the business does not just get the right people, but nurtures and capitalizes in them as well

These approaches deliver returns of investment because they identify people who perform; reduce the risk of employing people who cannot (or will not) perform; cut the costs of recruitment and development; and play a major part in driving forwards organizational change. In common with all people processes, recruitment is there to deliver tangible human and business benefits. Devoting a little time to considering the return on investment is not a nebulous luxury—it is essential to delivering the results the organization needs. It is also a powerful way of positioning Human Resources at the heart of the business.

INDUCTION

Every organization, large or small, should have a well-considered induction program. Designing an appropriate and cost-effective induction package is a complex task. The induction program has to provide all the information that new employees and others need, and are able to assimilate, without being overwhelming or diverting them from the essential process of integration into a team. The length and nature of the induction process depends on the complexity of the job and the background of the new employee. One size does not fit all—a standardized induction course is unlikely to satisfy anyone.

The purpose of induction is to ensure the effective integration of staff into or across the organization for the benefit of both parties. Tailor-made program will increase staff retention. A good induction program contains the following elements: (1). Orientation (physical)—describing where the facilities are; (2). Orientation (organizational)—showing how the employee fits into the team; (3). Health and safety information—this is a legal requirement; (4). Explain terms and conditions; (5). Explain details of the organization's history, its products and services, its culture and values; (6). Explain a clear outline of the job/role requirements.

The structure of an induction course depends not only on the size and nature of an organization but also on the type of recruit. The process begins at the recruitment stage and continues into employment. New recruits need to know the organization, the culture and the people, and their role. Ideally, all new employees should receive an individual induction program that reflects their specific needs. For a large company, this program would be a combination of one-to-one discussions and more formal group presentations, which may be given within an induction course.

PERFORMANCE MANAGEMENT

Executives must manage employee performance well in order for agencies to accomplish their missions and achieve their goals. Consequently, performance management is one the most important parts of a supervisor's or team leader's job. Developing skills in performance management is a wise investment for agencies—investments that will help them achieve their strategic goals. It can be achieved by:

a. Establishing a method for providing each staff with expectations for performance and periodic evaluation of performance;

b. Facilitating direct communication between supervisors and staff members on performance expectations and achievements;

c. Recognizing the accomplishments and define the educational needs of staff members;

d. Providing a reliable method of acquiring feedback on departmental operations

Performance management is an important component of the supervisor/staff member relationship. It facilitates the growth and development of individuals and achievement of institutional goals. It is a continuous process that begins during the initial hiring process and continues throughout the year. The actual performance review is a formal opportunity to review the progress made during the year and set goals. This process is in alignment with the company values, all staff should be aware of the expectations of their position as well as how they will be evaluated. Performance review is an ongoing process to help employees to understand the nature and quality of their performance, and to identify what they must do to improve and motivate them to improve.

Performance planning must clearly identify the results expected, as well as the behaviors and skills the employee is expected to demonstrate providing a specific action plan aimed at clear targets. Performance plans are to be consistent with position descriptions unless projects or duties are assigned temporarily. Performance plans (goals and objectives) are established by the supervisor, in consultation with the employee, at the beginning of each year. Supervisors aim to achieve mutual agreement, wherever possible, to build commitment to the action plans.

Performance plan documentation should be submitted to Human Resources for personnel files. Performance appraisal discussions are a year-end performance review of past performance and an opportunity to document the results of the year's performance management activities. The analysis of past performance provides a basis for planning next year's expectations and discussing development needs and career plans. Supervisors will review their assessments with the employee. The supervisor's responsibilities are to: communicate and clarify major job duties, priorities and expectations; establish and communicate performance standards; monitor employees' performance through observation, discussion, etc; document good and unacceptable performance; provide continuous coaching and constructive feedback in a timely manner; hold performance discussions (at least annually); correct poor performance and reinforce good performance; help employees to develop skills and abilities for improved performance; provide necessary information, resources and opportunity to allow accomplishment of key results.

Performance Management is an ongoing process of working towards performance expectations established in the planning phase. Together, supervisors and employees review the employee's performance on a periodic basis. If it's on track or exceeding expectations, the manager provides positive reinforcement to keep performance at a high level. If performance is lacking, the supervisor coaches the employee on improving problem areas. This involves developing strategies with the employee to determine appropriate action plans. The objectives of Performance Management are to: (1). Increase two-way communication between supervisors and employees; (2). Clarify mission, goals, responsibilities, priorities and expectations; (3). Identify and resolve performance problems; (4). Recognize quality performance; (5). Provide a basis for administrative decisions such as promotions, succession and strategic planning, and pay for performance.

Development of a performance management plan should be consistent with the following principles:

a. Performance management is considered a process, not an event. It follows good management practice in which continual coaching, feedback and communication are integral to success.

b. The Performance Management Plan is primarily a communication tool to ensure mutual understanding of work responsibilities, priorities and performance expectations.

c. Elements for discussion and evaluation should be job specific—not generalized personality traits. The major duties and responsibilities of the specific job should be defined and communicated as the first step in the process.

d. Performance standards for each major duty/responsibility should be defined and communicated.

e. Employee involvement is encouraged in identifying major duties and defining performance standards.

f. Professional development should be an important component of the plan.

g. The formal evaluation period should be long enough to allow for full performance and to establish a history such that evaluations are fair and meaningful. One year is a common evaluation period.

h. Documentation of performance will occur as often as needed to record the continuum of dialogue between supervisor and employee.

i. If formal ratings are included, they should reflect the incumbent's actual performance in relation to the performance standard for that major duty.

j. The supervisor should be evaluated on the successful administration of the plan and ongoing performance management responsibilities.

k. Training for supervisors and employees is encouraged and will be provided by Human Resources.

l. The Performance Management Plan should be consistent with federal and state laws which address non-discrimination.

The Performance review cycle has three basic components: planning, managing, and appraising performance. Performance planning is the process of identifying the desired performance and gaining employees' commitment to perform to those expectations. Managing employee performance includes:

a. Communicating. Establishing and maintaining effective communications with each employee not only requires good oral and written communication skills, but it also includes the ability to establish good working relationships. To communicate effectively with employees, supervisors must establish an environment that promotes an open door atmosphere, the sharing of ideas, and employee involvement in decision making processes.

b. Setting Goals. Setting long- and short-term goals with employees gives focus to employee efforts. When goal setting is done correctly, employees strive to accomplish those goals and feel confident in achieving them. When goal setting is done poorly, work does not progress as desired. Knowing how to set goals effectively is an important part of performance management. To do this well, supervisors need to be able to clarify expectations and to set realistic standards and targets.

c. Measuring Employee Performance. Credible measures of performance that employees understand and accept are critical for achieving high level performance. Measuring employee accomplishments, using both qualitative and quantitative measures, provides the information that supervisors and employees need in order to monitor performance.

d. Giving Feedback. Feedback should inform, enlighten, and suggest improvements to employees regarding their performance. Supervisors should describe specific work related behavior or results they have observed as close to the event as possible.

e. Coaching and Developing. Using their coaching skills, supervisors evaluate and address the developmental needs of their employees and help them select diverse experiences to gain necessary skills. Supervisors and employees create development plans that might include training, new assignments, job enrichment, self-study, or work details.

f. Recognizing. Effectively recognizing employees is another performance management competency. Being able to genuinely acknowledge a job well done is critical for strengthening employees' commitment to do their best. Supervisors should be skilled at using formal awards programs as well as using informal recognition techniques, including personal thank you and voicing verbal appreciation in staff meetings.

STAKEHOLDERS ASSESSMENT

Generally, performance appraisal has been limited to a feedback process between employees and superior. Now onwards, with the increased focus on teamwork, employee development, customer service, and employer's interest, the emphasis has shifted to multiple-input performance feedback, which is called 'Stakeholders' Assessment'. Assessment approaches with multiple rating sources provide more accurate, reliable, and credible information. Management should support the use of multiple rating sources as an effective method of assessing performance for formal appraisal and other evaluative and developmental purposes. The elements of stakeholders assessment consists of superior, peers, subordinates, customers, corporate interest, supplier and one's self.

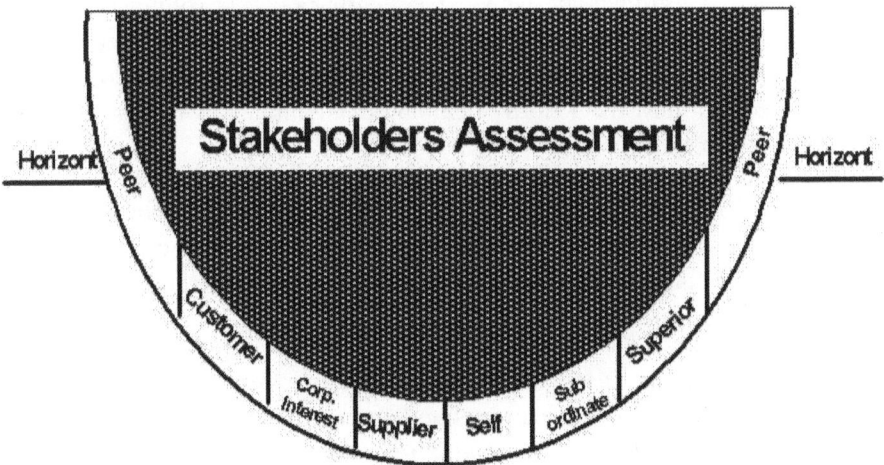

a. Superior. Evaluation by superior is the most dominant source of employee feedback. The evaluation includes both the scores of individual by supervisor and executive or by executive/senior executive and so on. Superiors should be able to observe and measure all facets of the work to make a fair evaluation.

b. Peer. Peer evaluation is almost always appropriate for developmental purpose, but attempting to emphasize them in term of pay, promotion, or job retention purpose. It is essential that the peer evaluators be very familiar with the team member's tasks and responsibilities. In cross-functional teams, this knowledge requirement may be a problem. In these situations, the greatest contribution the peers can make pertains to the behaviors and effort (input) the employee invests in the team process.

c. Subordinate. The subordinate-scoring provides particularly valuable data on performance elements concerning managerial and supervisory behaviors. However, there is usually great reluctance, even fear, concerning implementation of this rating dimension. On balance, the contributions can outweigh the concerns if the precautions noted below are addressed. The feedback from subordinates is particularly effective in evaluating the supervisor's interpersonal skills. It may not be as appropriate or valid for evaluating task-oriented skills.

d.   Customer. Customers are better at evaluating outputs (products and services) as opposed to processes and working relationships. They generally do not see or particularly care about the work processes, and often do not have knowledge of how the actions of employees are limited by regulations, policies, and resources.

e.   Supplier. Supplier is someone who has a working relationship in supplying a particular service. He/she provides appropriate quality and quantity of services to support the activities. The supplier may interact in professional and technical competence.

f.   Corporate interest. It's related to human resources records, i.e. code of conduct, harassment, discrimination, fraud and corruption, criminal act, absenteeism, warning letter, suspension, training outcome, involvement into company activities, performance certificate, etc.

g.   Self-assessment. The outcome of self assessment is open and honest communication between superior and employee. Self-appraisals should not simply be viewed as a comparative or validation process, but as a critical source of performance information. Self-assessment is particularly valuable in situation where the supervisor cannot readily observe the work behaviors and task outcomes.

Stakeholders' assessment is a wider approach to define the performance level of an entity. It can be done appropriately, if organization provides stakeholders of the entity as following: policy and procedure that are established to determine the level of performance, information or records that relevant to the entity (job description, training, competencies, talent, achievements etc), indicators/criteria to evaluate and grades, set goals for the entity and expectation, intervals of assessment, sufficient time to evaluate, and stakeholder competencies and relationships with the entity.

TRAINING

Successful people tend to continue receiving promotions until they eventually rise above their level of expertise or effectiveness. Then they stay stuck at this level, producing mediocre results and frustrating every one around them. Organization should:

a. Commit to a policy. (1). Help all people to perform their jobs effectively. To encourage everyone to perform their jobs to the highest possible level and will contribute, through the provision of appropriate training opportunities and an environment in which people are motivated, to undertake training and develop their skills and knowledge. Through this process we recognize that training and development will contribute to the furtherance of the company objectives; (2). Training budget is intended to be used in the most effective and efficient; (3). Identify training and development needs within the context of the department and the corporate business objectives; (4). Provide training and development solutions: using a range of training and development methods as appropriate including external consultants, internal mentoring, video etc.; providing advice and guidance in relation to training and development matters; encourage the sharing of expertise within the departments.

b. Give provision of training and development system: (1). Induction (Every new employee must attend a formal corporate Induction course which will be coordinated by the Training Department. In order to ensure that new staff become familiar with all aspects of their post as quickly as possible it is the responsibility of concern department Manager to organize for an appropriate person within the department to introduce the new employee to the work and procedures of the department); (2). Skills Development (technical skills, management development, team leader development, mentoring and coaching, customer care, presentation skills); (3). Allocation of Resources for External Training (budget allocation for technical training and professional development); (4). Training Records (corporate training record will be kept centrally by the training department); (5). Further Development (taking part in internal/external committees, taking on responsibilities that will develop the individual as well as the authority; or contributing to work related project teams); (6). Assistance for Further Education (consider requests for assistance towards further education course); (7). Monitoring and Evaluation (monitoring and evaluation by Training Manager and concern department Manager in order to assess its effectiveness)

COMPETENCY MANAGEMENT

Competency is defined as a cluster of related knowledge, skills and attitudes that affects a major part of one's job (a role or responsibility), that correlates with performance on the job, that can be measured against well-accepted standards, and that can be improved via training and development. Ensuring the staffs have the proper skills and competencies to consistently perform the tasks required of them is sometimes a daunting challenge. Managing and tracking individual skill levels in regulated environments is a continuous process. World-class organizations use competencies to articulate and leverage exceptional organizational performance. From a value-added perspective, competency-based management systems enable the realization of business strategy and provide a distinctive, enduring advantage for the organization. Competency Management involves: (1). Integrating competencies into training and development programs; (2). Assessing and building team competencies; (3). Reengineering performance management processes with competencies that account for the highest performance variance; (4). Determining the return-on-investment or economic value of competency initiatives; (5). Implementing competency-based organizational transformation and change strategies; (6). Assessing and developing leadership competencies; (7). Recruiting and selecting top performers; (8). Implementing succession planning and executive development processes; (9). Strengthen functional or technical competencies; (10). Implement competency-based, stakeholders' assessment and development planning; (11). Link the individual or team-based competencies with core competencies and strategic intent; (12). Design and implement a comprehensive competency-based system architecture and process.

CAREER DEVELOPMENT

Talented, engaged employees are the heart and soul of the organization. Turnover is costly. Recruiting a highly skilled workforce is tough and keeping your best and brightest is even tougher. Studies have shown that company-sponsored career initiatives increase job satisfaction and dramatically increase levels of employee commitment and engagement. The skills, competencies and career development activities defined in the model are based on values (respect, integrity, diversity, accountability and the public good) and business strategies.

Career development planning allows the organization to chart learning and development opportunities whether people want to stay in the current positions, are looking to make a lateral move or are considering positions of more responsibility. Career planning helps to keep people interested and engaged in their work. It also is a way for anyone to express his/her skills and interests to his/her manager, who can help provide him/her with opportunities and a good work match. Organizations are realizing the need to identify potential leaders and understand the skills, experience and career aspirations of all employees. The Managerial pathway will be of interest to those wishing to move to levels of management or leadership while those who follow the Professional pathway are typically more focused on specialized skill sets. The leadership career path model strives to emphasize that career development is not synonymous with "upward mobility".

In today's work environment more and more people are looking to be challenged in a continuous learning environment without necessarily moving "up the ladder". Lateral moves between and within pathways as well as upward movement between and within pathways are now very typical of career paths in today's work environment.

The company should make in partnership with staff in their continuing career development allows it to achieve maximum flexibility in meeting its current and future skills requirements. Therefore, the company should be committed to creating and fostering an environment that facilitates and enhances the skills training and career development of its staff. Staff will be provided with opportunities and time away from the job so that they may maintain and develop their skills, adapt to changing workplace needs and fulfill their employment potential within the company. Career development of staff is a primary means for the achievement of the company's employment equity goals and objectives; includes formal training, work experiences, job networking or formal courses of study to update and enhance the skills/knowledge necessary to make a continuing contribution to the work of the company, in current and future roles.

Coaching and mentoring are two of the most effective ways to grow careers. In today's dynamic work environment, organization needs the longer-term, more consistent relationship that career coaching and career mentoring provides. Following entities are responsible to:

a. Superior. Create and foster an environment that facilitates and enhances the skills training and career development of staff by: considering staff development initiatives in annually reviewing performance of employee; providing resources for staff training and development to ensure that skill levels of administrative staff are strong, broad and well-suited to the pursuit of the company's objectives;

b.   Human Resources. Administering and reporting on central funding support for staff training and development. Conducting training needs assessments and developing programs in consultation with the company community. Supporting individual career development through the provision of counseling, workshops and publication of career information. Posting job vacancies which represent career opportunities for staff in accordance with staffing policy. Providing information and consultation to managers on implementing staff planning and career development processes within their departments/ divisions. Providing training in management and supervisory skills

SUCCESSION MANAGEMENT

Succession management is a key strategy for addressing a number of critical Human Resource, i.e.: aging of the workforce, increasing retirement rates, tight labor market, limited competitiveness, and fast-paced changes in work. Every department's readiness for succession management will differ based on a number of factors, such as size, available resources, impending crisis for leadership and/or specialized technical skills, and the level of integration of the other Human Resources programs (e.g., performance management) that are so critical as supporting programs for implementing succession management.

Succession management is a structured effort by an organization to ensure leadership continuity in key positions and to retain and develop intellectual and knowledge capital for the future through: identifying positions and/or employees at risk, growing leadership capacity, bringing in diversity, including youth and experience, and encouraging individual advancement.

Succession management has evolved. In today's business environments, there are new and ever-changing demands for leadership talent in organizations.

Instead of developing one person for each key position, the focus is on developing many people with the capacity to be effective leaders in any number of positions, in any department. The organizational and departmental direction and business requirements will influence the type of skills required. Succession management will also be supported by and linked to the Human Resources programs and processes, such as performance management, recruitment, compensation, etc.

The terms succession planning and succession management are often used interchangeably, however they are different. Succession planning is defined as: Any effort designed to ensure the continued effective performance of an organization, department or work group by making provision for the development and replacement of key people over time. With the move to flatter management structures, succession planning is insurance for when key people leave an organization. With fewer layers of middle management available to fill these key roles it is important that potential successors are identified early and given appropriate training so that when the time comes for their move to more senior roles disruption is minimized. Organizations generally have a wealth of talent already working in different positions and levels throughout their business. This hidden resource needs to be identified and tapped as it is a key factor in effective succession planning. Workforce planning allows employees to know what skills and resources they already have at their disposal. People are company's most important asset and good workforce planning will give your business a clear performance and competitive advantage.

Succession management goes a step further—it is more encompassing. It is defined as: a deliberate and systematic effort by an organization to encourage individual advancement and ensure leadership continuity in key positions, including management, technical and professional specialist roles.

The need to extend beyond the focus on management and leadership roles is becoming more important as organizations take active steps to build high performance and high involvement work environments in which decision-making is decentralized and leadership is diffused throughout an empowered workforce.

Succession management is fundamental to organizational learning as it is aimed at preserving institutional memory and continuous improvement in individual and organizational effectiveness. Therefore, succession management will: provide a seamless service to the citizens of corporate, identify replacement needs as a means of targeting necessary training, employee education and development, provide increased opportunities for high potential employees, increase the talent pool of promote-able employees, contribute to implementing the organization's strategic business plans, help individuals realize their career plans within the organization, encourage the advancement of diverse groups in the future, improve employees' ability to respond to changing environmental demands, improve employee morale, and allow us to cope with effects of attrition (e.g., retirements, restructuring, etc.)

Succession management is fundamental to organizational learning as it is aimed at preserving institutional memory and continuous improvement in individual and organizational effectiveness, i.e. (1). Create a more comprehensive Human Resources planning system; (2). Communicate career paths to individuals; (3). Establish development and training plans; (4). Establish career paths and individual career moves; (5). Communicate upward and laterally the management organization

Succession management is about harnessing all the human resource systems of diversity management, recruitment & resource, leadership development, replacement rapping, career development. Foundation for succession management program is based on a philosophy of individual responsibility for career management and organizational support for personal development, i.e. commitment to people development, ensuring internal development and promotion, strategic human resource planning for the future, integration with performance management, leadership competencies

Identification

A key person or position is defined as one required to meet the departmental need in the future that exerts critical influence on organizational activities, operationally and/or strategically. Succession planning prevents potential succession gaps and assists in planning future staffing needs within the organization. Identification process includes:

a. Identify a key position or function required to meet the departmental need in the future is one that exerts critical influence on organizational activities—operationally, strategically, or both. As there are several corporate succession management programs aimed at developing senior leadership capacity, departments may choose to focus on supervisory and mid-management positions. However, it is important to keep in mind that key positions or functions may be found at other points in the organization chart, for example, professional or technical experts or specialists. A department may choose to implement succession management for these positions also.

b. Identify leadership competencies have been identified and are incorporated into the performance management process. These competencies are used in the identification of high potential employees and for development purposes. This process can also be used to identify specific technical requirements for a function or department. Corporate needs effective leadership at all levels to inspire and motivate employees, to lead successful change initiatives and to develop organizations and partnerships that can address current and future challenges. Leadership is strategic, aiming to transform an organization, to achieve a vision, as opposed to management, which ensures day to day operations work effectively and efficiently. Local government needs both good leadership and good management, but with the current challenges there is a particular need to develop leadership skills.

c. Identify individuals with advancement potential represent the corporate inventory of future leaders. They are usually individuals who are capable of advancing two or more levels beyond their present placement or individuals who have not reached their career plateau. Confidence exists that these individuals could move into a more senior leadership role. When identifying high potentials, consider our organizational values, leadership competencies, performance, and learning agility.

d. Identification should be based on a combination of looking at those characteristics that don't change much and can be detected early (e.g., the ability to learn quickly), and those that develop across time as the person learns to deal with new situations (e.g., business acumen or negotiation skills).

Development

It includes: identifying development required, providing development opportunities, developing performance goals, developing career development plan, coaching. Corporate should commit to the development of its employees:

a. All employees should have documented performance goals that include a development or competency goal. The goal should focus on the education or experiences required to achieve their results-focused goals. Managers and employees work together on the career development plans.

b. Considering a person's knowledge, skills and competencies, identify where development is required. It is important not to focus only on those areas where someone is weak, but also to consider how someone can further develop their strengths.

c.   Work with the employee to create a development plan to close the gaps and/ or strengthen existing skills and competencies.

d.   Develop goals that are aligned with the business plan and wherever possible, integrate development or competency goals that close any skill/competency gaps.

e.   Development opportunities could include a targeted job assignment, a project (departmental or inter-departmental), a formal training program, or an external activity.

f.   Continue discussion with the employee to exert a positive influence in their motivation, performance, awareness for improvement and development to help them be as effective as possible.

g.   Consider if goals are being achieved and gaps are being closed.

Evaluation

The talent review meeting, which is facilitated by Human Resources, is an opportunity to discuss individual reports and come to agreement on the list of "high potentials" within the department. Through these discussions and opportunities to share information on individual employees, the final list will be compiled. These sessions provide an opportunity to:

a.   Link the succession management process to the business strategy—consider what has changed inside the department or organization that might impact succession management

b.   Get everyone on the same page—not everyone will have the same idea of what it means to be "high potential". Through discussion, managers will establish common standards and bring multiple viewpoints together

c.   Give employees a sense of fairness—employees must feel succession management is being implemented in an objective way. It is not one person making the decisions, but a team of individuals across the department—even including other stakeholders

d. Make real action happen—through the conversations that take place; managers learn more about the capability of the people. This will lead to better assignment decisions

Human Resources should maintain a "talent" database. This should include information for each employee, such as their potential, performance level, career interests and goals, and retention risk. As a result of the talent review meetings there should be documented actions for every individual, such as a specific assignment, project, training course, etc.

8

CORPORATE COMPLIANCE

Corporate governance is the set of best practices that provides for the effective, open and visible management of an organization. While compliance with the applicable legal and regulatory rules is critical to effective governance, many of the new rules have been put in place due to the lack, or seeming lack, of visible corporate governance within many organizations. Good corporate governance practices lead to better compliance, but more importantly these behaviors lead to better organizational operation and increased shareholder and stakeholder confidence because of the increased visibility and monitoring that is put in place.

Corporate governance is a term that embodies all of the process, policies, procedures and records that an organization uses to make decisions and carry those decisions out. Corporate governance involves a set of relationships between a company's management, its board, its shareholders and other stakeholders. Corporate governance also provides the structure though which the objectives of the company are set, and the means of obtaining those objectives and monitoring performance are determined. Good corporate governance should provide proper incentives for the board and management to pursue objectives that are in the interests of the company and its shareholders and should facilitate effective monitoring.

The purpose of corporate audit and governance compliance is as follows:

a. Examine the entire gamut of issues pertaining to the Auditor—Company relationship with a view to ensuring the professional nature of the relationship; in this respect to consider issues such as (but not limited to) rotation of auditors/auditing partners, restrictions on non-audit fee/work, procedures for appointment of auditors & determination of audit fees, etc.

b. Examine measures required to ensure that the managements and auditors actually present the true and fair statement of the affairs of companies; in this respect to consider measures such as (but not limited to) personal certification by directors, random scrutiny of accounts, etc.

c. Examine if the present system of regulation of the profession of Chartered Accountants, Company Secretaries and Cost Accountants is sufficient and has served well the concerned stakeholders, especially the small investors, and whether there is advantage in setting up an independent regulator (along the lines of the recently passed Sarbanes-Oxley Act of 2002) and, if so, what shape should the independent regulator take.

d. Examine the role of independent directors, and how their independence and effectiveness can be ensured.

e. Strengthening the responsibilities of audit committees

f. Improving quality of financial disclosures, including those related to related party transactions and proceeds from Initial Public offerings

g. Requiring Boards to adopt formal code of conduct, Whistle Blower Policy, etc

h. Improving disclosures related to compensation paid to non-executive directors

i. Suggest suitable amendments to the listing agreement executed by the stock exchanges with the companies and any other measures

j. Improve the standards of corporate governance in the listed companies, in areas such as continuous disclosure of material information, both financial and non-financial, manner and frequency of such disclosures, responsibilities of independent and outside directors;

k. Draft a code of corporate best practices; and

l. Suggest safeguards to be instituted within the companies to deal with insider information and insider trading.

Corporate should substantially comply with most of followings:

a. Auditor-company relationship, i.e. a policy for external auditor independence, ensure best practice in financial and audit governance, establish audit committee, etc

b. Auditing the auditors, i.e. independent auditing quality board, audit standard, disciplinary mechanism

c. Independent Director, i.e. Chairperson and majority of board and audit committee should be independent director, non executive directors' remuneration, audit committee charter, performance management etc

d. Shareholder, i.e. communication strategy to promote effective communication with shareholders and encourage effective participation at general meetings, answer shareholder questions, shareholders right, etc

e. Stakeholder, i.e. involvement, communication, etc

THE AUDITOR-COMPANY RELATIONSHIP

a. Disqualifications for audit assignments—In line with the international best practices, includes: (1). Prohibition of any direct financial interest in the audit client by the audit firm, its partners or members of the engagement team as well as their 'direct relatives'. This prohibition would also apply if any 'relative' of the partners of the audit firm or member of the engagement team has an interest of more than 2 per cent of the share of profit or equity capital of the audit client; (2). Prohibition of receiving any loans and/or guarantees from or on behalf of the audit client by the audit firm, its partners or any member of the engagement team and their 'direct relatives'; (3). Prohibition of any business relationship with the audit client by the auditing firm, its partners or any member of the engagement team and their 'direct relatives'; (4). Prohibition of personal relationships, which would exclude any partner of the audit firm or member of the engagement team being a 'relative' of any of key officers of the client company, i.e. any whole-time director, CEO, CFO, Company Secretary, senior manager belonging to the top two managerial levels of the company, and the officer who is in default. In case of any doubt, it would be the task of the Audit Committee of the concerned company to determine whether the individual concerned is a key officer; (5). Prohibition of service or cooling off period, under which any partner or member of the engagement team of an audit firm who wants to join an audit client, or any key officer of the client company wanting to join the audit firm, would only be allowed to do so after two years from the time they were involved in the preparation of accounts and audit of that client; (6). Prohibition of undue dependence on an audit client. So that no audit firm is unduly dependent on an audit client, the fees received from any one client and its subsidiaries and affiliates, all together, should not exceed 25 per cent of the total revenues of the audit firm.

b. Prohibited non-audit services. Following services should not be provided by an audit firm to any audit client: (1). Accounting and book keeping services, related to the accounting records or financial statements of the audit client; (2). Internal audit services; (3). Financial information systems design and implementation, including services related to IT systems for preparing financial or management accounts and information flows of a company; (4). Actuarial services, e.g. (A). Broker, dealer, investment adviser or investment banking services; (B). Outsourced financial services; (C). Management functions, including the provision of temporary staff to audit clients; (D). Any form of staff recruitment, and particularly hiring of senior management staff for the audit client; (E). Valuation services and fairness opinion.

c. Independence standards for consulting and other entities that are affiliated to audit firms: No more than 25 per cent of the revenues of the consolidated entity should come from a single corporate client with whom there is also an audit engagement

d. Compulsory audit partner rotation: The partners and at least 50 per cent of the engagement team (excluding article clerks and trainees) responsible for the audit should be rotated every five years.

e. Auditor's disclosure of contingent liabilities. The Management should provide a clear description of each material liability and its risks, which should be followed by the auditor's clearly worded comments on the management's view. This section should be highlighted in the significant accounting policies and notes on accounts, as well as, in the auditor's report, where necessary.

f. Auditor's disclosure of qualifications and consequent action: Qualifications to accounts, if any, must form a distinct, and adequately highlighted, section of the auditor's report to the shareholders; these must be listed in full—what they are (including quantification thereof), why these were arrived at, including qualification thereof, etc; in case of a qualified auditor's report, the audit firm may read out the qualifications, with explanations, to shareholders in the company's annual general meeting; it should also be mandatory for the audit firm to separately send a copy of the qualified report

g. Management's certification in the event of auditor's replacement. Require a special resolution of shareholders, in case an auditor, while being eligible to re-appointment, is sought to be replaced. Also the explanatory statement accompanying such a special resolution must disclose the management's reasons for such a replacement, on which the outgoing auditor shall have the right to comment. The Audit Committee will have to verify that this explanatory statement is 'true and fair'. It is applicable only in circumstances where the statutory auditors are sought to be replaced. The Company's Act is yet to be amended by the government to seek special resolution of the shareholders in case of a replacement of an auditor. The audit committee consisting fully of independent directors recommends the appointment or replacement of auditors.

h. Auditor's annual certification of independence. The auditors before agreeing to be appointed, must submit a certificate of independence to the audit committee or the board of directors of the client company stating that the auditors are independent and have arm's length relationship with the client company, have not engaged in any non-audit services and are not disqualified from audit assignments by virtue of breaching any of the limits, restrictions and prohibitions. Public accounting firms should limit their services to their clients to performing audits and to providing closely-related services that do not put the auditor in an advocacy position. Such services might include developing novel and debatable tax strategies and products that involve income tax shelters and extensive offshore partnerships or affiliates.

i. Appointment of auditors. The audit committee of the Board shall be the first point of reference regarding the appointment of auditors. In discharging this fiduciary responsibility, the audit committee shall discuss the annual work program with the auditor, review the auditor independence and recommend to the board, with reasons, either the appointment/re-appointment or removal of the external auditor, along with the annual audit remuneration.

j. CEO and CFO certification of annual audited accounts. The CEO and CFO should state their knowledge and belief: (1). The signing officers have reviewed the balance sheet and profit and loss account and all its schedules and notes on accounts, as well as the cash flow statements and the Directors' Report; (2). These statements do not contain any material untrue statement or omit any material fact nor do they contain statements that might be misleading; (3). These statements together represent a true and fair picture of the financial and operational state of the company, and are in compliance with the existing accounting standards and/or applicable laws/regulations; (4). The signing officers are responsible for establishing and maintaining internal controls which have been designed to ensure that all material information is periodically made known to them; and have evaluated the effectiveness of internal control systems of the company; (5). The signing officers have disclosed to the auditors as well as the Audit Committee deficiencies in the design or operation of internal controls, if any, and what they have done or propose to do to rectify these deficiencies; (6). The signing officers, have also disclosed to the auditors as well as the Audit Committee instances of significant fraud, if any, that involves management or employees having a significant role in the company's internal control systems; (7). The signing officers, have indicated to the auditors, the Audit Committee and in the notes on accounts, whether or not there were significant changes in internal control and/or of accounting policies during the year under review; (8). In the event of any materially significant misstatements or omissions, the signing officers will return to the company that part of any bonus or incentive- or equity-based compensation which was inflated on account of such errors, as decided by the Audit Committee; (9). CEO (either the Executive Chairman or the Managing Director) and the CFO (whole-time Finance Director or other person discharging this function) discharging the function shall certify to the Board that: (A). They have reviewed financial statements an the cash flow statement and the directors report and that to the best of their knowledge and belief: these statements do not contain any materially untrue statement or omit any material fact or contain statements that might be misleading; these statements together present a true and fair view of the company's affairs and are in compliance with existing accounting standards, applicable laws and regulations; (B). There are to the best of their knowledge and belief, no transactions entered into by the company which are fraudulent, illegal or violative of the company's code of conduct or ethics policy; (C). They accept responsibility for establishing and maintaining internal controls and that they have evaluated the effectiveness of the internal control systems of the company an they have disclosed to the auditors and the audit committee, deficiencies in the design or operation of internal controls, if any, of which they are aware and the steps they have taken or propose to take to rectify these deficiencies; (D). They have indicated to the auditors and the audit committee; significant changes in internal control during the year; significant changes in accounting policies during the year and the same have been disclosed in the notes to the financial statement; and instances of significant fraud of which they have become aware and the involvement if any, of the management or an employee having a significant role in the company's internal control system.

Boards should be responsible for overseeing corporate ethics. A major challenge to corporations and their leaders is to create a "tone at the top" and a corporate culture that promotes ethical conducts on the part of the organization and its employees. The single most important factor in creating such a culture is the quality of corporate leadership, especially the "tone at the top" set by boards, CEOs, and senior management. Leaders must also put in place appropriate management systems and processes to achieve and regularly monitor these results. Ethical conduct should be encouraged and reinforced by including it as an important and explicit part of each employee's annual review.

Corporations should work to support responsible behavior and build environments in which employees are encouraged and feel safe to take the initiative to address misconduct rather than waiting until after the damage is done. Prevention is the best cure for malfeasance. If an independent investigation is reasonably likely to implicate company executives, the board and not management should retain special counsel for this investigation. Investigative counsel should be chosen by, and report directly to, the board and should not be one of the corporation's regular outside counsel or a firm that receives a material amount of revenue from the company.

AUDITING THE AUDITORS

a. Setting-up of independent Quality Review Board (QRB): which periodically examines and review the quality of audit, secretarial and cost accounting firms, and pass judgment and comments on the quality and sufficiency of systems, infrastructure and practices; the QRB should focus their audit quality reviews to the audit firms; QRB will be funded by their respective institutes in a manner that will enable it to discharge its functions adequately.

b. Propose disciplinary mechanism for auditors: (1). Company will establish a mechanism for employees to report to the management concerns about unethical behavior, actual or suspected fraud or violation of the company's code of conduct or ethics policy; (2). Mechanism must provide for adequate safeguards against victimization of employees who avail of the mechanism; (3). Mechanism must also provide, where senior management is involved, direct access to the Chairman of the Audit Committee; (4). Existence of the mechanism must be appropriately communicated within the organization; (5). The Audit Committee must periodically review the existence and functioning of the mechanism

INDEPENDENT DIRECTORS: ROLE, REMUNERATION AND TRAINING

a. Definition of an independent director: Independent directors are directors who apart from receiving director's remuneration do not have any other material pecuniary relationship or transactions with the company, its promoters, its management or its subsidiaries, which in the judgment of the board may affect their independence of judgment. He is not receiving, other than for service on the board, any consulting, advisory, or other compensatory fee from the issuer, and as not being an affiliated person of the issuer, or any subsidiary thereof. Further, all pecuniary relationships or transactions of the non-executive directors should be disclosed in the annual report.

The non-executive directors, i.e. those who are independent and those who are not, help bring an independent judgment to bear on board's deliberations especially on issues of strategy, performance, management of conflicts and standards of conduct. The corporate therefore lays emphasis on the caliber of the non-executive directors, especially of the independent directors. The board of a company has an optimum combination of executive and non-executive directors with not less than fifty percent of the board comprising the non-executive directors. The number of independent directors (independence being as defined in the foregoing paragraph) would depend on the nature of the chairman of the board. In case a company has a non-executive chairman, at least one-third of board should comprise of independent directors and in case a company has an executive chairman, at least half of board should be independent. The Chairman's role should in principle be different from that of the chief executive, though the same individual may perform both roles.

b.   Percentage of independent directors. 50% of the board of directors of any listed company, as well as unlisted public limited companies with a paid-up share capital, should consist of independent directors. The board of the company to have an optimum combination of executive and non-executive directors. In case of a Non-Executive Chairman, at least one-third of the board shall comprise of independent directors and in case of Executive Chairman, at least half the board shall comprise of independent directors). A director shall be considered to be an independent director only so long as his tenure on the board does not exceed, in the aggregate, a period of nine years, such period to be considered as commencing on or after the date this circular comes into force or the date of his first appointment as a director, whichever is later. After the expiry of the said period, the director may continue to be a member of the board and be eligible for reappointment on the expiry of his term, but shall not be considered to be an independent director.

c.   Minimum board size of listed companies. The minimum board size of all listed companies of which at least four should be independent directors. To ensure that the members of the board give due importance and commitment to the meetings of the board and its committees, there should be a ceiling on the maximum number of committees across all companies in which a director could be a member or act as Chairman.

A director should not be a member in more than 10 committees or act as Chairman of more than five committees across all companies in which he is a director. Furthermore it should be a mandatory annual requirement for every director to inform the company about the committee positions he occupies in other companies and notify changes as and when they take place.

The board should establish a structure that provides an appropriate balance between the powers of the CEO and those of the independent directors. Three principal approaches are recommended including: separating the offices of Chairman and CEO; having a non-executive Chairman and a Lead Independent Director; or, if the Chairman and CEO is the same person, establishing a Presiding Director position for leadership of the independent directors. Where boards do not adopt any of these approaches, they should disclose how their board structure provides the appropriate balance. Each board of directors should adopt processes to ensure that the ability of the independent directors to be informed, to discuss and debate issues they deem important, and to act objectively on an informed basis is not compromised.

The roles of Chairman, Lead Independent Director, and Presiding Director should be clearly defined. Where companies have a non-independent Chairman, the Lead Independent Director or the Presiding Director should have ultimate approval over information flow to the board, meeting agenda, and meeting schedules to ensure that the independent directors have sufficient time for discussion of all agenda items. Directors should display the character, independence, integrity, and will to assert their points of view. They must demonstrate loyalty exclusively to the corporation and its shareowners.

Membership of non-executives on the board should be limited to a maximum period of twelve years. The retirement of one-third of the board members every year, and qualifies the retiring members for reappointment. No more than one non-executive board member should have served as an executive member of the company. Boards of directors should develop procedures to receive and to consider shareowners' nominations for the board of directors as well as shareowner proposals related to serious business issues. Boards of directors should give serious consideration to adopting advisory shareowner proposals that receive a significant number of the votes cast. In the event that the board chooses not to implement a proposal that receives a substantial percentage, even if less than a majority of the votes cast, it should publicly disclose its reasons for its actions. The corporate governance framework should ensure the strategic guidance of the company, the effective monitoring of management by the board, and the board's accountability to the company and the sharcholders. Board members should act on a fully informed basis, in good faith, with due diligence and care, and in the best interest of the company and the shareholders. Where board decisions may affect different shareholder groups differently, the board should treat all shareholders fairly. The board should apply high ethical standards. It should take into account the interests of stakeholders.

The Board should fulfill certain key functions, including: (1). Reviewing and guiding corporate strategy, major plans of action, risk policy, annual budgets and business plans; setting performance objectives; monitoring implementation and corporate performance; and overseeing major capital expenditures, acquisitions and divestitures; (2). Monitoring the effectiveness of the company's governance practices and making changes as needed; (3). Selecting, compensating, monitoring and, when necessary, replacing key executives and overseeing succession planning; (4). Aligning key executive and board remuneration with the longer term interests of the company and its shareholders; (5). Ensuring a formal and transparent board nomination and election process; (6). Monitoring and managing potential conflicts of interest of management, board members and shareholders including misuse of corporate assets and abuse in related party transactions; (7). Ensuring the integrity of the corporation's accounting and financial reporting systems, including the independent audit, and that appropriate systems of control are in place, in particular, systems for risk management, financial and operational control, and compliance with the law and relevant standards; (8). Overseeing the process of disclosure and communications.

The board should be able to exercise objective independent judgment on corporate affairs. Boards should consider assigning a sufficient number of non-executive board members capable of exercising independent judgment to tasks where there is a potential for conflict of interest. Examples of such key responsibilities are ensuring the integrity of financial and non-financial reporting, the review of related party transactions, nomination of board members and key executives, and board remuneration. When committees of the board are established, their mandate, composition and working procedures should be well defined and disclosed by the board. Board members should be able to commit themselves effectively to their responsibilities. In order to fulfill their responsibilities, board members should have access to accurate, relevant and timely information.

d.   Disclosure on duration of board meetings/committee meetings: the minutes of board meetings and Audit Committee meetings must disclose the timing and duration of each such meeting, in addition to the date and members in attendance.

The Board meeting shall be held at least four times a year, with a maximum time gap of four months between any two meetings. As a part of the disclosure related to Management, as part of the directors' report or as an addition there to, a Management Discussion and Analysis report should form part of the annual report to the shareholders. This Management Discussion & Analysis should include discussion on the following matters within the limits set by the company's competitive position: industry structure and develop-ments; opportunities and threats; segment-wise or product-wise perfor-mance; outlook; risks and concerns; internal control systems and their adequacy; discussion on financial performance with respect to operational performance; material developments in Human Resources/Industrial Rela-tions front, including number of people employed. Disclosures must be made by the management to the board relating to all material financial and commercial transactions, where they have personal interest, that may have a potential conflict with the interest of the company at large (for e.g. dealing in company shares, commercial dealings with bodies, which have shareholding of management and their relatives etc.)

e. Tele-conferencing and video conferencing. If a director cannot be physically present but wants to participate in the proceedings of the board and its com-mittees, then a minute, and signed proceedings of a teleconference or video conference should constitute proof of his or her participation. Accordingly, this should be treated as presence in the meeting(s). However, minutes of all such meetings should be signed and confirmed by the director/s that has/have attended the meeting through video conferencing. The minutes of the Board meetings of the unlisted subsidiary company shall be placed at the Board meeting of the listed holding company. The management should peri-odically bring to the attention of the board of directors of the listed com-pany, a statement of all significant transactions and arrangements entered into by the unlisted subsidiary company.

f. Additional disclosure to directors. Corporate should transmit all press releases and presentation to analysts to all board members. This will further help in keeping independent directors informed of how the company is pro-jecting itself to the general public as well as a body of informed investors. The Board shall periodically review legal compliance reports prepared by the company as well as steps taken by the company to cure instances of non-compliance. Following disclosures should be made in the section on corpo-rate governance of the annual report: all elements of remuneration package of all the directors i.e. salary, benefits, bonuses, stock options, pension etc; details of fixed component and performance linked incentives, along with the performance criteria; service contracts, notice period, severance fees; stock option details, if any—and whether issued at a discount as well as the period over which accrued and over which exercisable. Senior management shall make disclosures to the board relating to all material financial and commercial transactions, where they have personal interest that may have a potential conflict with the interest of the company at large (e.g. dealing in company shares, commercial dealings with bodies, which have shareholding of management and their relatives etc).

The corporate governance framework should ensure that timely and accurate disclosure is made on all material matters regarding the corporation, including the financial situation, performance, ownership, and governance of the company. Disclosure should include, but not be limited to, material information on: (1). Financial and operating results of the company; (2). Company objectives; (3). Major share ownership and voting rights; (4). Remuneration policy for members of the board and key executives, and information about board members, including their qualifications, the selection process, other company directorships and whether they are regarded as independent by the board; (5). Related party transactions; (6). Foreseeable risk factors; (7). Issues regarding employees and other stakeholders; (8).Governance structures and policies, in particular, the content of any corporate governance code or policy and the process by which it is implemented.

Information should be prepared and disclosed in accordance with high quality standard of accounting and financial and non financial disclosure. An annual audit should be conducted by an independent, competent and qualified, auditor in order to provide an external and objective assurance to the board and shareholders that the financial statements fairly represent the financial position and performance of the company in all material respects. External auditors should be accountable to the shareholders and owe a duty to the company to exercise due professional care in the conduct of the audit. Channels for disseminating information should provide for equal, timely and cost-efficient access to relevant information by users. The corporate governance framework should be complemented by an effective approach that addresses and promotes the provision of analysis or advice by analysts, brokers, rating agencies and others, that is relevant to decisions by investors, free from material conflicts of interest that might compromise the integrity of their analysis or advice.

Independent directors on audit committee of listed companies

Audit Committees should consist exclusively of independent directors. A qualified and independent audit committee should be set up by the board of a company. This would go a long way in enhancing the credibility of the financial disclosures of a company and promoting transparency. The audit committee should have minimum three members, all being non executive directors, with the majority being independent, and with at least one director having financial and accounting knowledge; the chairman of the committee should be an independent director; the chairman should be present at Annual General Meeting to answer shareholder queries; the Audit Committee should invite such of the executives, as it considers appropriate (and particularly the head of the finance function) to be present at the meetings of the Committee but on occasions it may also meet without the presence of any executives of the company. Finance director and head of internal audit and when required, a representative of the external auditor should be present as invitees for the meetings of the audit committee; the Company Secretary should act as the secretary to the committee.

The audit committee should meet at least thrice a year. One meeting must be held before finalization of annual accounts and one necessarily every six months. The quorum should be either two members or one-third of the members of the audit committee, whichever is higher and there should be a minimum of two independent directors. The audit committee should possess the following powers: to investigate any activity within its terms of reference; to seek information from any employee; to obtain outside legal or other professional advice; to secure attendance of outsiders with relevant expertise, if it considers necessary.

The audit committee's role should include the following: oversight of the company's financial reporting process and the disclosure of its financial information to ensure that the financial statement is correct, sufficient and credible; recommending the appointment and removal of external auditor, fixation of audit fee and also approval for payment for any other services; reviewing with management the annual financial statements before submission to the board, focusing primarily on: any changes in accounting policies and practices; major accounting entries based on exercise of judgment by management; qualifications in draft audit report; significant adjustments arising out of audit; the going concern assumption; compliance with accounting standards; compliance with stock exchange and legal requirements concerning financial statements; any related party transactions i.e. transactions of the company of material nature, with promoters or the management, their subsidiaries or relatives etc. that may have potential conflict with the interests of company at large; reviewing with the management, external and internal auditors, the adequacy of internal control systems; reviewing the adequacy of internal audit function, including the structure of the internal audit department, staffing and seniority of the official heading the department, reporting structure, coverage and frequency of internal audit; discussion with internal auditors of any significant findings and follow-up thereon; reviewing the findings of any internal investigations by the internal auditors into matters where there is suspected fraud or irregularity or a failure of internal control systems of a material nature and reporting the matter to the board; discussion with external auditors before the audit commences, of the nature and scope of audit. Also post-audit discussion to ascertain any area of concern; reviewing the company's financial and risk management policies; looking into the reasons for substantial defaults in the payments to the depositors, debenture holders, share holders (in case of non-payment of declared dividends) and creditors.

Every board should be composed of a substantial majority of independent directors. This goes beyond proposals by the New York Stock Exchange to have only a majority of independent directors. Every board should tailor the mix of directors' qualifications for its particular requirements. Each board should collectively have knowledge and expertise in business, finance, accounting, marketing, public policy, manufacturing and operations, government, technology, and other areas that the board believes are desirable. Every board should establish a nominating/governance committee composed of independent directors. This committee should monitor all governance matters for the board, as well as be responsible for nominating qualified candidates to stand for election.

Each board should develop a three tier director evaluation mechanism. This should include evaluation of the performance of the board as a whole, the performance of each committee, and the performance of each individual director, as necessary. At a minimum, director evaluation should ensure that each director meets the board's qualifications for membership when the director is nominated or re-nominated to the board. A statement in summary form of transactions with related parties in the ordinary course of business shall be placed periodically before the audit committee. Material individual transactions with related parties or others which are not on an arm's length basis should be placed before the audit committee, together with management's justification for the same companies should formulate and communicate a strategy specifically designed to attract investors known to pursue long-term holding investment strategies. In this way, the corporation may be able to reduce the volatility in trading of its shares and build a stronger shareowner base. Also, such a shareowner base would allow companies to focus on their strategic business rather than on meeting quarterly earnings targets to satisfy short-term traders who are apt to display little interest in governance.

The policy makers should find ways to create incentives for investors to hold for the long term, perhaps such as increasing the differential tax rates for long-term and short-term holders.

g.   Audit committee charter. The Board annually certifies whether and to what extent each of the functions listed in the Audit Committee Charter were discharged in the course of the year. This will serve as the Committee's 'action taken report' to the shareholders. The disclosure shall also give a succinct but accurate report of the tasks performed by the Audit Committee, which would include, among others, the Audit Committee's views on the adequacy of internal control systems, perceptions of risks and, in the event of any qualifications, why the Audit Committee accepted and recommended the financial statements with qualifications. The statement should also certify whether the Audit Committee met with the statutory and internal auditors of the company without the presence of management, and whether such meetings revealed materially significant issues or risks. This recommendation is complied with. Infosys has a charter for the Audit Committee. Also the annual report of the company contains a report of the audit committee duly signed by the chairman of the committee. It shall be obligatory for the board of a company to lay down the code of conduct for all board members and senior management of the company. All board members and senior management personnel shall affirm compliance with the code on an annual basis.

The audit committee shall have minimum 3 members. All the members of the committee shall be independent directors. All members of the committee shall be financially literate and at least one member shall have accounting or related financial management expertise. The chairman of the audit committee shall be an independent director. The chairman of the audit committee, or in his absence, a designated member of the audit committee who is an independent director shall be present at the annual general meeting to answer shareholders queries. The audit committee should invite such of the executives, as it considers appropriate to be present at the meetings of the committee. The audit committee should meet at least four times in a year and not more than four months shall elapse between two meetings. The quorum shall be either two members or one-third of the members of the audit committee whichever is greater, but there should be a minimum of two independent members present). The audit committee shall have the powers which should include the following: to investigate any activity within its terms of reference; to seek information from any employee; to obtain outside legal or other professional advice; to secure attendance of outsiders with relevant expertise, if it considers necessary.

Auditing standard: The Board would be required to cooperate on an ongoing basis with designated professional teams of accountants and or other advisory groups convened in connection with standard-setting. The Board will have authority to amend, modify, repeal, and reject any standards suggested by the groups. The Board must report on its standard-setting activity on an annual basis, and adopt an audit standard to implement the internal control review. This standard must require the auditor evaluate whether the internal control structure and procedures include records that accurately and fairly reflect the transactions, provide reasonable assurance that the transactions are recorded in a manner that will permit the preparation of financial statements, and a description of any material weaknesses in the internal controls.

The Audit Committee shall review the following information: management discussion and analysis of financial condition and results of operations; statement of significant related party transactions submitted by the management; management letters/letters of internal control weaknesses issued by the external auditors; internal audit reports relating to internal control weaknesses; and the appointment, removal and terms of remuneration of the Chief Internal Auditor. Where in the preparation of the financial statements, a treatment different from that prescribed in an accounting standard has been followed, the fact shall be disclosed in the financial statements, together with the management's explanation as to why it believes such alternate treatment is more representative of the true and fair view of the underlined business transaction.

Audit Committees should be vigorous in complying with the numerous new requirements imposed by the Sarbanes-Oxley Act and by the proposed listing standards of the New York Stock Exchange. Boards should not underestimate these new requirements with respect to Audit Committees and should devote sufficient resources and time to implement its requirements. Members of the Audit Committee must be independent and have both knowledge and experience in auditing financial matters. Also, the board should understand the obligations under the Act that the company must disclose whether or not one or more members of the audit committee qualify as financial experts within the meaning of regulations promulgated pursuant to the Act and, if not, why not.

h.   Remuneration of non-executive director. The statutory limit on sitting fees should be reviewed, although ideally it should be a matter to be resolved between the management and the shareholders. The present provisions relating to stock options, and to the 1 per cent commission on net profits, is adequate and does not, at present, need any revision. However, the vesting schedule of stock options should be staggered over at least three years, so as to align the independent and executive directors, as well as managers' two levels below the Board, with the long-term profitability and value of the company. The company shall publish its compensation policy and statement of entitled compensation in respect of non-executive directors in its annual report. Non-executive directors shall be required to disclose their stock holding in the listed company in which they are proposed to be appointed as directors, prior to their appointment. All remuneration paid to non-executive directors, including independent directors, shall be fixed by the board and shall be agreed to by shareholders in general meeting. Limits to be set on the maximum number of stock options that can be granted to the non-executive directors, including independent directors, in any financial year and in aggregate. The Stock options granted to non-executive directors shall vest after a period of at least one year from the date of grant of the stock option. The shareholders approve the maximum amount up to which commission could be paid to non-executive directors.

The Board should set up a remuneration committee to determine on their behalf and on behalf of the shareholders with agreed terms of reference, the company's policy on specific remuneration packages for executive directors including pension rights and any compensation payment. To avoid conflicts of interest, the remuneration committee, which would determine the remuneration packages of the executive directors should comprise of at least three directors, all of whom should be non-executive directors, the chairman of committee being an independent director.

The board of directors should decide the remuneration of non-executive directors. All elements of remuneration package of individual directors should be summarized under major groups, such as salary, benefits, bonuses, stock options, pension etc. The Compensation Committee should exercise independent judgment in determining the proper levels and types of executive compensation to be paid unconstrained by industry median compensation statistics or by the company's own past compensation practices and levels. The Committee should also be mindful of the differences in compensation levels throughout the corporation in setting senior executive compensation levels. The Compensation Committee should retain any outside consultants who advise it. The outside consultants should report solely to the Committee. Performance-based compensation tied to specific goals can be a powerful and effective tool to advance the business interests of the corporation. The use of performance-based compensation tools should be encouraged in a balanced and cost-effective manner.

The Compensation Committee should establish, with the concurrence of the board, performance-based incentives that support and reinforce the corporation's long-term strategic goals set by the board (examples of these goals include cost of capital, return on equity, economic value added, market share, quality goals, compliance goals, environment goals, revenue and profit growth, cost containment, cash management, etc.). The award of these incentives should be linked to achievement of specific strategic goals. The Compensation Committee should be responsible for all aspects of executive officers' compensation arrangements and perquisites, including approval of all employment, retention, and severance agreements. The Compensation Committee should approve any compensation arrangement for a senior executive officer involving any subsidiary, special purpose entity or other affiliate, and such compensation arrangements should be disclosed in filings with the SEC. Compensation policies should encourage a meaningful financial stake in the corporation through long term "acquire and hold" practices by key executives and directors. This practice provides an additional incentive to serve the long-term best interests of the corporation.

Compensation decisions should be based on the effectiveness of various forms of compensation to achieve company goals and their respective relative costs, rather than simply on their accounting treatment. The costs associated with equity-based compensation should be reported on a uniform and consistent basis by all public companies in order to provide clear and understandable comparability. Fixed-price stock options should be expensed on financial statements of public companies. The costs associated with equity-based compensation should be reported on a uniform and consistent basis by all public companies in order to provide clear and understandable comparability. In addition, the Compensation Committee must disclose in conspicuous ways the effective costs passed on to shareholders through dilution or share repurchases to limit dilution.

Companies should make conspicuous disclosure of the size, costs, and effects of stock options on both earnings per share after dilution and the proportion of future shareholder value that such equity compensation plans would provide to executives and employees. A corporation's public disclosures should include a conspicuous statement highlighting both earnings per share after dilution and the proportion of future shareholder value that equity-based compensation plans would provide to executives and employees. Executive officers should be required to give advance public notice of their intention to dispose directly or indirectly (e.g., by hedging or other similar arrangement) of the corporation's equity securities. In this connection, the Compensation Committee, with the assistance of experts as required, should develop and publish appropriate methods by which disclosure of such intentions must be made. The transactions made by designated officers of the company are being disclosed to all the stock exchanges within a specified period.

i.   Exempting non-executive directors from certain liabilities: Executive directors are, and ought to be, more liable than their non-executive or independent counterparts. Independent directors should be indemnified from litigation and other related costs. It would be prudent for companies to purchase a reasonable amount of directors' and officers' (D&O) insurance. This should cover independent directors even after they have ceased to be directors, if the offences relate to the period when they were directors. Such policies pay for the cost of litigation and pecuniary penalties, if any, and hence mitigate the corporate and individual risk of being an independent director.

j.   Training of independent director: all independent directors should be required to attend at least one such training course before assuming responsibilities as an independent director, or, considering that enough programs might not be available in the initial years, within one year of becoming an independent director. An untrained independent director should be disqualified after being given reasonable notice. There should be an orientation program for each member of the Audit Committee. Members of the Audit Committee should participate regularly in continuing education programs. Compliance with the Sarbanes-Oxley Act will require scrutiny and evaluation by top management and the board of issues such as the company's control environment, business risks, information and communication systems, and monitoring processes. All the new members of the Board, goes through a structured induction program. The company has not put in place any continuing education programs. All companies should have an internal audit function. This should be established regardless of whether it is an "in-house" function or one performed by an outside accounting firm that is not the firm that acts as the company's regular outside auditors. Public companies should revise their internal controls to reflect a broad risk-based approach and to support the certification process for both financial reports and internal controls. The internal auditor should have a direct line of communication and reporting responsibility to the audit committee. Audit Committees should consider rotating audit firms when there is a combination of circumstances that could call into question the audit firm's independence from management. The existence of some or all of the following circumstances particularly merit consideration of rotation: (1). the audit firm has been employed by the company for a substantial period of time, e.g., over 10 years; (2). one or more former partners or managers of the audit firm are employed by the company; and (3). significant non-audit services are provided to the company—even if they have been approved by the audit committee. The Audit Committee should, if necessary, retain professional advisors to assist it in carrying out its functions. These professional advisors should have no other ties to the company. Because of the scope and magnitude of their responsibilities, Audit Committee members may require additional expertise as well as additional staff assistance to fulfill their new responsibilities.

SHAREHOLDERS

A company should aim primarily at maximizing shareholder value in the long-term. Companies should clearly state (in writing) their financial objectives as well as their strategy, and should include these in the Annual Report. Major decisions which have a fundamental effect upon the nature, size, structure and risk profile of the company, and decisions which have significant consequences for the position of the shareholder within the corporation, should be subject to shareholder's approval or should be decided by the Annual General Meeting (AGM). Antitakeover defenses or other measures which restrict the influence of shareholders should be avoided. In addition to the regular channels, electronic means should be used by the company to provide shareholders with price-sensitive information. The proceeding of the Annual General Meeting is web cast live on the Internet to enable shareholders across the world to view the proceedings. The archives of the video are also available on the company's home page for future reference to all the shareholders. Shareholders shall have the right to elect members of at least one board and shall also be able to file a resolution for dismissal. Prior to the election, shareholders should be able to suggest candidate members of the board. Shareholders should have control over potential equity dilution resulting from compensation practices. Existing equity compensation arrangements should not be materially modified, including the re-pricing of options, without shareholder approval. The corporate governance framework should protect and facilitate the exercise of shareholders' rights, i.e.:

a. Basic shareholder rights should include the right to: (1). Secure methods of ownership registration; (2). Convey or transfer shares; (3). Obtain relevant and material information on the corporation on a timely and regular basis; (4). Participate and vote in general shareholder meetings; (5). Elect and remove members of the board; and (6). share in the profits of the corporation.

b. Shareholders should have the right to participate in, and to be sufficiently informed on, decisions concerning fundamental corporate changes such as: amendments to the statutes, or articles of incorporation or similar governing documents of the company; the authorization of additional shares; and extra-ordinary transactions, including the transfer of all or substantially all assets that in effect result in the sale of the company.

c. Shareholders should have the opportunity to participate effectively and vote in general shareholder meetings and should be informed of the rules, including voting procedures that govern general shareholder meetings: (1). Shareholders should be furnished with sufficient and timely information concerning the date, location and agenda of general meetings, as well as full and timely information regarding the issues to be decided at the meeting; (2). Shareholders should have the opportunity to ask questions to the board, including questions relating to the annual external audit, to place items on the agenda of general meetings, and to propose resolutions, subject to reasonable limitations; (4). Effective shareholder participation in key corporate governance decisions, such as the nomination and election of board members, should be facilitated. Shareholders should be able to make their views known on the remuneration policy for board members and key executives. The equity component of compensation schemes for board members and employees should be subject to shareholder approval; (5). Shareholders should be able to vote in person or in absentia, and equal effect should be given to votes whether cast in person or in absentia.

d. Capital structures and arrangements that enable shareholders to obtain a degree of control disproportionate to their equity ownership should be disclosed.

e. Markets for corporate control should be allowed to function in an efficient and transparent manner that includes (1). The rules and procedures governing the acquisition of corporate control in the capital markets, and extraordinary transactions such as mergers, and sales of substantial portions of corporate assets, should be clearly articulated and disclosed so that investors understand their rights and recourse. Transactions should occur at transparent prices and under fair conditions that protect the rights of all shareholders according to their class; (2). Anti-take-over devices should not be used to shield management and the board from accountability.

f. The exercise of ownership rights by all shareholders, including institutional investors, should be facilitated.

g. Shareholders, including institutional shareholders, should be allowed to consult with each other on issues concerning their basic shareholder rights as defined in the Principles, subject to exceptions to prevent abuse. The corporate governance framework should ensure the equitable treatment of all shareholders, including minority and foreign shareholders. All shareholders should have the opportunity to obtain effective redress for violation of their rights. All shareholders of the same series of a class should be treated equally, which includes (1). Within any series of a class, all shares should carry the same rights. All investors should be able to obtain information about the rights attached to all series and classes of shares before they purchase. Any changes in voting rights should be subject to approval by those classes of shares which are negatively affected; (2). Minority shareholders should be protected from abusive actions by, or in the interest of, controlling shareholders acting either directly or indirectly, and should have effective means of redress; (3). Votes should be cast by custodians or nominees in a manner agreed upon with the beneficial owner of the shares; 94). Processes and procedures for general shareholder meetings should allow for equitable treatment of all shareholders. Company procedures should not make it unduly difficult or expensive to cast votes. Insider trading and abusive self-dealing should be prohibited In case of the appointment of a new director or re-appointment of a director the shareholders must be provided with the following information: a brief resume of the director; nature of his expertise in specific functional areas; and names of companies in which the person also holds the directorship and the membership of Committees of the board. Information like quarterly results, presentation made by companies to analysts may be put on company's web-site or may be sent in such a form so as to enable the stock exchange on which the company is listed to put it on its own web-site.

The half-yearly declaration of financial performance including summary of the significant events in last six months, should be sent to each household of shareholders. a board committee under the chairmanship of a non-executive director should be formed to specifically look into the redressing of shareholder complaints like transfer of shares, non-receipt of balance sheet, non-receipt of declared dividends etc. there should be a separate section on Corporate Governance in the annual reports of companies, with a detailed compliance report on Corporate Governance the company should arrange to obtain a certificate from the auditors of the company regarding compliance of mandatory recommendations and annexure the certificate with the directors' report, which is sent annually to all the shareholders of the company. The same certificate should also be sent to the stock exchanges along with the annual returns filed by the company.

The company has in place a communication policy addressed to the needs of all investors. As a policy, the company does not differentiate between small and large investors. Shareowners, particularly long-term shareowners, should act more like owners of the corporation. They should have the ability to exercise their right to participate more readily in the corporation's election process through involvement both in the nomination of directors and in proposals in the company's proxy statement about business issues and shareowner concerns regarding governance of the corporation. The process of mergers and takeovers should be regulated and compliance with these regulations should be supervised. If a shareholder's stake in the company passes a certain threshold, that shareholder should be obliged to make an offer for the remaining shares under reasonable conditions, that is, at least the price that was paid for the control of the company.

Companies should immediately disclose information which can influence the share price as well as information about those shareholders who pass (upwards or downwards) 5% thresholds. There should be serious penalties in case of non-compliance. Auditors have to be independent and should be elected by the general meeting. Shareholders should be able to place items on the agenda of the AGM. Shareholders holding not less than one-tenth of the paid-up capital of the company are entitled to requisition a general meeting, and place items on the agenda.

The company has in place a communication policy addressed to the needs of all investors. As a policy, the company does not differentiate between small and large investors. Shareowners, particularly long-term shareowners, should act more like owners of the corporation. They should have the ability to exercise their right to participate more readily in the corporation's election process through involvement both in the nomination of directors and in proposals in the company's proxy statement about business issues and shareowner concerns regarding governance of the corporation. Members of the board and key executives should be required to disclose to the board whether they, directly, indirectly or on behalf of third parties, have a material interest in any transaction or matter directly affecting the corporation.

STAKEHOLDERS

The corporate governance framework should recognize the rights of stakeholders established by law or through mutual agreements and encourage active co-operation between corporations and stakeholders in creating wealth, jobs, and the sustainability of financially sound enterprises.

a.   The rights of stakeholders that are established by law or through mutual agreements are to be respected.

b.   Where stakeholder interests are protected by law, stakeholders should have the opportunity to obtain effective redress for violation of their rights.

c.   Performance-enhancing mechanisms for employee participation should be permitted to develop.

d. Where stakeholders participate in the corporate governance process, they should have access to relevant, sufficient and reliable information on a timely and regular basis.

e. Stakeholders, including individual employees and their representative bodies, should be able to freely communicate their concerns about illegal or unethical practices to the board and their rights should not be compromised for doing this.

f. The corporate governance framework should be complemented by an effective, efficient insolvency framework and by effective enforcement of creditor rights.

REFERENCES

1. Eric Stevens, Corporate Governance: What Enterprise Content Management Was Meant For, Sarbanes-Oxley Journal, SimplexKnowledge Company, 2005

2. Shann Turnbull, Corporate Governance: Its scope, concerns & theories, Graduate School of Management Macquarie University, Sydney, (Abstract, Published in: Corporate Governance: An International Review, Blackwood, Oxford, vol. 5, no. 4, pp. 180–205), Forthcoming, October, 1997

3. Greg Pritchard, Corporate Governance, CPA Audit LLP, UK, 2005

4. Michael Kellogg, Dictionary, WordReference.com, Virginia-USA, 2005

5. James Manktelow, Introduction: Why you need to get your message across, Mind Tools Ltd of Signal House, Station Road, Burgess Hill, West Sussex, RH15 8DY, United Kingdom, 2005

6. Brent Baccala, Connected: An Internet Encyclopedia, 3rd Edition, Freesoft, USA, 1997

7. Joe Charlaff, A Roadmap for Corporate Brainstorming, United Jewish Communities, New York-USA, 2005

8. Bob Nelson, Bottom-Up Brainstorming, Prism Business Media Inc, 2001

9. Robert B. Reed, Communication: The Medium, Robert B. Reed, 2000–2006

10. Natasha Spring, Teambuilding, CW Bulletin, CW Bulletin CW Bulletin CW Bulletin International Association of Business Communicators, CA—USA, 2006

11. Bill Dutton, Prof., Alphanumeric Pagers, University of Southern California, USA, 2005

12. Lisa Bryan, How to Design a Brochure: Make Your Brochure Do Its Job, Digital Women, USA, 1998

13. David D. Clark, An Insider's Guide to the Internet, Armony, Texas-USA, 1999

14. Suler, J.R, e-Mail Communication and Relationships, Elsevier Academic Press, England, 2004

15. Christopher Wedde, Call Centers Privacy Statement, Lund Boat Company, Lake Forest, Illionis, USA, 2006

16. Gerry McGovern, Intranet communication versus traditional communication, 2002

17. Joel Orr, PhD, What is an extranet? And why should you care?, UK Construction Industry Net, UK, 2003–2005

18. Judith Fleeno & Silicon Reef, Which Comes First: the Intranet or the Extranet?, The Open Group, California-USA, 1998

19. Rachel Chertkoff, Alphanumeric Pagers, the University of Southern California, USA, 1998–2006

20. Houghton Mifflin, The American Heritage® Dictionary of the English Language, Fourth Edition, Houghton Mifflin Company, Maryland-USA, 2000

21. JJ Murphy, The Concepts of Vision & Mission Revisited, The Negotiation Academy, London-UK, 2003–2006

22. Susan M. Heathfield, Human Resources Policy and Procedure Directory, About Inc., USA, 2006

23. Lixing Wan, Corporate Gift Company, Wave Dancing, LLC, Iowa City, IA-USA, 2003

24. Graham Douglas, Innovation—Top Down or Bottom Up?, Mansueto Ventures LLC, New York-USA, 2005

25. Sandy Bradford, Implementing an employee handbook: Make sure your company's employee handbook functions effectively, National Roofing Contractors Association, IL-USA, 2006

26. Andrew Liveris, Corporate Report: Introduction, The Dow Chemical Company, USA, 2005

27. Kevin Sweeney, Transparency and Social Report of Companies, CSRwire, LLC, USA, 2005

28. Michael Glynn, Practice Alert No. 2002–2: Use of Specialists, The American Institute of Certified Public Accountants, USA, 2006

29. Howard Rohm and Larry Halbach,
    A Balancing Act: Sustaining New Directions, Balanced Scorecard Institute, USA, 2006

30. William Baue, Ford's Latest CSR Report Increases Transparency by Using GRI Guidelines, SRI World Group, Inc., USA, 1998–2006

31. Cornelius von Baeyer, What's Workplace Ethics?, Workplace Ethics Consultancy, Ontario-Canada, 2006

32. Caroline Steel, Change Management and Communication Plan, The University of Queensland, Brisbane, Australia, 2004

33. Gerry Richmond, Write a Business Plan: Planning Your Business Success, Garry Richmond, USA, 2004

34. Phillip J. Windley, Ph.D., The Discipline of Product Management, Office of the Governor-State of Utah, USA, 2006

35. T.J. Becker, Branding: Delivering on a Promise, Edward Lowe Foundation, Michigan-USA, 2006

36. Hermann Simon, Core Competencies For Power Pricing, The Journal of Professional Pricing, Germany, 1998

37. Martin Payne, Differential pricing: the way forward, Through the Loop Consulting Ltd, USA, 2002

38. Alexander Reppel, Understanding The Consumer, The Privacy Marketing Review, Germany, 2003

39. Ken Rigby, Technical Management—a pragmatic approach, 2nd Edition, Kend Rigby, UK, 2003

40. Paul Thornton, Environmental Policy, South Herts Waste Management Ltd, London-UK, 2004

41. Clive Bone and Mark Law, Bone and Robertson, 4 Onslow Gardens, Management Action Notes, UK, 2006

42. Panos Varangis, Abstracts of Current Studies: International Economics, World Bank, USA, 1996

43. Joel Spolsky, Fog Creek Compensation, Joel On Software Discussion Group, USA, 1999–2006

44. John G. Brau, Employee Incentives and Career Development, The Quorum Group, Texas-USA, 1997–2003

45. Werther & Davis, Human Resources and Personnel Management, McGraw-Hill, Inc. New York, NY, 1996

46. Carter McNamara, MBA, PhD, Project Management, Authenticity Consulting, LLC, USA, 1999

47. Gerard M Blair, Planning a Project, The University of Edinburgh, UK, 2002–2006

48. Michael Grose, Leadership Code, Michael Grose Presentations Pty Ltd, Australia, 2006

49. Alan Eastwood, Code of conduct, Salford City Council, UK, 2006

50. Todd Presnell, Business Law Today: A higher standard, American Bar Association, USA, 2005

51. Carl Geppert and partner, How the global communications industry is tackling margin enhancement, KPMG LLP, USA, 2002

52. Philip K. Akalp, Esq, Corporate Minutes & Recordkeeping, My Corporation Business Services, Inc., USA, 2001–2002

53. Naresh Chandra Committee, Report of the Committee on Corporate Audit and Governance, Manupatra Information Solutions Pvt. Ltd., India, 2006,

54. Sheila M. Rioux, Ph.D., and Paul Bernthal, PhD, Executive summary, Succession Management Practices, Development Dimensions International, MCMXCIX

55. Ron Hellbusch, Succession management planning, American Public Works Association, USA, 2001

56. Sanjeev Sharma, Recruitment Management System—Finding the ROI on Recruitment, BPOIndia.org, 2001

57. Jean Richards and Clare Hogg, Induction, Helios Associates Ltd, UK, 2006

58. Mark Henricks, Management Training Program: Golden Rules, Baker Communications in Houston, Texas, USA, 2003–2006

59. Pam Matheson, Career Path Model, Province of Nova Scotia, Canada, 2001

60. Michael G. Finlayson, Training and Career Development Policy, The Office of the Governing Council, Ontario-Canada, 1995

61. Eric Stevens, What Enterprise Content Management Was Meant For, Simplex Knowledge Company, 2005

978-0-595-40160-4
0-595-40160-0

www.ingramcontent.com/pod-product-compliance
Lightning Source LLC
Chambersburg PA
CBHW020733180526
45163CB00001B/216